PRAISE FOR

THE TURNAROUND 2

"Every business owner needs *The Turnaround 2* in their library. Bob's blueprint for success will benefit any size organization. I have incorporated most of the sales best practices garnered from Bob in my company and have seen excellent results. If your company needs a 'Total Makeover' with management, finance, operations, human resources, or sales, you must read this book over and over. I can't wait for Bob Curry's next turnaround book!"

—Michael Seifert, Digital Director, Fox Television Stations

"As a fan of Bob Curry's books, I have now read all three: *From Red to Black*, *The Turnaround*, and *The Turnaround 2*. This most recent book, The Turnaround 2, is an easy-to-read true story about a contemporary turnaround Bob did this past year. The 6.3-million-dollar off-road supply business discussed in this book was in severe financial trouble and ready to close their doors permanently. Bob worked with the owners to give the business a complete makeover, upgraded the management team, and hired an accounting manager to update the financial and operational reporting. Bob's best practices helped improve the company's marketing and sales management and grew the sales from 6.3 to 8.0 million dollars. The business's bottom line improved from a loss of $100,000 to a profit of more than $500,000 in twelve months.

"Throughout the book, Mr. Curry inserts 'gray boxes,' highlighting the important changes and best practices implemented during the turnaround engagement that helps all readers understand what he was attempting to accomplish and why. *The Turnaround 2* is an enjoyable book to read and understand as a CEO. My suggestion is to read this book, and then read it again, so you did not miss a word of what Bob has to say! Enjoy!"

—Anthony Rolon, CEO, Tribeca Marketing

"In *The Turnaround 2,* the reader gets a unique perspective perched on Bob Curry's shoulder. He offers a view into the world of reengineering the machinery of operating a business. Worksheets, motivational messages, and tactile exercises all bring the reader into the fascinating world of evaluating one's own business from an extraordinary point of view. From the subconscious safety of reading another's business evaluation, the material encourages readers to have a self-engaging dialogue, exploring ways to improve the operations of their business, which often becomes invisible to business owners immersed in day-to-day operations.

"I found the book enjoyable, as the style of writing draws the reader into the conversation, while always having you thinking, *Hmm, is this something for me?* I highly recommend this book and look forward to the next."

—Michael Miller, Chairman & Founder, The Institute
for Scientific Validation

"Reading Robert (Bob) S. Curry's Losses to Profits series is like getting a master's degree in business management (MBA) without leaving your home. Seriously! You'll learn Bob's secrets to building a great management team, creating and using financial reports, marketing, and selling your products or services. It's all here! Bob Curry is a very successful business turnaround coach who has turned around more than seventy distressed businesses. *The Turnaround 2* is the third book in the Losses to Profits series.

"Like a good novel, each book in the series tells the engrossing story of a real-life business turnaround. You'll root for the struggling good guys (the owners and the hard workers) as Bob takes on their company's myriad woes. I turned the pages quickly to find out who goes and who stays and what happens next! In each engagement, Bob wins the team over with his clearheaded thinking and expertise. If you own or manage a business, you need to read these books!"

—Valerie Kay, Former Director, Creative Services I Field Marketing,
Advantage Sales and Marketing

"Employee morale was low at my eight-year-old IT company. I had an overpaid employee who thought he owned the place, and the business was about to tailspin out of control. I hired Bob to turn my company around, and within six months, all the employees were happy, the bad apples were gone, and overpaid contractors/vendors were replaced. I went from working eighty hours a week to having free time to spend with my kids. Bob will not only evaluate the finances of your business but also 'see through' the staff and instinctively know where to make the changes to get your business profitable and running as it should.

"My experience with Bob Curry was similar to the true-life examples he writes about in his Losses to Profits series. All three of his business turnaround books are like fun-to-read college textbooks on how to improve your business to make more money and have a strong, sustainable business. *The Turnaround 2* is a great book for business owners because Bob makes it easy to apply his turnaround policies, procedures, and business practices to your own business. You will enjoy the read and then start making positive changes to your company."

—Reginald R. Andre, President/CEO, ARK Solvers, Inc.

"What an amazing, enjoyable, and insightful book! I never thought a business book could be both entertaining and educational. Robert's writing style is so simple yet detailed to an extent that you feel that you are sitting right next to him. That is why you feel emotionally connected to him and all the people involved in the turnaround. Through his words you can tell that he is such a nice guy who has high morals and that he has changed the lives of so many people around him for the better. His job is literally saving companies from going under and, in the process, he ends up creating a great corporate culture, saves so many jobs, and establishes meaningful and lasting connections with the employees and their families.

"I'm so glad he has written another book, and I will start reading it right away. I was so upset when this one was finished! Thanks, Robert, for sharing all your insights—I can't wait to read the other books you have written and hope you continue sharing all the turnarounds you will be working on in the future."

—Adolf Kabban, Director at Deloitte Restructuring Services

"Cover to cover! I know it's a bit cliché, but I couldn't put it down until I finished it. Not only is Bob's writing style detailed yet easy to read, his client-study format has you feeling like you're sitting in an office with him talking out your own business problems. It is rare to be both entertained by what you are reading and, at the same time, learning vastly insightful information. It is 'How-to' with a flare. You are guaranteed to glean applicable 'PIRs' (as he calls them) that will affect the bottom line of your business if you choose to use Bob's turn-around skills as described in the book.

The Turnaround 2 focuses on managing people, improving the company culture, and strengthening financial reporting. Bob's skills at implementing good business practices rather than just fixing problems lead the reader to the "why" behind the issues businesses face, and seamlessly guides them through making impactful changes. The step-by-step process that Bob lays out in the book makes molehills out of mountain-size problems and, like the book says, Profits out of Losses. In short, this is an excellent book and I highly recommend it. If his book were a class, I would give Bob an A+."

—Bob L. Harris, Esq.

PRAISE FOR
THE TURNAROUND

"This is a true 'From Red to Black' story that every business executive should read and use as a reference manual to grow their business, improve their management skills, and increase the profits of their company. Bob Curry's first book, *From Red to Black,* was focused on improving the management's leadership skills, productive business operations, and hiring the best employees. Throughout *The Turnaround*, Bob's second book in the From Losses to Profits series, he has highlighted the 'Best Practices' that he used to grow the company's sales, improve the productivity of the management team, and take a company from losses to profits.

"This book is easy to read and makes a 'bookmark' obsolete. You will not be able to put this book down until you have read the last page. Keep a notebook close to record Bob's 'best business practices' while you read this book. Mark my words, you will read this book more than once . . . it is a great resource to learn more about how to make a business more profitable."

—Kathy Anthony, Vistage Florida Chair–
Executive Coach & Facilitator

"*The Turnaround* is brilliantly written by one of the best in his field, Robert Curry. This book is about an incredible turnaround of a distressed 48-million-dollar company that was headed for bankruptcy and how it grew to $130 million in sales and $4 million in profits in nine months. It is about growing sales and improving the management of a company to improve profits. A must-read for business executives and anyone looking to improve sales and profits."

—Dr. Joe Pace, Performance Psychologist and Chairman
of the Board–Global Education, The Pacific Institute

"Within the first few pages of this book, you'll realize Robert Curry is among the elite business turnaround experts in America. The book is very interesting because it tells the story about a company Bob took over and how he grew the company from $48 million and losing almost a million dollars in the prior year to $130 million in the first nine months, making the company very profitable.

"In this book, Mr. Curry describes the 'Best Practices' that were used to grow the business and to make the managers and employees accountable. This is definitely the type of book that once you start reading it, you cannot put it down until you finish the last chapter. Bob is the kind of guy you want on your team and with this recent book, *The Turnaround,* you can now have a peek into his million-dollar-business strategies."

—Shirley Solis, Peak Performance Coach and Family Catalyst

ALSO BY ROBERT S. CURRY
BUSINESS RECOVERY SPECIALIST

FROM RED TO BLACK:
How to Turn a Business Around

THE TURNAROUND:
How to Take a Business from Red to Black

TO PROFITS

The
TURNAROUND
2

FROM LOSSES

HOW **"ABC OFF-ROAD SUPPLY"**
WENT FROM RED TO **BLACK**
A True Story

ROBERT S. CURRY
BUSINESS RECOVERY SPECIALIST

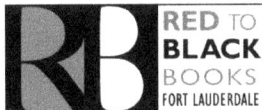

RB RED TO
BLACK
BOOKS
FORT LAUDERDALE

Disclaimer: This book is designed to provide accurate and authoritative information regarding the subject matter covered. The publisher and author are not engaged in rendering legal advice or any other professional services to the reader. If legal advice or other assistance is required, the services of a competent professional should be sought. The reader should be aware that laws and rules applicable to their situation may differ from the information in this book. It is the responsibility of the reader to seek professional guidance whenever necessary. The author and publisher are not responsible for any adverse effects or consequences resulting from the use of the information in this book.

The Turnaround 2 is based on a real client. However, actual names and identifying characteristics have not been used, and any resemblance to a specific individual or company is coincidental.

Published by:
Red to Black Books
Fort Lauderdale, Florida

Copyright © 2020 by Robert S. Curry

ISBN-13: 978-1-7327891-2-8

Printed in the United States of America.

To my wife, Esther Curry—
my best friend, partner, lover,
advisor, and supporter.

CONTENTS

INTRODUCTION

"If you hire people just because they can do a job, they'll work for your money. But if you hire people who believe what you believe, they'll work for you with blood and sweat and tears."

—Simon Sinek, Organizational Consultant

FOR MANY YEARS, I HAVE BEEN DOING TURNAROUNDS OF distressed companies to make the businesses profitable. I believe that the main reason companies are distressed is that the business owners do not know how to hire and manage a strong management team. Many business owners do not realize how important it is to have and maintain a qualified team of managers to oversee their employees. Most entrepreneurs believe they are doing a decent job of building a quality management team to lead their companies. But there are many reasons my potential clients have never achieved their goals before engaging a turnaround specialist. Some of the explanations are:

+ Ownership and management do not know how to recruit and hire top performers.

+ Managers do not keep their superstar employees happy to prevent them from considering leaving the company to work for another employer.

+ Unfortunately, many companies have poor financial and operational reporting available for the president and the management

1

team. Good reporting would help them better understand which member(s) of the management team and their employees are doing a great job and who are the nonperformers. Owners don't understand the value of spending the right amount of money on hiring a reliable, qualified, and talented controller/CFO.

Those are probably the top three reasons and the most important, but also:

✦ In many companies, the owners have relationships/friendships with the members of the management team. Therefore, they do not objectively evaluate their performance and demand better results from them or their organizations.

✦ Many business owners are too busy working in their business rather than on their business. This issue stops them from being aware of how vital a professional-level management team is to the success of their company.

✦ From my experiences, a high percentage of business owners set the hiring salary below the market range for the position and then have problems finding qualified people to hire at the lower wage.

✦ Many business owners are nonconfrontational and "stick their head in the sand" rather than deal with their problems.

✦ Many entrepreneurs are too naive to understand how stronger and more productive managers could impact the success of their company.

✦ Some business leaders and members of management teams are poor communicators. Poor communication skills by senior managers of the organization cause vulnerable relationships with their team. This problem also results in a disconnect of the manager from the day-to-day activities in the company.

✦ Many entrepreneurs do believe that their company's profitability depends upon staffing their organization with top-tier employees. The unfortunate issue is very few middle-market, and smaller companies (companies with $25 million in sales or less) have the talent on staff to recruit, interview, hire, onboard (help a new hire adjust to social and performance aspects of the position), and maintain those quality employees.

✦ Many companies have business owners who are not knowledgeable about managing a company using the best business practices. This problem sounds like a straightforward issue, but it is not.

✦ One of the most common reasons businesses fail is they do not know their customer, their market space with their products or services, or both.

✦ Many business owners do not know how to read a simple financial statement. Most business owners manage their company by the balance of cash in their checking accounts.

Numerous companies have, for example, an electrician or an off-road supply expert or an HVAC guy managing the business rather than a "businessman" operating the electrical firm, off-road supply business, or HVAC company. The HVAC guy knows how to install an air conditioner, but he may not know how to manage a business. The electrician knows how to wire a home, but he may not know how to run his company. I am rarely hired by a company that has a leader who is a "businessman" managing the organization. Most of my clients have been senior executives who were very good at their trade (HVAC, engineer, etc.) and decided to start their own companies because it looked so easy. Unfortunately, if the owner does not have any business education or experience, he ends up hiring someone like me to turn around his distressed business.

If you own a business and can identify with any of the problems listed earlier, please have a notebook next to you as you read this book. You are going to need to take notes as you are reading the story about the turnaround of ABC Off-Road Supply. I promise you:

✦ You will learn a lot about how vital a quality management team is to the success of your business.

✦ If you do have a business education and experience, the information in this book will remind you of what you learned in the past about best business practices but have not used with your company.

For those companies that have a weak management team and are losing money every month, you should know that making personnel changes is very difficult and costly. When I work with a company in a turnaround engagement, I always take an aggressive approach and terminate the weaker manager(s) or employee(s) early in the consulting job. Bad employees, unlike a good bottle of wine, do not get better with age. I have always felt that it is not a wise business decision to invest the company's funds on a poor-performing manager or staff member.

Making personnel changes is expensive and stressful for everyone at the beginning of the turnaround process. The company owners must understand that all the employees are stressed during management changes. With most of the distressed companies I have worked with during a turnaround engagement, the first change I make is to terminate the weaker manager(s) and hire a stronger leader. Making these types of personnel changes sends a message to the rest of the employees who remain employed by the company: "Work hard, work smart, or find a new job."

When I start a turnaround engagement, I first interview each member of the senior management team, beginning with the president.

If the president's background is in finance where most of his job experience was as a controller or CFO, I am not that concerned about having a top-tier talented controller/CFO on the management team. If the president was a former CFO, he is going to know enough about the finance department even if the current CFO is not that strong. But if the president was a former VP of sales, then I am very concerned about the strength of the current CFO. Most sales-experienced presidents do not know what a qualified CFO does for a living. I find that if the president was not a CFO before he became president, he does not even know how to interview or evaluate a candidate for the CFO position.

Most companies have four key senior positions reporting to the president: VP of sales, VP of operations, CFO, and VP of information technology. Each manager has an essential function for the success of the company. Each manager is like one of the four legs of a chair. If one leg on the chair is weak, the chair is going to fall. Just like the management team, if one of the managers is weak, the whole team could fail.

Throughout my years of managing companies as the President/ CEO or doing turnarounds and business coaching, I have found that the best companies always have something in common. The most profitable companies are those with the least amount of employee turnover. They are the companies that take their time to hire the best employees rather than hiring the first person with a résumé to fill the position quickly.

Profitable companies are also the ones with the most significant budgets for employee training. Companies that invest in their employees have less turnover and better-qualified staff. These are the successful organizations that focus on "employee development." Companies that "invest" in their people are the businesses that attract top-tier employees and keep them on their payroll for many years. Employee turnover is an extremely costly business expense that the best companies experience less because they treat their people well. By creating an "employee-based" corporate culture of recognizing and developing the best employees at every level, these companies ultimately generate a significant gap between their organization and its competitors. Even when their competitors try to recruit and hire the company's top managers, the best employees do not leave because of their company's corporate culture. When a company invests in its people, the employees don't leave because they know that the "grass is not greener" at other companies.

A good friend of mine recently told me a story that supports the "invest in your employees" theory because it makes businesses more profitable. My friend was talking to the CEO of a chain of hospitals. The CEO shared that when there is patient-care employee turnover in the hospital, it costs the hospital between $40,000 and $50,000 to replace that employee. The management decided to offer their employees a tuition-reimbursement benefit to help solve the employee turnover problem. There were two very positive results after they started the tuition-reimbursement benefit. First, the employees who took advantage of the tuition-reimbursement benefit stayed with the hospital between five and seven years longer. Second, the hospital also had better-educated employees working as part of their workforce. By offering their employees the tuition-reimbursement benefit and reducing the employee turnover, it saved the hospital millions of dollars in payroll expenses.

When I am assessing a client's corporate culture and the strength of their managers, I analyze their commitment to hire the best and invest in their employees. I ask the series of questions to follow. The answers to these questions indicate whether the company has committed to hire only the best possible employees and invest in training and personal development for the company's management and staff.

✦ What are the company's mission and vision, and is management focused on living up to their corporate culture statements?

✦ Does the company have written corporate goals that connect to these cultural statements?

✦ Does the company have timely, accurate, and simple-to-read weekly or monthly financial and operational reporting?

✦ Does the reporting give the president and senior management team accurate information to measure employee productivity?

✦ Does the company have well-documented policies, procedures, and goals for recruiting, hiring, and onboarding new employees?

✦ Is the company recruiting top-tier management and employees who have the skills and ability to advance the quality of the management team and their staff?

✦ Can the managers make sound business decisions for each functional area of the organization by using the information in the financial and operating reports? Or, on the contrary, does the finance department issue monthly reports late that get filed in a binder and stored on the manager's credenza. Are the financial statements never reviewed because they are way too long, very complicated, a cosmetic mess, and impossible to read and understand?

✦ Are the managers willing to leave a vacancy open for months, if necessary, until they find the right outstanding candidate?

✦ Is the human resources department investing the time and money to recruit qualified top-tier candidates? Or are they like most companies who delegate that function to the managers who have no idea how to recruit and hire high-quality candidates? Or is the company hiring the first warm body that shows up at the front door? You know, the candidate who needs a job and has a résumé that lists their professional experience saying that he or she qualifies for the position, whether or not the information on the resumé is accurate.

✦ Does the company maintain consistent demanding standards for everyone in the organization? Or just the opposite: Is management willing to tolerate a weak division manager, a floundering sales force, or a poorly functioning department head?

✦ Does the president formally review the results of each manager's performance semiannually or annually? Do the managers evaluate the performance of their direct reports to determine if each employee is meeting their individual goals?

✦ Does the company make progress each year with the management team for each department? Or is the next year going to have the same old managers doing the same old boring things and producing the same lackluster, mediocre results?

✦ What is the company's budget for employee training and development?

As we all know, times have changed, and the old-style methods of managing an organization have also changed. The process of recruiting, interviewing, hiring, onboarding, and developing employees has transformed in the past decade. An organization that promotes employees based upon job seniority no longer works, as it used to years ago. With businesses being more competitive due to the internet, companies must now have a top-tier management team to be successful in today's business environment. Internet marketing, technology, and price pressures from companies like Amazon demand a strong management team—or the company will fail.

These changes require business owners to either change or eventually file for bankruptcy protection. The president of each organization should regularly evaluate the company's management group to understand if there are any weaknesses. Then there should be a plan developed to resolve them. A management evaluation should be done either quarterly or at least twice a year. Owners must address the deficiencies with training classes at a minimum or replacement of the employee in the worst case.

Working with distressed companies, I have almost always taken an aggressive approach to stop the company from bleeding cash. My mission is to build a strong management team to keep the company profitable in future years. I hope that you enjoy this book. This true story is about a successful business turnaround.

Throughout this book, comment boxes like this one highlight the critical issues concerning the ABC Off-Road Supply turnaround. In these boxes is information about the "Best Business Practices" that were used to help ABC Off-Road Supply turn around and be profitable. These business practices are critical to the success of any business, including possibly your company. I added these boxes so that you can easily find this crucial information after you've finished reading this book and wish to use the best practices in your own business.

Chapter 1

A TURNAROUND IN UTAH

"If you can't fly then run, if you can't run then walk,
if you can't walk then crawl, but whatever you
do you have to keep moving forward."

—MARTIN LUTHER KING JR.,
AMERICAN CHRISTIAN MINISTER AND ACTIVIST

ON WEDNESDAY, DURING THE THIRD WEEK OF JANUARY, I received the following email:

> **Subject:** Turnaround in Utah
>
> Hello Bob,
> Our leadership team just finished reading your first book, *From Red to Black.*
>   Our company is 14 years old, and profits avoid us while the revenue exceeds $6 million. We see the value of your book and your turnaround skills. Please let me know if this is worthy of a phone call.
>
> Regards,
>
> Scott
> Operations – ABC

I was surprised and excited about the email because it was the first lead for a turnaround engagement I had received from someone because they had read one of my books. I planned to return the email after I did a little research about the company.

I googled the name of the company, reviewed its website, and its Facebook, Twitter, LinkedIn, Instagram, and YouTube accounts. I found the information about the company on their website and social media accounts fascinating. Unfortunately, the company's message was all over the map. There was no clear, focused "statement" about the company's business. There were just pictures and videos with jeeps and trucks in an "off-road" environment. Each of their social media accounts had pictures of jeeps, pickup trucks, and SUVs, all "jacked up" with lift kits, flashy lights, big bumpers with winches, roof racks, decals all over the vehicles' bodies, and all with massive tires and fancy wheels. Most of the vehicles had lifts installed and a step immediately below the passenger doors. No human being could raise his or her leg high enough to get into the truck without using the footstep. The vehicles in the pictures looked powerful and ready to climb up or descend steep, rocky off-road hillsides.

When I clicked on their website, there were vehicles at a location called "Moab" in Utah. I googled "Moab" and found that it is a city on the southern edge of Grand County in southeastern Utah on the western side of the United States. Moab is the county seat and the largest city in Grand County. Its estimated population is 5,000. Every year, the area attracts many tourists, mostly visitors to the nearby Arches and Canyonlands national parks. Moab is a popular location for "off-roaders" who come for the annual Moab Jeep Safari. According to the websites I read about this town, "off-roading" is the local culture. When you think about "4-wheeling," you think *Moab*. The landscape and scenery are indescribable, and the number of trails is amazing.

The videos showed these jacked-up vehicles climbing 90-degree rock formations. I watched the videos continuously because they were very entertaining, but the off-roading did look dangerous at times. I had never seen anything like this before. I wondered what the value of the company's website was other than watching "big jeeps and trucks" going places that I had never dreamed they could go. I got the impression that whoever designed ABC Off-Road Supply's website was a "rookie" rather than an expert at building professional websites. I finally located the sales area of the site. It appeared to be cluttered, confusing and challenging to search for the different products that the company had for sale.

I now had a feeling about the personality of the company through their presence on social media and the company's website. The company sells off-road parts and supplies to "off-roaders" all over the world from their website. They also have a large garage in Utah with at least a dozen bays where they install these off-road parts on customers' vehicles.

Next, I searched LinkedIn to see if any of the executives in the company had a profile posted. Brian (GM and owner), Jordan (VP of procurement services), and Scott (Operations) all had profiles. Scott's profile stated that he was responsible for the following:

✦ Building dreams in all areas of life for employees, customers, vendors, and off-road enthusiasts.

✦ Inspire a culture of change, improvement, leadership, and teamwork.

✦ Lead and manage all areas of operations throughout the organization.

✦ Building a culture of well-being, growth, and success throughout the organization.

✦ Developing a workflow, processes, and procedures that reflect the dreams of the organization.

✦ Develop, implement, and deliver an experience that exceeds customer expectations.

✦ Align financials with company directives and strategies.

✦ Implement inventory management with an integrated software solution.

✦ Develop leadership and management roles with support, training, and mentoring.

✦ E-commerce alignment with enhanced performance strategies.

✦ Human resources development.

✦ Develop a handbook, standards, guidelines, organization struc-
ture, and corporate policy.

Scott's list of responsibilities looked like he copied them from a
college textbook. My impression was that if a manager could accomplish this list of duties, his title would be either "Supreme Leader"
or "Superstar"! I was looking forward to meeting Scott someday.
I wanted to see if he had the personality to accomplish all these
tasks for a $6 million company that was currently losing money.
My thoughts were that if Scott did achieve everything on his list, he
probably would not have needed to contact a turnaround specialist.

Brian's and Jordan's profiles on LinkedIn did not reflect Scott's
brand of creative imagination. Theirs simply listed their jobs, their
education, and what looked like current photos of themselves.

Being satisfied that I knew enough about the company to have
an intelligent conversation with the owners, I answered Scott's email.
In my return email, I told him that I would be happy to schedule
a phone call to discuss the situation about their business, which he
had referred to as the "Turnaround in Utah." We planned the phone
call for later that day, which was suitable for both parties.

* * *

My phone rang precisely at 6:00 PM. I saw that the phone number was from the "801" area code, so I knew the call was from Scott.
I answered the phone, and Scott introduced himself and said that
Brian and Jordan, the two owners of the business, were also on the
call. Scott thanked me for agreeing to take the call, and then he talked
nonstop for about thirty, maybe thirty-five minutes. He described
his version of the current financial and operating situation of this
off-road supply company.

I had a tablet in front of me on which I had listed ten questions before the call. When Scott finished talking, I would ask the

owners my questions. I grabbed a second tablet to take notes as Scott explained the company's status in extreme detail. As he spoke, I checked off each question he had answered before I was able to ask it. Finally, when there was a pause from Scott's apparently prepared speech, I seized the opportunity to ask the balance of my questions. There were only four left on my list. At this point, I was still not sure what Scott's role was with the company, even though I had read his extreme profile with this title: "Operations." I hesitated to ask that question because I guessed his reply would take another thirty minutes. I moved on to the other items on my list.

I said, "Brian, could you please describe the management team currently working for you and Jordan?" I turned on the speaker on my phone because I wanted my hands free so that I could take notes as he talked.

"Bob, I oversee the sales and marketing departments, and Jordan manages the purchasing, shop, and warehousing functions," he replied. "I have a sales manager who supervises our five salespeople. We have a service manager who oversees the twelve technicians in the shop and the two 'tire-busters.' The service manager reports to Jordan."

I asked, "How many employees do you have working for your company, and what do they all do?"

Brian replied, "We have twelve techs in the shop, two tire-busters, a service manager, and four guys handling all the inventory. We have three drivers, two ladies in purchasing, five salespeople, and a sales manager. Then, there is one guy handling the internet stores, one employee doing the shop-productivity reporting, a bookkeeper, one young lady who does the marketing, and a maintenance guy. Scott, Jordan, and I are responsible for all those employees. I am not sure how many that is, but that is the whole team."

I made a list of the employees while Brian was talking, and it totaled 38. I still did not know what Scott did for this company, but I decided not to ask that question yet.

I then said, "Please tell me about the bookkeeper."

Brian replied that Carole, the bookkeeper, was a part-timer. She was there for three half days a week and had been with the company

ABC Off-Road Supply
Chart of Organization

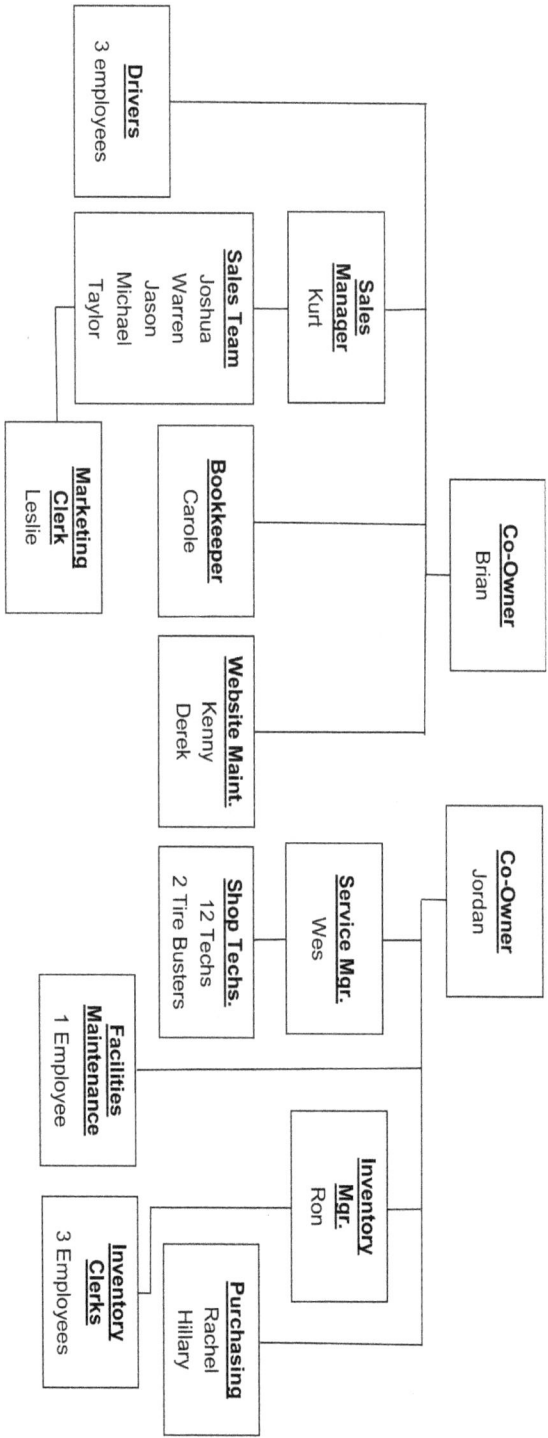

Drivers
3 employees

Sales Manager
Kurt

Sales Team
Joshua
Warren
Jason
Michael
Taylor

Marketing Clerk
Leslie

Bookkeeper
Carole

Co-Owner
Brian

Website Maint.
Kenny
Derek

Shop Techs.
12 Techs
2 Tire Busters

Service Mgr.
Wes

Co-Owner
Jordan

Facilities Maintenance
1 Employee

Inventory Mgr.
Ron

Inventory Clerks
3 Employees

Purchasing
Rachel
Hillary

38 Employees

2 – Owners		4 – Warehouse Labor	
3 – Department Managers		2 – Tire Busters	
5 – Salesmen		3 – Drivers	
1 – Bookkeeper		1 – Marketing Clerk	
2 – Purchasing / A/P		2 – Website Maintenance	
12 – Shop Technicians		1 – Facilities Maintenance	

for several years. He added that she was looking forward to retiring as soon as possible.

"Brian, I hate to tell you, but you cannot run a 6-million-dollar company with a part-time bookkeeper managing your accounting department. There is no way she would be able to keep the financial department current working twelve to fifteen hours per week!"

There was a long pause—a very long awkward moment.

Then I asked, "This is the third week of January, have you seen your December reports or the year-end financial statements yet?"

Scott chimed in, "We have not even seen the June income statement and balance sheet. I believe Carole is so busy doing the payroll, payroll taxes, sales taxes, paying the bills, and reconciling the checking account and credit cards that she does not have time to work on preparing the financial statements."

I sat back in my chair and said, "Gentlemen, I will be honest with you: You cannot manage a 6-million-dollar company without monthly financial statements, let alone not having an income statement and balance sheet for over seven months. You cannot properly manage a company without an operating budget, which is your plan on how you are going to manage the finances and operations of your company. Your bookkeeper probably knows that, and that is, perhaps, the reason she wants to retire and get away from your company."

I wish I could have seen the expressions on their faces after those comments. Unfortunately, I couldn't because we were talking on the phone. I guessed that they were looking at each other red-faced with embarrassment.

Next, I asked, "I have another question. How much inventory do you currently have in your warehouse?"

Jordan, the owner responsible for purchasing and the warehouse, answered this one. "I am guessing, between 350,000 and 750,000 dollars."

I thought for a moment about Jordan's answer. I realized these men did not have a clue how much inventory they had in their warehouse. I asked, "Are you telling me that you don't know within 400,000 dollars how much inventory you have in your warehouse?"

"Yes, sir, that is what I am saying," Jordan replied. "We do not have an on-hand inventory balance report in our accounting software. We use QuickBooks. We have too much inventory for the capacity level of QuickBooks. The software cannot handle an inventory as large as ours."

"Jordan, do you have an inventory or warehouse manager?" I asked.

"No," he replied quickly, "we have a guy that is in his mid-twenties that manages the inventory and warehouse."

I leaned closer to the phone and said, "So, you have a young clerk managing your 750,000 dollars of assets in your company, is that right?"

"Yes, sir, that is correct. But when you say it like that, it sounds like we have made a horrible mistake," Jordan said.

"I did not say that, sir, but I have to admit, I am thinking it! So, let me ask you a different question. What is the labor rate that you charge for the shop technicians?"

"We charge 92.50 per hour," Brian answered.

I then asked, "What does your competition charge?"

"Between 125 and 135," he replied.

"Why is your labor rate 42.50 per hour less than your competition?" I asked.

Brian explained, "Bob, that is because I don't think that our technicians are worth 135 dollars per hour."

Wow, that answer surprised me. I made myself a note about the low labor rate for service. I would need to deal with this issue if Brian and Jordan hired me to turn this company around. I asked Brian if the bookkeeper did any cash flow projections or a weekly flash report.

"I don't think so," he replied, "at least she never showed me any reports other than the financial statements from six or seven months ago."

"Jordan, is there any security over the company's inventory?" I asked.

"No," he replied.

I stopped asking questions because I could tell I was not going to enjoy any of the likely answers, plus I think I was embarrassing Brian and Jordan. I decided to wait to get the rest of my questions answered once I visited their facilities.

After a moment, Jordan said, "Mr. Curry, we have all read your two books. We understand that you know how to manage businesses to be profitable. Brian and I are off-road vehicle guys trying to run a 6-million-dollar business. Bob, our company is failing. We need your help. We need your help to learn how to manage this company as a business. We want to be two business guys running an off-road company rather than off-road guys running a business. We know how to take a jeep apart and put it together again. But we do not know the best practices on how to manage this business profitably."

Brian spoke next. "Bob, if we do not make a profit this year, I am going to shut down this business and move on to a new career. I cannot afford to invest any more money into this business and watch the cash go down the drain daily. Scott shared your books with me, and I took the time to read them both. Your books are great and have given me hope that this company can be successful. I know that we need your help to turn this company around. Reading your two books have convinced me that you are the person who can help us make this business profitable. Mr. Curry, I have three children, as does Jordan. This business is critical to the financial health of both of our families. If those stories in your two books are accurate, I know that you can turnaround our company. I do not know how busy you are right now, but we need your help. So, sir, can you come to Utah and help our company be profitable and cash-flow positive?"

Wow, the two owners were selling their company's needs to me rather than my having to sell my turnaround skills to them, the potential customer. I had never had a problem with closing turnaround engagements with company owners who needed my help. But this company's owners stated that they knew I could turn their company around because they read my books. The fact that these two business owners "stripped down naked" and were being 100 percent honest scored major points with me. I found it fascinating that they did not even ask me what it was going to cost them for my services.

We finished the call after I told Scott, Brian, and Jordan that I would review the situation and get back to them within twenty-four hours. Scott again thanked me for my time, and we ended the phone call. After I hung up, I sat there and thought about this challenge. For the next thirty minutes, I updated my notes about the company. I knew that if I accepted this engagement, it was not going to be easy. I had already done more than seventy-five turnaround engagements, and each job had its unique problematic situations but not much different from the problems this company was facing. Once I had gathered all my notes, it took me less than one minute to decide to accept this engagement because I knew I could do it and be successful.

* * *

One of the major issues in the decision about accepting or turning down a turnaround consulting job is whether the owner(s) will follow my direction to improve the profitability of the company. I know that it is not easy for owners to manage a business for many years and then engage a consultant to come into their company and make material changes to the organization. It was crystal clear that Brian and Jordan needed help and knew that they needed help. It was my impression that they would take my direction to improve the success of their company. They wanted success so badly that it hurt, but they didn't know how to get it. After my short phone call with them, I liked them already.

A long time ago, I decided I would never accept a turnaround engagement for a business owner I did not like. My reason for this is that I do not want to make any "jackasses" wealthy with my turnaround skills. I had a situation years ago where I did a successful turnaround, but the owner attempted to renege on the contract. I had saved him from bank foreclosure on his company *and* home. When it was time for me to receive my bonus from the bank that had hired me for the turnaround, the owner tried to stop my reward payment and reroute the money to his checking account. It was right then that I decided I would not work for another "jackass"!

I am now at the age that money is not as important as it was when I was between the ages of twenty-two and fifty. I have enough money now that I can live comfortably for the rest of my life and support my family. If I don't like the business owner of a prospective company's turnaround engagement, I do not accept the turnaround, regardless of the financial compensation. I did not think that would be the case with Brian and Jordan. I felt very comfortable with the integrity of these two owners. I planned to schedule a trip to Utah in the next two weeks to start a "Turnaround in Utah."

* * *

The next day, I checked the flights to Salt Lake City and the hotels in the town close to the client's facility. I also told my wife, Esther, that I was accepting a turnaround engagement in Utah in January.

"Bob, you have zero winter clothes in your closet," she said.

"Hmm, I didn't even think about that," I replied. "You are right—Utah's weather probably is a tad bit colder than Fort Lauderdale in January."

I googled the average weather in Utah for January, and the computer said it was between 21 and 37 degrees. The weather in Fort Lauderdale, Florida, is 58 to 76 degrees that time of the year. Esther was right. I needed to do some shopping for warm clothes to start this turnaround. A quick trip to the local mall with my wife and VISA card took care of my wardrobe problems. Since I am colorblind, I never buy any clothes without my wife picking them or confirming my selection. I did that once and failed miserably.

Immediately after Esther and I returned from the mall, I developed a proposal and emailed it to Scott, Brian, and Jordan. Then I called Scott and told him that I was accepting the consulting job, and I had just sent him the proposal. I asked him to review it with Brian and Jordan.

"Please, if they agree with the terms and conditions, then ask them to please sign it, scan it, and email it back as soon as possible," I said.

Scott said that he would have it signed and returned within fifteen minutes. I shared with him that I would be flying into Salt Lake City International Airport, landing on Sunday, January 27, at 9:54 AM.

With great enthusiasm, Scott said, "Wonderful, Bob! I will pick you up from the airport so we have some time to talk before we get to ABC Off-Road Supply. We will have a vehicle for you to drive while you are in Utah, so don't worry about renting a car. Lastly, but most important, how do you like your coffee from Starbucks in the mornings?"

Scott's Starbucks question took me by surprise. But then I thought that it made sense for his personality according to his LinkedIn profile. "I usually order a hot venti nonfat vanilla latte in the morning," I told him.

"Okay, Bob, I am looking forward to you visiting our company. I am so excited. I know that this is going to be fantastic. I am going to learn so much from you! Have a great day. Thank you for accepting this turnaround."

I hung up the phone and just had to laugh. Scott was a different kind of guy. As Scott promised, fifteen minutes later, I received an email from him with the signed proposal that served as the contract agreement for this turnaround.

Now, I had to develop my turnaround plan. Unfortunately, I had limited information about the client. I sat down at my desk with a tablet and my laptop. I always keep a tablet next to me so that when I am working and think of something I need to do or remember, I write it on the tablet. That way, I don't forget it and can continue with my work. By writing my thoughts down on the tablet, I can relax, knowing that I will remember everything, mainly because I wrote it down.

After working for about ten minutes, I had more written on the tablet than I did on the computer. I had only been on the phone with the two owners and Scott for forty-five minutes. I did learn a great deal of information about the company and what needed immediate attention at the beginning of the turnaround. This was my list of tasks:

✓ The company needs a new "sales-friendly" website.

✓ A manager-level person needs to be in charge of receiving, warehousing, and picking, packing, and shipping the inventory to customers.

✓ The company needs to hire an accounting manager to replace the part-time bookkeeper.

✓ I need to understand Scott's responsibilities and determine how he can best help the company.

✓ I need to increase the labor rate for the shop technicians to the current market rate ($125 to $135).

✓ Financial statements need to be updated. They must always remain current in the future.

✓ The company needs to have security over its inventory, so the off-road parts do not disappear on employees' trucks. The goal is to sell every off-road part to a customer, not allow it to be stolen by an employee.

✓ There needs to be an operating budget for the year.

✓ The on-hand inventory balances need to be recorded within the accounting software and accounted for properly.

✓ A physical inventory needs to be taken, so the company knows how much stock it owns. By doing a physical inventory count, this will help me reconcile an accurate inventory balance and the total for the cost of goods sold for the year.

✓ The two owners, Brian and Jordan, need to be trained to be "business-men" rather than two guys who know how to install a lift kit on a pickup truck running a business.

The eleven issues listed above had to be solved during the turnaround, but they were not part of the "turnaround plan." If I resolved these business issues, the chances are that those and other problems would occur again and again. The turnaround plan is a list of tasks that need to be accomplished that solve the issues that caused the problems I noted. Solving these eleven items I had learned about the company from the phone call would be easy. But the secret to managing a successful turnaround is to dig into these problems to determine why they occurred in the first place. The "why" is the most important part of the turnaround. The turnaround plan goal is to solve the issues that caused the problems that have not been resolved by the existing management team. The turnaround plan mostly has to do with determining the quality of the management team and then fixing their weaknesses. My goal is always to have managers in place who can recognize potential problems and solve them before the issue becomes problematic. Turnarounds all have to do with the management team—not the issues that are caused due to weak management.

Chapter 2

THE FIRST DAY
ON THE JOB

*"My experience has shown me that the people who are
exceptionally good in business aren't so because of what
they know but because of their insatiable need to know more."*

—MICHAEL GERBER, AMERICAN AUTHOR AND FOUNDER
OF A BUSINESS SKILLS TRAINING COMPANY

THE FLIGHT FROM FORT LAUDERDALE TO SALT LAKE CITY
International Airport took off Sunday at 6:45 AM and arrived at 9:50
AM. The trip was five hours in the air, but we gained two hours
flying east to west. Unfortunately, the only direct flight to Utah was
at 6:45 AM. For that early of a morning flight, I had to be at the
airport at 5:30 AM. That meant that I was up out of bed, showered
by 4:00 AM, and out the door at 4:45 AM. There were many other
connecting flights to Salt Lake City from Fort Lauderdale, but only
with connections. Most of the flights were at least seven and a half
hours long. I am six-foot-three, so sitting in an airplane seat for
almost eight hours does not work well for me.

I decided to travel to the client's location on Sunday for my first
visit so I could get the lay of the land. My goal was to be on the job
Monday at 8:00 AM to start the turnaround. I knew that this trip
was going to make it a very long day for me. I do not handle time
changes very well when I am traveling. It takes me a few days to
recover from the change in time zone. There's a two-hour difference

between Utah and Florida. I decided that this trip would only be for three days (onsite from Monday to Wednesday) because I was not sure what I would find when I visited my new client.

Scott had texted me the day before and told me to send him a text message once the plane landed, and I had gotten my luggage. As soon as I saw my suitcase on the baggage carousel, I sent a text to Scott and told him I was ready to be picked up. I went outside to the passenger pick-up area #7. The cold weather hit me in the face like a sledgehammer. It was 15 degrees with strong winds of at least 20 mph, and snow piled up everywhere. I could not believe how cold it was, and the wind made it feel like it was 30 degrees colder than the actual temperature.

* * *

Sure enough, Scott was there waiting for me in his pickup truck, which was jacked up at least six inches. When he saw me, he jumped out of the pickup, grabbed my suitcase, and put it in the backseat. Scott was wearing only a flannel shirt and jeans. I could not believe that was all he was wearing with the temperature being that cold. I opened the passenger door and jumped into the front seat. He got back into the truck and reached over to shake my hand and said, "Welcome to Utah!"

"Where is your coat?" I asked.

He pointed in the backseat and said that he only wears it when it is cold outside. I guess because I was coming from Fort Lauderdale to Salt Lake City in January, I was cold because there was a 60-degree change in temperature between the two cities. The considerable difference in temperature made it feel much colder to me. The other reason was—it was cold, freezing cold outside, period.

Scott was probably fifty years old. He had red hair, but since I am colorblind, the red hair was just a guess. Scott was about five-foot-nine and weighed maybe 240 pounds, with much of the weight at his waistline. When he was sitting in the driver's seat of his pickup, his belly was about an inch away from touching the steering wheel.

Scott had a smile on his face most of the time as he talked. Scott smiled a lot because he talked a lot. He pointed at the coffee cup in the drink holder in the center console and said, "Bob, that is your hot venti non-fat vanilla latte from Starbucks."

I was pleasantly surprised. "Thank you, Scott, you did not have to go out of your way for me!"

"Yes, I did, sir. I want you to be very comfortable while you are in Utah. That way, you will do the turnaround of ABC Off-Road Supply for Brian and Jordan. Getting you a cup of coffee is no big deal. I am glad to do it for you."

"Well, thank you, Scott, it is appreciated." I picked up the cup and took a big sip of the hot latte. It tasted great and warmed up my hands. The hot latte was, indeed, just what I needed. "Thank you again for picking me up. I feel safe in this big ole jacked-up pickup truck with these huge wheels."

Scott laughed. "I needed this truck this morning to get out of my driveway. Yesterday, it snowed twenty inches, and I did not have the time to shovel the snow off my driveway to clear a path to the street. But with this lifted pickup truck and the wide wheels, I can pretty much go anywhere in the snow." I sipped my latte as Scott continued to talk. "I am thrilled you traveled on Sunday because it will give us time to talk. I can give you the background of the company and many of the employees."

I thought that he had already done that on the phone call last Wednesday, but apparently, he had a lot more to say.

"First, let me tell you about Brian. He is a very nice guy but gets stressed and frustrated all the time. His frustration shuts him down, plus it also shuts the whole sales team down when Brian is in one of his moods. He knows off-road industry products exceptionally well, but Brian does not know how to manage people. This guy is an excellent salesman but terrible at managing employees. I am hopeful that he will learn how to be an outstanding professional manager with you at the company. He needs to grow in this area, or the company is never going to be successful like he wants it to be."

By this time, Scott was on a six-lane highway going north toward Ogden, according to the street sign. Cars were flying by us, which was a little scary because the freeway still had some snow on the concrete.

Scott continued, "Then, there is Jordan, the other owner. Jordan is just the opposite of Brian. He is very even-tempered and never gets upset about anything. Brian is fortunate to have Jordan as a partner because when Brian gets all worked up, Jordan can settle him down quickly. Jordan is a very bright guy, and so is Brian. They both have very high IQs. Their problem is that they do not know how to run a business. Every decision they make is trial and error! I think we are seeing too many errors that are causing the company to bleed cash. Every week is a challenge to have enough money to make the payroll. You can always tell Brian's high-stress level on Tuesday, Wednesday, and Thursday. It's because he needs to pull some miracles out of his hat to have enough funds to make payroll."

I voiced what I already knew: "It sounds like you have two off-road supply guys managing the business, rather than a couple of businessmen running an off-road supply company."

Scott agreed wholeheartedly.

Unfortunately, many of my turnaround clients fall into the same category as Brian and Jordan. They knew the technical side of the business, like installing a lift kit on a Jeep Gladiator, but neither of them knew the business side of how to manage a $6.3 million off-road supply company. This turnaround would have to include teaching the owners how to run a multimillion-dollar business that needed to grow to be profitable. This task was not going to be easy!

Scott continued his sermon about ABC Off-Road Supply: "Wes is the current service manager. He has been in that position for about three months. There was a different service manager before Wes that

Brian and Jordan fired before they rehired Wes. Wes worked for the company a few years ago, also in the service manager's position. Unfortunately, Wes's problem was that he could not keep up with the work required to manage twelve service bays. Wes saw the hand-writing on the wall that he was probably going to get fired soon, so he gave notice and left."

I remained silent, taking all this in, and finished the last sips of my latte.

"When they fired the old service manager," Scott went on, "Brian called Wes to offer the service manager job back. Wes said that he would accept his old service manager job since he was currently unemployed. Wes told Brian that he would work again for ABC Off-Road Supply for one year, and then he was going to retire."

This decision to temporarily bring back a weak manager (Wes, for a maximum of one year) to fill the service manager position should not have been an option for ABC Off-Road Supply. As mentioned in the introduction to this book:

Is the company recruiting top-tier management and employees who have the skills and ability to advance the quality of the management team and their staff? The answer to this question was a resounding "No!" The owners' decision to do so caused the company to be weaker.

Are the managers willing to leave a vacancy open for months until they find an outstanding candidate, if necessary? The answer to this question was also a resounding "No!"

I kept my thoughts to myself and let Scott go on without interruption.

"I am guessing that Wes is probably sixty-three or sixty-four years old, and it seems to me that he has already retired. Unfortunately, he still shows up at work every day and collects a big salary.

He is unquestionably not the answer to the service manager position for this company. If I owned the company, I would immediately start searching for Wes's replacement."

That sounded like a very wise plan, indeed, but again, I said nothing.

"Carole is the bookkeeper. She's almost seventy years old, and she also needs to move on. Carole has only one speed: very, very slow. She likes Brian and Jordan but gets frustrated about everything because there is such a total lack of organization at ABC. Brian's stress about not having enough funds to make the weekly payroll downloads on her and causes her anxiety. Like the sales team, when Brian gets stressed, so does Carole."

So far, Scott had described two managers (Wes and Carole) at the company and stated that he would terminate them both and hire replacements. That made it "zero for two" on the management team so far.

"Next is the sales manager, Kurt. Kurt has been with the company for about twelve years. He started in the shop and then eventually moved over to the sales department. Kurt became the sales manager because Brian is such a poor manager, especially with the sales team. In my opinion, Kurt is also a weak sales manager, but he is better than Brian. Kurt is very even-tempered. He does not get excited about anything. He does not sell, but he has good off-road product knowledge from working in the shop. Kurt is a big guy, six-foot-three, and weighs over 300 pounds. Everyone likes him. Yeah, he is a nice guy, but he's not motivated at all.

Scott's description of Kurt as a sales manager was not good. Kurt sounded more like "sales support" for the sales team than a sales manager. I had a strong feeling that, for this company to turnaround, sales were going to have to grow. If Scott's description of Kurt was even close to accurate, Kurt was not going to be the sales manager for ABC Off-Road Supply for much longer.

"He is married with two young kids. His wife is a nursing supervisor and makes an excellent living, especially for the Ogden area. The cost of living in Salt Lake City or the Ogden area is not that expensive. I believe that if Kurt had it his way, he would quit his job, stay at home, and be "Mr. Mom" for his family. When Kurt takes a week off work for vacation, I don't think anyone on the sales team even notices that he is gone."

* * *

This situation was all starting to make sense now, which explained why the company is losing money. Over the twenty-plus years, I have been doing turnarounds, and the universal problems are the same for every one of my clients. It does not matter the type of business (service, manufacturing, healthcare, distribution, retail, wholesale, education, etc.), the product, or even the location of the organization. The only thing that matters that makes a company successful (or unsuccessful) is the quality of the management team. If the company has a pedestrian management team, the business loses money, apparently just like ABC Off-Road Supply was doing. If a company has a quality management team running the business, the enterprise will be successful and profitable. There is nothing more essential to make a business a success than the quality of the company's managers.

So far, Scott had described the service manager, bookkeeper, and sales manager, who were all "D-quality" managers, at best. I wished that I had a tablet and pen to take notes, but that was not necessary. The information Scott was sharing with me was pretty much unforgettable. Also, I was not sure how good Scott was at assessing the company's talent. My usual turnaround plan starts by interviewing every manager. My goal is always to get a feel for the quality of the management team. Scott's opinions were not going to influence my thoughts or feelings about these people who I would soon be interviewing. But if they were as bad as he described them, the interview process would not last very long.

Unfortunately, one of the major speed bumps in starting my consulting engagement with ABC Off-Road Supply was not having access to current monthly financial statements. Typically, if the company's financials are up to date and accurate, I can diagnose the company's problems in a matter of minutes. Once I review the statements, I then go attack the "low-hanging fruit" problem areas first. Not having financial statements would delay my progress for this turnaround. I hate speed bumps that slow me down!

I started thinking about what my plan of attack ("turnaround plan") was going to be with this client, while Scott continued to talk away. But I was so deep in thought that I was no longer hearing him, but that did not seem to bother him. I imagined him thinking, *Hmm, is Bob listening to me? Obviously not, but that's okay. Eventually, he will refocus and start listening again.* What seemed important to Scott was that he had a great chance to talk in the privacy of his pickup truck with the turnaround consultant who was going to fix ABC Off-Road Supply's business problems. Also noteworthy to him was that he would be part of the team to accomplish that goal.

Scott made some turns off the major highway, and suddenly, we were pulling into the ABC facility. He pulled his truck up next to a little Lexus sitting in front of one of the big garage doors. The car had about ten inches of snow piled up on it, so it was hard to determine the make or model of the vehicle. Scott put his truck in park, reached in the backseat, and grabbed an ice scraper to clean the snow and ice off the Lexus. After he grabbed it, I thought that he was going to get out and clean off the car, but I was wrong.

Scott continued to talk for another thirty minutes. He focused on all the problems the company was experiencing, according to him. Honestly, I heard about ten minutes of his comments and zoned out for the other twenty minutes. Finally, he opened his door, got out, and cleaned off the car. I got out, retrieved my suitcase from the backseat, and stood there in the cold, watching Scott finish cleaning off the car in his flannel shirt. I was so cold in my beautiful new Tommy Bahama parka that I wanted to climb back into the front seat of the pickup, but I didn't. I decided that if Scott could clean the snow off the car in his flannel shirt, I could stand there in my new parka to wait for him to finish.

Once the Lexus was clean, he handed me the keys and pointed north. Scott then gave me directions to my hotel. He stood there talking like it was 75 degrees out. I was shaking like I was stark naked. Scott could make a short story long and a long one even longer. We shook hands, and then he gave me a little "man hug."

Finally, I got into the front seat of the car after putting my suitcase in the backseat. Scott jumped into his pickup and sped off south on Main Street in Ogden. I turned on the heater to blast hot air. All I could think of was that Scott had to be very cold with no coat, but he didn't show it. I found the hotel, checked in, and spent the balance of the day making notes from our conversation—er, I mean, from Scott's monologue.

* * *

The next morning, I got up early and had an excellent breakfast at the hotel. Unfortunately, I had a terrible night's sleep because of the two-hour time change from Eastern Standard Time to Mountain Time. I had on a T-shirt, a dress shirt, a bulky sweater, and wool slacks. My goal was not to be cold while I was at the client's facility. I knew that I was going to have to spend time in the shop and warehouse, and I was sure that those locations were going to be semi-cold at best! Knowing that I did not sleep well, I drained two cups of coffee during breakfast and brought another to-go cup of coffee with me.

Scott told me that the doors of the company opened to the public at 9:00 AM, but many of the shop technicians would arrive between 7:30 and 8:00 AM. I decided that 8:15 AM was going to be my ETA (expected time of arrival) for my first visit to ABC Off-Road Supply.

When I arrived at the ABC facility, I was the first car in the parking lot. I decided to leave the car running with the heater on while I checked the door to the shop to see if it was open. Sure enough, the door was locked. I got back into my warm car and sipped my hot coffee. Thirty minutes later, two guys dressed like auto mechanics parked their jacked-up pickup trucks and entered the garage area of the building.

The company's facility was an old Dodge dealership that had closed for some time before Brian leased it to open ABC Off-Road Supply. In the parking lot were huge piles of snow stacked up high. Someone had plowed the lot early that morning to make room for customers and employees to park their vehicles. In the front of the former dealership, there was an old Dodge sign still on the building. High on a pole was an "ABC Off-Road Supply" sign, 15 or 20 feet higher than the Dodge sign.

After the two techs entered the shop, I decided to wait until Brian, Jordan, or Scott arrived before I went into the old dealership facility. At 8:45, sure enough, Scott's pickup truck pulled into the parking lot next to my parked Lexus. I got out and grabbed my backpack, which had my laptop computer inside. This time, Scott had on a big, thick turtleneck sweater and a pair of jeans. He carried a winter coat with him under his arm just in case it got cold in Utah that day. After we shook hands and he welcomed me to ABC Off-Road Supply, we entered the garage area door to this old dealership.

As we walked further in the building, I scanned the shop area, which looked like a dump. My first impression was terrible. I thought that if I had a truck or jeep, I would not bring it to ABC Off-Road Supply. I learned later that day that the shop was the cleanest area of the facility.

When I walked into the shop that first day, the place looked like an unmanaged mess. There were empty cardboard boxes, dirt, and tools everywhere with pools of oil on the bay floors. This area screamed to me that the service manager and every tech who worked there were not doing their jobs.

When a business looks like this, I believe lazy employees and poor management are the cause of the problem. There was not one good reason the shop should look that bad. What made the problem worse was that when a shop gets to this terrible point, it will only get worse. That's because everyone at this company believed that it was okay not to keep his bay area clean. The reason all the techs were letting their bay areas look like dumps was because the service manager was doing nothing to solve the problem. In essence, management had confirmed that the condition of the shop was not a problem because they had done nothing to have it cleaned up.

Scott walked me to an office off the front showroom of the facility. He told me that this was where I would be setting up shop to turn this business around to be profitable. Scott was proud of the job he did cleaning up the office for me, the new turnaround consultant. He had gone to the Staples and bought a desktop printer, a coffee maker, and all the office supplies he thought I would need.

When he showed me the office, he had one of those, "Scott smiles." I thanked him for being so considerate to set up the office with a professional touch. After I put my backpack on the desk, he asked me if I would like the "fifty-cent tour" of the facility. In my short trip from the shop to this office, I had a horrible feeling that no one on earth could turn this company around. But I knew I had to be positive, so I told Scott that I would love a tour of the facility.

* * *

My office was down a short hallway off the front showroom. There were four other small offices on the left and right side of the corridor, each filled with junk. If I translate the term "junk," it is old, used parts that were taken off customers' vehicles. Later, I learned that Brian and Jordan did not like to get rid of these old, used parts because the company had sold used parts in the past. Brian did not want to throw anything away if he could sell or use it in the future on a customer's vehicle. The unfortunate thing is, if they find an actual need for the used parts, they have no idea where to find it in the warehouse. Neither the new nor the used parts were in the accounting software.

The weak management team, as described by Scott, was a significant problem with ABC Off-Road Supply's profitability. After the weak management team, the next most significant challenge was the company's inventory. The only way they could find where a part was in the warehouse that they needed for a customer's vehicle was an inventory clerk's memory. This issue created a considerable profit leakage because they were continually searching for a specific part. Many times, they couldn't find the part. Therefore, to resolve that problem, they would just purchase a new one. This delay caused inefficient labor hours searching for parts plus an additional delay for finishing the customer's vehicle. The postponement was because the tech had to wait to receive the newly purchased off-road part.

As we passed by the four offices, Scott said, "Don't pay any attention to these offices; we are cleaning them soon."

That comment reminded me of the scene in the movie *The Wizard of Oz*. The "wizard" told Dorothy, the Tinman, the Scarecrow, and the Lion, "Don't pay any attention to the guy behind the curtain!" Scott did not want me to pay attention to the mess in those offices or anywhere else in the company.

We walked out to the front showroom, which was large enough to display at least four or five off-road vehicles. The showroom had floor-to-ceiling glass windows on the roadside of the big room. This showroom was a perfect place to show off-road vehicles to ABC's customers. There were hundreds of cars driving past the dealership daily for potential customers to see these vehicles. The problem was, there were *no* cars on display—only an overabundance of big rubber tires and fancy wheels.

I told Scott to wait for a minute; I wanted to get a notebook out of my backpack to take some notes during our tour. After retrieving a tablet and pen, I made notes about the dirty offices down the hallway from my office. Then, next, I noted that the front showroom was dirty, and the windows were filthy to the point that it was hard to see through them. I wrote down that the showroom should be displaying off-road vehicles, not tires and wheels. On the far north end of the showroom, there as a little cutout area that had an old jeep parked in it. It looked to be forty or fifty years old and had army decals on the hood of the vehicle. I wrote a short note that the jeep did not belong in the showroom. I was not sure how that jeep fit in on the front showroom of this off-road supply company. ABC Off-Road Supply was not in the business of selling old vehicles that need a ton of work done before it would be roadworthy.

This front showroom was a valuable part of the business. Management was doing *nothing* to make it a useful marketing area for the company. They treated the showroom more like a tire and wheel warehouse rather than an expensive piece of real estate to market to more customers. Then having an old jeep in the front showroom made no sense at all. The jeep had no sales or marketing value for ABC.

We walked out of the front showroom to the main retail area of the company. In this area, the sales team (five salesmen and a sales manager) would welcome and serve the customers. This area had three rows of shelving with off-road products for sale. There were also two more rows of tires and wheels. The one thing that I noticed when entering this room was the incredible amount of cardboard, brown cardboard. On the retail shelving, about 30 to 40 percent of the products were still in cardboard boxes, which looked terrible. Many of the products did not have a price tag. Much of the inventory was covered in a layer of dust. My initial thought was that these poorly displayed products were not selling because of the dusty shelves and cardboard boxes.

The main retail space was just one more neglected area of the company. The retail showroom looked dirty and mismanaged. There was a sales manager and five salespeople in the room for more than eight hours a day. They walked past the dusty and unpriced products daily and did not see the poor condition of the showroom like I did in the first five seconds of my visit. The poor condition of the showroom proved the fact that employees only do what managers demand of them. I noted on my tablet a solution for getting the retail showroom cleaned up very soon.

* * *

By now, the five salespeople and the manager were standing in their places behind the sales counter. Scott led me behind the counter to introduce me to each of the salespeople and Kurt, the manager. He first introduced me to Kurt and asked him to introduce me to the rest of his team.

Scott told Kurt that my name was Bob Curry and that I was the new "acting CEO" of the company. When Scott announced that my title was "acting CEO," I gave him a surprised look. I am sure that Kurt also noticed my surprise.

Kurt and I shook hands, and he welcomed me to ABC Off-Road Supply. Next, he introduced me to Michael.

Michael was probably in his early forties with dark hair, clean-shaven, glasses, and a little on the heavy side. He had been with ABC for less than a year and had a "salesman-type" personality. It was easy for Michael to talk to the customers. He did have good "off-road" product knowledge per Kurt. Michael was there to make money, and that was his focus. This salesman had a wife and three small children at home, so he needed to make money to support his family.

Michael had a professional background in photography and excellent experience with social media, which I learned later. When I was introduced to Michael, he was very polite and asked me the first question: "Where are you from, Bob?" When I told him that I lived in Fort Lauderdale, he shook his head like he was shocked that someone from South Florida would travel to Utah to get involved with an "off-road supply" business such as ABC Off-Road Supply. Michael then told me that he had read both of my books and indicated that he was impressed with my stories. He asked if both stories in the books were about real companies.

"Michael," I replied, "I graduated college with an accounting degree, passed the CPA exam two years later. I also went to graduate school and received a master's degree in taxation. Do you think that an *accountant type* like me could make up those stories?"

"Hmm . . . good point, I guess that makes sense. So, I take it that both books are true stories about your turnarounds?"

"Yes sir, every word in the books was 100 percent true from the first word to the last."

Michael said, "Well, sir, I am impressed!"

Scott just stood next to me and smiled.

Kurt moved down the sales counter and then introduced me to Warren. Warren was not his real first name—it was Kurt, Kurt Warren. No one in the company called him Kurt because the sales manager's name was Kurt. They must have all believed that there was room for only one "Kurt" on the sales team. Therefore, Kurt got labeled "Warren."

Warren was about five-foot-six and bald. He was probably the friendliest person I had ever met. He was easy to talk to and sincere as the day is long. Warren had a six-inch beard hanging down from his chin. Just about 100 percent of the time when he spoke, his right hand was stroking his beard. The beard was gray and, in my opinion, made him look ten years older than his age.

Warren, "not Kurt," welcomed me to ABC Off-Road Supply. He asked me how long I expect to be visiting the company. I told him that my first goal was to get through today. He laughed and said that I was a funny guy. He added that he and I would get along well while I was working at ABC, and I believed him. I could not imagine Warren not getting along with anyone because of his sincere, friendly personality.

"Bob," he suddenly said, "you have been staring at my beard. Do you like it?"

"Unfortunately, I don't!" I replied. "I think that it makes you old and homeless."

"Mr. Curry, we just met, and you are telling me that I look homeless?" he asked, somewhat incredulous.

"No, Warren, what I said is that the beard makes you look much older than your age and homeless, not just homeless."

"Are you hinting that you want me to cut my beard?" He was still stroking his beard.

"I would suggest that you cut it off unless you are comfortable with looking older and homeless to your customers," I replied.

"Bob, are you serious? I cannot tell if you are kidding around or serious."

"I can understand that since we have just met. Therefore, I will be candid with you. I am honestly suggesting that every one of the salesmen who work for ABC Off-Road Supply look well-groomed, polished, and professional."

"Mr. Curry, are you saying that I am not polished or look professional?"

"Warren, please take a selfie of yourself today. Then, tomorrow morning, shave the beard off. Once you shave, take another selfie. You will see the difference, and you will be able to see what your customers see when they walk up to the sales counter."

"Okay, Mr. Curry, I will shave my beard before I come to work tomorrow morning."

"Deal, my friend, and thank you," I said, delighted.

"I am doing it exclusively for you because my wife likes the beard," he added.

When I first met the sales team, I was surprised by how poorly they dressed and their overall grooming. I believe that salespeople should always look professional. I have been in car dealerships and met with salespeople, service people, and technicians who worked on the vehicles. These ABC Off-Road Supply salespeople were dressed and groomed two levels below any of the people I had met at other dealerships.

Warren, like the other four salesmen, all looked like they really did not care about their appearance to the customers. Every one of the salesmen who work for ABC Off-Road Supply needed to look well-groomed, polished, and professional—without exception.

"Warren, I can see that you are one of the good guys. It has been my pleasure meeting you!"

Warren gave me a big smile as Kurt, Scott, and I moved down the sales counter to meet the next salesperson.

There was no sales training for the sales staff at ABC Off-Road Supply. There was an excellent opportunity to enhance the sales team's sales performance if they were all professionally trained on how to groom, dress, greet a customer, answer the phone, close a sales order with a customer, and so on.

Kurt next introduced me to Jason. He was probably in his early forties. Jason had a receding hairline and kept his blond hair short.

He was trying to grow a beard. He did not have an outgoing, friendly personality like Warren. Jason seemed to be uncomfortable meeting and introducing himself to customers, including me. He was 180-degrees opposite of Warren, the guy standing next to him five days a week at work. One would think that some of Warren's friendliness would have rubbed off on Jason. One would be wrong. Jason had been with the company for less than a year and was probably the second weakest salesperson of the group.

Standing next to Jason was Joshua, the top salesperson of the five. Joshua had been with the company for over twelve years and was an excellent salesperson. Joshua averaged almost $100,000 in sales each month, while the rest of the sales team averaged roughly half that total. Joshua's motivation, like some of the other salesmen, was to make a lot of money. Joshua had figured out how to sell off-road products to customers and make a big commission check at the end of each month. Joshua's one weakness, even though he is the top salesperson, was that he would get grumpy at times. He needed Brian's and Jordan's attention every so often to get him out of his cranky slump.

After meeting Warren and Joshua, I thought again about Jason. Jason was between the top-selling salesperson and the friendliest (Warren), and unfortunately, he picked up zero of their qualities.

Then there was Taylor, the fifth salesperson of the group. His physical sales position was on the back counter next to Brian. Brian hired Taylor a couple of months earlier to sell tires and wheels to customers. He had worked for a local tire store and was their top salesperson. Unfortunately, Taylor's sales skills did not travel with him from his old company to ABC. His monthly sales total was not even covering his salary. He seemed to be a little bit like a square peg in a round hole at ABC Off-Road Supply. He was more of an "order-taker." The four guys on the front counter got the first shot at the customers walking through the front door. Because Taylor did not have a robust sales-type personality, he was okay with taking the next customer in the door when the other four salesmen were busy with customers or on the phone.

After I chatted a little with Taylor, he said, "Bob, I enjoyed your first book, and I am halfway through your second book."

I said, "Thank you, Taylor, for reading my books. I appreciate it!"

Scott spoke up and said, "Bob, the company purchased copies of both of your books and made all the managers and salespeople read them. Brian, Jordan, and I all thought that it would be valuable for each sales associate on the team to read your books. Most of these people know nothing about managing a business or growing sales. Your two books have great business and sales management stories that all have valuable lessons to learn. Brian told all the salespeople that they would not get their next commission check until they all completed reading your books."

"Scott, where is Brian? I need to thank him for buying and distributing my books to his employees."

"He is in the Dominican Republic right now on vacation. He will be returning to work tomorrow."

I thanked Kurt for introducing me to his team and shook each salesperson's hand. I told them that I was looking forward to getting together with them one on one soon to learn more about sales at ABC.

* * *

Next, Scott led me into the shop and introduced me to Wes, the service manager. Wes was about five-foot-six and had a very thick mustache that almost covered his whole mouth.

Wes looked up at me and said, "Welcome to ABC Off-Road Supply, Mr. Curry."

I answered, "Thank you, Wes, and please call me Bob. Mr. Curry was my father."

He smiled. "Okay, Bob, will do! How can I help you?"

"Wes," I said, "I would like you to introduce me to your techs working in the shop if you don't mind."

"Sure, no problem, follow me."

Scott, Wes, and I walked to the first bay on the left side of the shop. There were eight bays in this area; only six of the lifts were in the air with vehicles. Wes walked up to the technician (Joshua) in the first bay and waved for him to come over to meet me.

Unlike the sales department not allowing two "Kurts" in the sales area, it was okay to have two "Joshuas" in the company since one was a salesperson, and the other was a tech. Joshua put down his tools and grabbed a clean rag to wipe off his hands.

Wes said, "Bob, this is Joshua, one of our best techs. Joshua, this is Bob Curry, the guy who wrote the two books you recently read. . . . You *did* read them, didn't you?"

With a wide smile, Joshua quipped, "Do you think I would say no in front of you and the author? Yes, sir, I read both of your books." He reached out his right hand to shake my hand and said, "Where are you steel-tipped shoes? If you are going to be in the shop, you need to wear proper attire."

Joshua was in his mid-thirties, bald, and about five-foot-nine. I got the initial impression that he was a cocky guy but knew what he was doing under a car with a wrench in his hand.

"By the way," he said to Wes, "I am not one of the best techs in this shop, I am *the* best tech at ABC Off-Road Supply." Then to me, he added, "Mr. Curry, I enjoyed *listening* to your books. I purchased the audio versions of both. I listened to them on my way to and from work each day in my truck."

I was going to ask him what he thought of the books, but I figured the question would generate a sarcastic answer, so I did not ask. Instead, I said, "Joshua, this is my first day on the job with this company. I was not sure if I needed steel-toed shoes, but I will have them in the future if I return to ABC Off-Road Supply after this visit."

"How long are you in town on this visit?" he asked.

"I am here until Wednesday, sir," I told him.

"Mr. Curry, you haven't accepted the turnaround engagement yet?" he asked me but looked at Wes and Scott.

"I don't have an answer to your question yet," I said, recapturing his gaze. "But when I do, I will let you know."

"Just so you know," he said a little sheepishly, "I was just kidding about the steel-toed shoes. I hope you did not take offense." He paused for a second, and then asked what seemed to be a burning question, "Are you going to write another book with ABC Off-Road Supply as the topic of the turnaround? If you do, are you going to put me in the book? You know, Joshua, the tech with the best skills at ABC Off-Road Supply?"

"Joshua, I am not thin-skinned," I assured him. "And in this case, you were right. I should have thought through this engagement better and packed the proper shoes to walk this shop."

With that, I shook his hand and thanked him for his time. I intentionally did not answer his question about writing a book about ABC. I looked at Scott, who had a distressed look on his face.

Scott said, "Bob, if you don't mind, let me show you the rest of the facilities, and I will introduce you to the rest of the techs later."

"Scott, you are in charge of this tour this morning, I am fine with your decision."

I knew that his stress was from my comment that I had not made my decision about taking on this job yet. I thanked Wes for his time and followed Scott to wherever he was about to take me.

* * *

At the south end of the shop, there was a stairway to the second floor. Scott asked me if I wanted to go up to the second-floor storage area for used parts.

"Sure, Scott, let's see everything; don't leave any rock unturned."

Once we got up the top of the stairs, Scott pushed the door open and walked in. I walked in behind him and started shaking my head. I could not believe what I saw. There was warehouse racking in the big room with a plethora of old parts on the shelves. None of the inventory was tagged or organized.

"Scott, is the inventory on the computer?"

Scott hesitated and finally answered, "Bob, none of the inventory stock that you are going to see today is on the computer. We have pretty much made the decision that we are going to purchase software in the next two weeks to enter all the on-hand balances of both new and used inventory into the computer. The software is called 'BCD Inventory Software.' We have reviewed the programs, checked their references, and I believe that it is the best software out there for these types of products."

"Scott, who is going to do the implementation? Also, is this software compatible with QuickBooks?"

"Hmm, good question, Bob. I will have to check on that."

"And Scott, who is going to do the implementation and the training of the employees for the inventory software?" Before he answered the question, I had a vision that this was going to be a complete disaster.

"Well, Bob, now that you are here, you would be the project manager to install the software and train the staff on how to use it."

"I know nothing about this inventory program. Why would you think that *I* would handle the project?"

Scott just looked at me with a perplexed expression. The stress I was feeling about ABC Off-Road Supply had just doubled. This place was totally out of control. I started thinking that my trip to Utah had been a total waste of time and money. I knew that this place was awful, but I had no idea it was in such a terrible, terrible condition.

"Okay, my friend, where are you going to take me next?" I asked.

He told me we would be going first to warehouse 1 and then to warehouse 2.

"Lead the way," I said.

Halfway down the steps, Scott stopped and asked, "Bob, you *are* going to accept this turnaround engagement, right?"

"Let's check out the warehouses, and then we can talk about the future."

"Okay, Bob," he said with a sigh, "but I must tell you, you are stressing me out!"

At the bottom of the steps, Scott turned right and went into the warehouse 1 as I followed. The first thing I noticed was that there were no security cameras or a fence to secure the inventory. There was nothing that would stop the employees from stealing the company's expensive parts inventory. Since the company had not maintained inventory balances on the computer, the owners had no idea if employees were taking (stealing) the stock and how much.

My guess was, YES, YOUR EMPLOYEES ARE STEALING THE COMPANY'S INVENTORY!

It does not get any worse than this. It was like management was saying, "Do you need some of our inventory? Please take some because we don't care." There were zero security and internal controls to protect the company's $750,000 of inventory assets. Inventory shrink caused by poor internal controls is a very costly hidden expense.

Imagine if you walked into a local bank and right in the middle of the lobby was a stack of $750,000 in cash. (The high end of the estimated inventory in the ABC Off-Road Supply's warehouses as stated by Jordan on our initial phone call.) Imagine further that the bank lobby had no security cameras, no guards in the building, and nothing to protect the cash (like a safe) from theft. Also, imagine that the bank did not know how much money was in the stack of cash. That is very similar to how ABC Off-Road Supply was protecting its inventory.

It is true that almost every tech and salesperson who worked at ABC had an off-road vehicle at home or drove one to work daily. I was not accusing any employees of stealing from the company. My point was only that there was a good opportunity for employees to take the vehicle parts off the warehouse racks, and no one would ever know that the inventory was missing. All they needed to do is grab the parts from either warehouse. ABC's inventory situation was similar to the bank with all the money in the middle of the lobby unprotected. Employees steal from their employers because they can.

Scott introduced me to Ron, the employee responsible for the inventory. I shook his hand and introduced myself. Ron said that he was glad that I came to ABC Off-Road Supply because, according to him, "WE NEED YOUR HELP!"

Ron was in his late twenties but looked younger. He had a trimmed mustache and beard, but it did not look good on him. I believe he grew the beard to try to look older. Unfortunately, his attempt was not working. He was very light-complexioned. His skin color made him look sort of "baby-faced." Ron was the type who looked like he was always in a hurry. He had been with the company for a year.

Jordan had hired Ron as an inventory clerk. Ron took the responsibility of managing the inventory department even without receiving a formal promotion. Neither Brian nor Jordan realized Ron's value. I liked Ron. He had a great passion for his job. I would treat him as a valuable employee if this young man worked for a company I managed. I believed he had potential and would grow with the company. Ron was hungry to learn more and professionally mature in his position. He wasn't what I would call "young and dumb," but he needed to grow professionally.

Since Ron had joined the company, he had gotten married and bought a home. His motivation was to work hard and develop into a management position with the company. His goal was also, most importantly, to make more money to support his family and new home. I believed if Ron had a mentor, he would develop into a trustworthy inventory manager for this company.

It was one of Brian's and Jordan's weaknesses. They did not recognize the value of how Ron could grow into a valuable manager and be there for many years to run his department. As I said earlier, the company's inventory was the second most significant problem in the company, with the management team ranking first.

In contrast, Brian and Jordan had hired Scott and had no idea what value he was going to bring to the company. Scott was like a third "Brian or Jordan" with no idea of how to manage this company into profitability.

I asked Ron about what he did for ABC. First, he introduced me to the other two workers in the department. Both workers were part-time college kids. They were responsible for receiving the products and placing them in the warehouse racks in the proper location. Then later, they would pick, pack, and ship the inventory for ABC internet orders. They would also pick the parts for the work on the vehicles in the shop.

Ron said that they had a tough time keeping up with the customer orders. As we were talking, Ron and I walked around the warehouse so I could ask questions to get a feel for what was going on. I needed to know if the warehouse function of the company was under control or if it required my attention. Quickly, I figured out the answer to my question: it needed my immediate attention.

I asked Ron about the warehouse racking that had all kinds of miscellaneous products on the shelves with paperwork taped to the parts.

Ron put his head down like he was ashamed to answer my question. He said, "That is where we store all the inventory from customer returns that are to be sent back to the vendors for a variety of reasons. Unfortunately, we have not had the time to keep current with returning these products."

"So, Ron, this is a big stack of money sitting here. By not returning this inventory, it hurts the company because it reduces our available credit with the vendors. The company is bumping into its credit lines, forcing us to pay for current purchases on a COD basis."

Ron said softly, "Yes, sir."

There was another warehouse rack that looked like the vendor returns area. I asked Ron, "Are these more vendor returns here?"

"No, sir, those products are customer pick-ups. When a customer comes in to purchase a product, and if we do not have the product in stock, the purchasing department buys the part to satisfy the customer's order. When the product comes in, and we receive it, we store it on these racks. Once we put the product in these racks, we notify the salesperson, and he is supposed to call the customer to let them know that we received the product. At that time, the customer should come in to pick up the product."

"Ron, that whole process should probably take five days, worst case, correct?"

"Yes, sir."

"Then, when the customer comes in, the salesperson comes back and gets the product from this rack, and gives the customer their products, is that right?"

"Yes, sir, that is exactly right."

When a company is not keeping current with sending back their customer returns to their vendors, they are exposing the company to "profit-erosion" problems. First, many vendors will not accept a return to vendor (RTV) for a product that was purchased more than 30 days before the return date. If a company does not keep up with its RTVs, that company will end up with inventory they may not be able to resell, causing inventory shrink. Second, if the company is not staying current with RTVs, then the company is not receiving credit for the vendor return. This problem may cause the company to be hitting their credit limit with that vendor. When your company is bumping up against its credit limit with vendors, the vendors put your business either on credit hold or COD terms. Credit hold and COD terms with vendors always damages the company's cash flow. The warehouse team must process RTVs weekly.

I looked at the inventory, and the sales orders taped to the product boxes. I reviewed about 10 sales orders and found the products were received dating back to seven months ago. I asked Ron, "Why are there sales orders for July of last year still here?"

"Bob, the problem is that our salespeople are too lazy to come back here. All they need to do to clean up this rack is to call the customer to tell them to come to pick up their products."

I gave Scott a look that said, *This is crazy*. He shook his head as if he could not believe what was going on here either. Having a lazy sales team is terrible. This sales team was dropping the ball and hurting the company's reputation with the customers. I stood there for a second to decide how I would handle this issue.

I looked at Ron and Scott, and said, "Stay here, I will be right back."

I walked back to the sales floor and got Kurt, the sales manager. I asked him to follow me to the warehouse. I told him that I had a question for him to clear up an issue for me. Kurt knew something was up, and it probably was not going to be a good thing. Once we arrived back at the customer pick-up rack, I asked Kurt about the products stored on the shelves.

ABC's customers would come into ABC to purchase products for their vehicles. The salesman would write up the order, and the customers would pay for the products in full. If the product was not in their inventory, the salesman would deliver the sales order to the purchasing department. Purchasing would buy the product from the vendor. The vendor would then ship the product to ABC's warehouse. The warehouse staff would receive the inventory and put it on the "customer pick-up rack." This process typically took three to five days.

For the salespeople to leave the customers' orders on the warehouse shelves for longer than a week, let alone up to seven months, was crazy. This type of lack of performance by a sales staff is horrible. This problem should have impacted their monthly commission checks to pay for their laziness. It must have been embarrassing to call a customer to inform them that their order from seven months earlier was in the warehouse.

Brian's solution to this problem was not to give the salespeople their monthly commission check until they called every customer for each pick-up order and had a note of when the customer would pick up the part. Personally, if a salesman had a product on the customer pick-up rack from an order from seven months ago, I would have a hard time keeping that salesperson on the payroll!

"Bob, these are products ordered by our sales team for customers. Once the products are received, the salespeople are supposed to call the customer to pick up their products."

"Kurt, how can we have parts with sales orders dating back to July, over seven months old?"

"Bob, unfortunately, we have one of the laziest sales teams in Utah, maybe even in the whole United States."

"Hmm, Kurt, please remind me who is responsible for managing the salespeople."

"Mr. Curry, these shelves will be cleaned up within forty-eight hours."

"Great, Kurt, I wish I would have thought of that! While you are here, are there going to be other disasters I am going to find this week like these customer pick-ups?"

"Sir, I hate to say it, but yes."

"Okay, Kurt, let's you and me meet one on one tomorrow and talk. In the meantime, you keep a tablet with you all day today. Every time you think of something that I would classify as a *problem* at ABC Off-Road Supply, I want you to write it down so we can talk about it. My goal for you would be to have a bullet-point list of issues tomorrow for when we talk. Also, Kurt, I like managers who use my favorite phrase."

Kurt asked, "What phrase is that, Bob?"

"It's called: *I have a problem; I have a solution.* Do you understand what I am saying, sir?"

"Yes, sir, I understand."

"Great, Kurt, thank you for your time."

* * *

I made several notes on my tablet about the warehouse area and the staff. I told Ron that I planned to sit down one on one with him soon to discuss how we can improve the warehouse operations. Ron shook my hand and said that he looked forward to the opportunity.

I looked at Scott, and he said, "Okay, Bob, we are off to warehouse 2."

Kurt left the warehouse and returned to the sales area. He had looked a little intimidated while we were talking, but that was okay with me. Still, it was a bit surprising to see a six-foot-three, 300-plus-pound guy intimidated, but I guess that happens.

Before Scott and I walked to warehouse 2, three salespeople came back to the customer pick-up racks with tablets to record information from the sales orders. I guess Kurt must have figured out that these products on the shelves were an immediate problem that needed the salespeople's attention. I was pleased that Kurt had reacted so quickly. I thought that maybe there was hope for this company's turnaround.

The tour with Scott so far had been terrible, and it was about to go downhill even more. As we went through a hallway leading to warehouse 2, Scott stopped to tell me to get ready. "This is going to be bad."

I gave him a puzzled look and asked, "How could it get any worse than my last thirty minutes of the tour?"

Scott did not answer my question. He opened the swinging vinyl door, and we entered. Scott and I stepped into the 5,000-square-foot warehouse. Once we entered, we could not walk more than three steps in any direction.

Off to my right, there was a 1964 Ford Mustang up on the lift about six feet in the air. Scott said that Brian had purchased the Mustang over a year ago. His goal was to refurbish the car and give it to his girlfriend, Leslie. He liked the car because both the car and his girlfriend were born the same year. I stopped to think, *This is a beautiful gift for Leslie, but obviously, Brian does not have the time to work on the car and get this company profitable.*

Plus, it was not possible to get within twelve feet of the Mustang because of all the crap everywhere. The car looked in horrible condition. To get that Mustang in driving condition would be a significant project. Brian had a romantic dream about this car, but there were just not enough hours in the day for him to make this rehab project a priority.

There was old inventory and junk piled everywhere. Whoever

had moved this inventory into the warehouse just set down pallets of different products wherever they could fit it with the Bobcat forklift. Whoever was responsible for the ridiculously poor condition of this warehouse should have been fired immediately.

Scott started to crawl over pallets of product, attempting to get to the middle of the room. I was not sure why he was doing that because I had seen enough from my point of view. Nevertheless, I followed him. Once we were in the middle of the room, Scott started explaining what I was seeing. Then Jordan, who I had only spoken to on the phone, walked through the warehouse door. Scott waved to him to come over and join us. Jordan climbed over the pallets like a pro who had done this many times before. When he arrived next to us, Scott formerly introduced us, and we shook hands.

Jordan said, "Bob, welcome to Utah. I see that you found the worst area in the whole company."

"Jordan, I believe that Scott saved the best area until the end of the tour."

Jordan looked down and said softly, "There's that pallet of the leveling kits that I bought last week. I just had to send the vendor another 20,000-dollar order because the warehouse guys could not find this pallet."

I just shook my head. I never imagined a company could be this much out of control and stay in business for so long.

Jordan said, "Do you want to have lunch today? I have to go cancel that order with the vendor now since I found this pallet."

"Lunch would be great," I said agreeably. "I look forward to it and our chat."

Scott told me to follow him as we made our way out of the warehouse 2. First, I sat down on one of the pallets of products and made notes about what I had just seen. After I finished writing, I followed Scott into the area by Brian's office. We wound down a hallway to a set of steps leading to the second floor. At the top of the steps was a sizeable but unfinished conference room. Scott told me that Brian was in the process of finishing the room so that he could hold company meetings on the second floor. As Scott continued talking about

Brian's plans for the space, I zoned him out. My head was spinning from everything I had seen in the last thirty minutes. Finally, Scott stopped talking.

"Scott, this place is crazy!" I exclaimed. "I cannot believe that this company is still in business. This place is a *mess*! The inventory in this company is ridiculous. Those racks of customer pick-ups and vendor returns are out of control. The two showrooms look terrible. I bet the customers walk through the front door and have an awful impression of ABC Off-Road Supply. Not seeing financial statements for seven months is as bad as it gets. The shop, where the company makes most of its money, is a dump, probably hasn't been cleaned up in months."

Scott was quiet. For once, he did not know what to say.

"Scott, you don't need a turnaround guy, you need a magician to fix this business."

Scott remained quiet.

"I want to go spend some time in my office to put together my thoughts about this business before I have lunch with Jordan and meet Brian tomorrow morning."

"Is there anything I could do to help you?" Scott asked.

"Yes," I said without hesitation. "Do you have a big bottle of vodka?"

Scott broke into a laugh and said, "Yes, there is a bottle in Carole's office!"

I looked at him like he was kidding, but he wasn't.

"I guess you were joking about the vodka," he said with a hint of a smile.

"Yes, of course!" I replied with a straight face, which had him worried until I gave him a wink.

"All joking aside," Scott said, "before you head off to your office, tell me you are going to take this job and turn this company around."

"Seriously, I don't think that anyone could turn this company around—and I mean no one!"

* * *

I went back to my office and pulled out my laptop. I started typing everything that I saw that morning that I viewed as a problem, which was just about everything. I wrote up my notes in the format: *I have a problem, I have a solution!* I stopped for a minute because I was wondering what Scott was doing all the time he had been working at ABC. The issues I had on my list of bullet point problems were so undeniable that anyone with any business experience should have identified each. If Scott knew what he was doing, he would have started working on the resolutions on day one of his employment. Unfortunately, Scott had not done that, which told me a story about his skills and abilities.

Precisely at noon, Jordan walked into my office and said, "Bob, are you ready for some lunch?"

"Sure, Jordan, what is the plan?"

"Do you like sushi?"

"Yes, sir, I pretty much eat anything, including sushi."

"Scott is going to join us if that is okay with you?"

"That is fine with me."

I grabbed my parka and papers and followed Jordan. I had printed the problem list and solutions I had been working on for the past two hours to prepare for this lunch meeting. Jordan walked into the showroom, and I followed him to where Scott was waiting for us. I zipped up my coat because I knew it was freezing outside. Jordan's big blue jacked-up pickup truck was just outside of the front door, already running. He had pulled his truck around to the front door and left the vehicle running to warm up before he came to get me.

Married with three children, Jordan was thirty-four years old and over six feet tall. He was a good-looking guy of Taiwanese descent. He was easy to get along with and had a high IQ—in other words, he was quite astute. If I were ever going to build another company from scratch, I would consider hiring Jordan. Sure, his company was a mess, but he had a great personality, and I am sure that he would be very easy to work with as a partner.

At lunch, Jordan asked us if it was okay if he ordered lunch for the three of us. I said that was fine with me, and Scott agreed. After Jordan placed the order, I gave him and Scott a copy of my three-pages-long, double-spaced list of issues.

Jordan glanced at the task list, gave each page a once-over, and then commented, "Bob, you have been here for three hours, and these are the only problems you found?"

I peered at Jordan and knew he was kidding. I kept the list in front of me even after the platters of sushi arrived. As we talked, Jordan made some notes on his copy of the list and the notes app on his phone.

After we all had our fill of sushi and I was done discussing every point on my list, Jordan asked me a question: "Since you found all these problems in your first three hours on the job, could you please take the time this afternoon and resolve them? I am sure that if you solve all these problems by five tonight, ABC Off-Road Supply will be profitable by then."

"Jordan, I would do that, but it would leave me nothing to do on Tuesday and Wednesday! Besides, I created this list from a forty-five-minute tour with Scott. If we focused on all the real problems with this organization, my list would be ten to twelve pages long, single-spaced. I will continue documenting the issues and my suggestions for the solutions this afternoon. When Brian returns in the morning, we can all sit down and talk about the future."

"Bob, that sounds great. Now, let's get you back to the office so you can get in front of your computer."

"Jordan, thank you for lunch. The sushi was excellent!"

Back at the ABC facility, I spent the rest of the afternoon working on my list, continuing to put it into an *I've got a problem, I have a solution* format. While I wanted this list for my meeting the next morning, more important to me was my goal to prioritize the list of this company's problems. I made copious notes on how I was going to attack each of those issues efficiently.

Chapter 3

MEETING WITH THE OWNERS

"Successful people do what unsuccessful people are not willing to do. Don't wish it were easier; wish you were better."

—JIM ROHN, AN AMERICAN ENTREPRENEUR

TUESDAY MORNING, I WOKE UP VERY EARLY (4:30 AM) AT THE hotel because of my inability to adjust to the change in time zones. I did not mind waking up so early because it gave me more time to prepare for my meeting with the two owners later that day. But more important, it gave me time to organize and prioritize all the problems I had discovered the day before.

At 7:00 AM, I was showered, dressed, and ready for breakfast. My hotel offered free breakfast each morning, so I took my laptop with me to breakfast to continue working while I enjoyed a good cup of coffee, some eggs, and a couple of strips of bacon. At 7:45, I went out to the parking lot, found my Lexus, and started it up. I put the window defrosters on high. It looked like it had snowed at least six inches during the night. It was cold outside, even though I was wearing my brand-new parka, which my wife had picked out exclusively for this turnaround in Ogden, Utah. I went back inside to finish up.

I have always believed that the more organized you are, the more efficient you are. When you organize yourself, you can accomplish substantially more. I love having a checklist of tasks that I need to do. Each hour, I check off the finished items on the list.

Usually, when I am working, I keep a tablet next to me to jot down notes, so I can continue working and not be interrupted. When I write down my notes, I can continue to focus. When I finish what I am working on, I go back to my handwritten notes and develop a new plan.

During the second semester of my senior year in college, I participated in an internship with a "Big 8" public accounting firm. The partner of the firm gave me some valuable advice on my first day. I still remember what he said and have lived by it for the past forty-plus years.

He told me that most accountants are unorganized. The result of being disorganized is that it takes you half the time to find the information, and the other half of the time to do the work. "So, Mr. Curry," he said, "if you stay organized, you can accomplish twice as much work because you do not have to take time to find what you are looking for before you do the task assigned."

At 8:00, I finished my breakfast, put my computer in my backpack, and was back in my car traveling to ABC. Warming up my car with the defrosters worked well, which was an excellent decision. All the snow had melted off the front and back windshields. Ten minutes later, I arrived at my client's facility. Surprisingly, there were about two dozen employee cars and trucks in the parking lot. I got out of my car and walked into the shop. I looked around, and every bay had a vehicle on the lift with a technician below working. The previous day at 8:15 AM, there was not a soul in the whole building. I was a little confused about what had caused such a material change with all the technicians coming to work much earlier this morning.

I walked into the sales area, all five salesmen and Kurt were there, each working on some paperwork. I was not sure what was going on, so I asked Kurt. "Good morning, Kurt! How are you doing this cold morning?"

"Bob, I am doing great. Thank you for asking."

"Kurt, what are all the salesmen doing here so early?"

"They are getting every one of their customer pick-ups organized. Then they are going to be calling the customers to come to get their parts before noon today."

"Why are they here so early this morning?"

"They all like their jobs, and everyone wants to continue to work here after today."

"Hmm . . . now I understand, you provided them some motivation to clean up the customer pick-up racks in the warehouse."

"Yes, sir, that would be accurate!"

"Good, Kurt. I like a manager, especially a sales manager, who can motivate the sales team."

I said good morning to each member of the sales team and went to my office to prepare for my meeting with Brian and Jordan.

Surprisingly, Scott was in one of the four offices located in the hallway by my office. I later learned that the night before, Scott and two warehouse guys had relocated all the used inventory that had been stored in there. Then they rented and used a rug scrubber on the carpet, cleaned the whole office with Windex, Lysol wipes, and furniture polish. They moved Scott's personally owned desk that he had brought from his home into the office. There were already live phone lines and computer hookups in the room. That office had gone through a significant transition between 5:00 and 8:00 PM the night before.

Scott was sitting at the desk, working away an hour earlier than he had arrived at the company yesterday. *Hmm,* I thought, *another positive change at ABC!*

Scott turned around, quickly stood up, and said, "Good morning, Bob, how did you sleep last night? And, by the way, your Starbucks latte is sitting on your desk."

"Scott, you are too much. Thank you, sir. You did not have to stop and get me that. And to answer your question about how I slept last night, I was up at 4:30 AM working. I am well prepared for my meeting with Brian and Jordan this morning. And, Scott, *when* did you clean up this office?"

"I decided yesterday afternoon that I wanted my office to be close to yours," he told me. "I want to watch you do your magic on this company. I want to learn about what you do for a living."

"Scott, you know that already," I replied. "I do turnarounds and write books on the topic."

"Yes, I know that, but I want to *see* you do your job. I don't want to miss anything. So last night, I stayed late and cleaned up this office so I could work close to you going forward."

I gave him a nod. "By the way, I noticed that many of the shop techs and the whole sales team were here this morning much earlier, at least an hour earlier than yesterday. What happened?"

Scott let out a little laugh. "If you can't figure it out, your lunch meeting with Jordan yesterday woke him up. When he got back to the office after lunch, Jordan called an emergency management meeting. At that meeting, he lit some fires under some of the guys' fannies and motivated them to start doing their jobs, effective immediately. Chances are, you will also see some other changes around the company soon."

"Well, my friend, that is great news. I like change! Thank you again for the latte."

"Not a problem, my friend!" Scott said.

I headed to my office to take off my parka and get the day at the office started.

* * *

At 9:00 AM, Jordan, Brian, and Scott walked into my office together. I stood up from my desk.

Brian stuck out his hand for a shake as he introduced himself. As we shook hands, he said, "Bob, it is a pleasure to meet you. I loved reading your two books. I have looked forward to meeting you ever since I finished the second one."

"Thank you, Brian, and thank you for reading my books. The truth is that after all my years of doing turnarounds, I decided I have not been able to help enough business owners because I can only do four or five turnarounds every year. That motivated me to write my books so that maybe I could help *thousands* of business owners much like yourself."

"Well, Bob, your books have helped me realize what opportunity we have here at ABC Off-Road Supply once we clean up all our problem areas. I did not think that we could do this turnaround by ourselves, even after reading both of your books. Scott suggested that we give you a call to solicit your help. I thought that there was no way we could convince you to travel to Ogden, Utah, in January. But I was wrong, and here you are. Thank you for agreeing to come here to help us to make this business profitable."

"Aside from the change in time zone and the cold weather, it is my pleasure to help you," I told him honestly.

Brian smiled and continued, "Jordan sent me the list that you gave him at lunch yesterday, along with his comments from your discussion. After reading everything, it is obvious that you have a good grasp of our current problems. If it is okay with you, could we meet now and go over the details of your list again. I would like to have a complete and thorough understanding of what you are going to try to accomplish."

"Sure, Brian, I am okay with meeting now, but I want you to know that I have only been at your company for one day. This list is probably only a fraction of the items I will be working on in the future."

"I understand!" Brian replied.

Brian had been on a week's vacation with his girlfriend in the Dominican Republic. He had a nice tan from spending time in the sun all week. Brian, as I later learned, was forty-two years old. At five-foot-ten and about 160 pounds, he was a nice-looking guy with black hair and a well-manicured beard with some gray highlights, mostly by his chin. He usually wore an intense expression, mainly because he was stressed most of the time.

Jordan and Scott brought their laptops to the meeting to take notes, and Brian had a white tablet and a pen.

"Okay, then let's get started," I said.

My notes were organized and up on my laptop computer, as I had already been preparing to meet with the owners of the company. I told the three guys I had prioritized my list from most important to least important, so the order of my list would be different from theirs. I made new copies of the list and handed my list to each of them so we could all review the problems in the same order.

"The top priority for me is to interview the management team to determine who is doing their job and which managers shouldn't be working for this company any longer."

Brian, Jordan, and Scott all had "wow" looks on their faces as I read my first note.

"Gentlemen, please understand that I believe with a strong management team, your company will be profitable. I also believe that with a weak management team, you are going to lose money every month and fail. So, I hope that you understand how important it is to have the right managers working for the company; in fact, it is paramount. Do you have any questions?"

All three shook their heads no.

ABC Off-Road Supply had four very weak managers (service manager, sales manager, warehouse manager, and the bookkeeper) working for them. Plus, I still had no idea what one of the employees—Scott—did there daily. Usually, it takes only one or two bad managers to bring a company down, and then it lands in the hands of a turnaround specialist or a bankruptcy attorney. Incredibly, this company was still in business with *four* inadequate managers.

I went on, "We need to recruit and hire a new accounting manager so that we can get the financial statements current. Brian, how long do you think Carole is going to stay before she retires?"

"She will stay as long as we need her," he said, "but the sooner we find her replacement, the better."

"Okay, that's a top priority then. We need up-to-date financial statements to manage this business—and we need them soon."

There is not one good reason this company should not have had financial statements produced by the accounting department. Having timely and accurate financial reporting—income statement, balance sheet, sales reports, labor-efficiency reporting for the shop, weekly flash report, etc.—is an absolute necessity for a company with over $6 million in sales and thirty-eight employees. This company was in financial trouble because they did not have financial and operational reports to use to help management make sound business decisions.

I moved on to the next item. "The amount of inventory you have in this company is crazy high—completely too much. We need to reduce the amount of inventory and get the on-hand balances on the computer. These are two different problems: too much inventory and the inventory not being on the computer. My gut tells me that you have at least 50 percent too much inventory in this building to satisfy the customer orders of this business."

The excess inventory at ABC Off-Road Supply was a real problem. The level of stock had drained the cash from the business, causing the owners significant stress. If this company had $250,000 less in inventory, they would have a quarter of a million dollars sitting in their bank account to satisfy the cash needs of the business. The company would increase the inventory turns, improving the profitability of the owners' investment in the company. Also, they would need less warehouse space to store the inventory.

Many bad things can happen when a company has too much inventory and only one good thing. The list of bad things includes: the inventory gets lost, damaged, or stolen, or it becomes obsolete. The inventory ties up too much of the company's funds. The one good thing is: The inventory gets shipped to the customers on time.

When five bad things can happen to inventory in the company's warehouse and only one good thing, I would recommend being much more careful about the dollar value of stock in my warehouse. When the purchasing department can order inventory on day one and receive the product on day two or three, there is not a great need to have a huge dollar amount of stock in the company's warehouses.

This company had invested way too much money in inventory, and they did not have a software system to keep track of all the stock in the warehouses.

The solution was to stop all stock replenishment orders and only buy against customer orders. The goal was to reduce the inventory dollar value by $300,000 to $350,000. The reduction in inventory would increase the cash available for paying down the vendor debt.

The company needed to invest in inventory software to help control the investment in off-road parts for the business. The new software would improve the efficiency of the warehouse staff to store, pick, pack, and ship the products to ABC Off-Road Supply's customers.

"I am guessing that your employees are probably stealing inventory from your company daily," I told Brian and Jordan. "We need to have cameras and fences around the inventory racks, so only the warehouse employees have access to the parts inventory."

They didn't argue, so I continued, "The front showroom should be a *showroom* for ABC vehicles, not a tire and wheel storage area. We should get 98 percent of those tires stored somewhere else. Then we should have four or five beautiful jeeps, pickups, and SUVs in the showroom displaying all the off-road supply products that are sold by this company."

They nodded, and all three took notes. I gave them a moment before I went on.

"The front showroom should always be clean and look perfect. The windows should be cleaned and kept that way daily. We should mount televisions on the back walls playing videos all day, showing our customers what incredible off-road vehicles look like while climbing all the trails at Moab."

I could see them picturing that in their minds.

The management team had been mismanaging their front showroom. The building was in an "A+" location on Main Street in Ogden, Utah. The company could show four to five off-road vehicles in the showroom as a "sales support" for the sales team with their customers. The company had an excellent opportunity to display as many as twenty-five off-road vehicles in the front of the property. By displaying vehicles with off-road products, every car that passes by the ABC facility will see the jeeps and pickup trucks. This alone will generate more customers to stop in the store to make their trucks and jeeps look like the ones on display.

"The sales area in the main showroom looks terrible," I said. "The shelves and products are all dirty and dusty. The layout of the inventory is unorganized. There is way too much cardboard showing on the shelves. All the products should be removed from the boxes, correctly priced, and nicely displayed. We should also mount televisions on the back wall behind the sales counter for our customers to see several different examples of off-road vehicles.

"Each salesperson should be dressed and groomed professionally. I want our customers to have great respect for our salespeople. Proper clothing and grooming are essential, and my initial impression is that none of the salespeople cares much about their appearance. It is hard for me to believe that customers are going to come into our retail showroom and spend 12,000 to 15,000 dollars on their vehicles if the sales staff looks homeless."

None of them took offense to what I said, and then I asked Brian, "Does the sales team have sales quotas to meet monthly?"

"No, sir."

"Does the company have monthly sales contests to make the guys compete against each other to grow their sales?"

"No."

"Do you post the month-to-date sales totals by salesperson on a whiteboard somewhere, so everyone knows who is doing well and which salesperson is having a bad month?"

"No, sir."

"Have you provided this group with any sales training?"

"No, sir."

"Well, we have a lot of issues to work on in the future in the sales area at ABC Off-Road Supply."

This situation was shocking to me because Brian was such an excellent salesman. His monthly sales total doubled and tripled the sales for most of the sales team. He was a "relationship" type of salesman. Whenever he made a sale to a customer, they immediately became his friend. He had an impressive way about him that put customers at ease and got them to trust his judgment.

I have found that salespeople always need motivation from management to be more productive and sell more. If the sales manager leaves the sales team alone, each salesperson tends to go at his own pace. The sales manager can use several motivational methods to generate some excitement (and sales). For example:

- Each salesperson should have a monthly and quarterly sales quota.

- There should be weekly sales reporting to keep the sales team updated on their and the other salespeople's month-to-date results.

- The sales commission plan should be a "tiered" plan where the salesperson is paid a higher percentage of the gross profit as their monthly sales increase. The more they sell, the higher their commission percentage and the dollar amount of their commission check!

- There should be weekly or monthly sales contests to motivate the sales team to compete to win the competition.

- There should be a daily ten-minute stand-up meeting each morning to review the previous day's sales results and the current day's goals.

- Scheduling and implementing sales training should help each of the salespeople improve their sales skills.

- The salespeople should be assigned customer sales targets to force them to call on the more prominent clients. Unfortunately, many salespeople are "order takers." The sales management should force the sales staff to become "hunters" rather than "farmers."

- There should be extensive sales reporting done by management to track phone calls made, phone calls received, wholesale sales appointments, closing rate, average sale, etc.

- There should be a weekly sales meeting with accountability reporting at the meeting for every salesperson.

With those problems addressed, I went on to the next. "ABC Off-Road Supply website needs work. Over the weekend, I reviewed it in detail. If we are going to generate new customers, the website must be more interesting and quicker. When I was going from page to page, the whole website speed was slow. When the website moves slowly, we lose customers."

Brian chimed in, "Bob, I have a whole story to tell you about the website. I hired a new firm and paid them 10,000 dollars upfront to upgrade our website, but they have achieved nothing yet. This topic is a whole conversation we need to have later; it is too long to discuss now."

"Okay," I said and made myself a note on my computer, so I would not forget to talk to Brian about the website. "Who do you use to purchase AdWords and promote the website?" I asked.

"We use a local guy who has done an okay job," Brian replied. "Our traffic to the website is better this year than in past years. Honestly, I don't know how to measure the local guy's performance other than sales growth."

"So, that begs the question, are your internet sales greater this year than last year?"

"Hmm, I don't know," Brian responded. "I will check and have the information available for tomorrow's management meeting. Would you like me to arrange a meeting with our marketing guy, David?"

"Yes, this week is going to be too busy to meet him on this trip. Let's schedule and meet with him on my next trip."

"Okay, I will make that happen."

"I plan to be here every other week, probably from Monday through Thursday, throughout this turnaround."

"That would be great," Brian said.

"I assume your marketing guy regularly sends you Google Analytics reports showing the traffic to the website."

"Yes, he does. I will forward the reports to you. Bob, please send me your email address, and I will forward you the last five reports."

I made a note to send Brian my email address. "Has he showed you the different AdWords he has used in the past and the results of each?"

"No, sir. He refused to show me the AdWords details because he says that they are his *secret sauce*, and he will not share them."

I made myself another note to deal with the marketing guy about the AdWords details. I quickly decided that if he used that stance with me, he would soon become ABC's ex-marketing guy. "Do you know what he is charging you for his services?"

"I pay him 5,000 a week. I don't know how much of that is for the AdWords and how much is for his fees." *Hmm*, I thought, *that is a problem!*

"Okay, we will focus on this marketing area on my next visit. But between now and then, I want to see all the information you can provide me concerning marketing."

Brian said, "Understood, sir."

"The outside of the building needs to be cleaned up. We should only display vehicles in front of this building that has ABC Off-Road Supply installed products. You should make the rest of the employees park in the lot behind the building. The building needs a coat of paint, and the sign needs to be lit up and cleaned. We need every potential customer who drives down Main Street to see the ABC Off-Road Supply facility. At night, when the sun goes down, no one can see this business. There should be spotlights installed inside the showroom over all the vehicles. That way, people can see off-road vehicles as they walk or drive past the building in the evenings and throughout the night. And the second reason people driving past the showroom don't see any off-road vehicles is that there are no vehicles parked there, which is pretty amazing! Gentlemen, we need four of five lifted vehicles in the front showroom as quickly as possible. I know that it will make a difference with the traffic to the store and our closing rate with our customers."

"The shop needs to be cleaned and maintained in the future. Right now, it looks terrible. I will not get into the details because I believe you understand what I am saying. Plus, we need new signs mounted on the walls in every bay about safety and the proper appearance of their bay area. I don't know what logic this company is using to purchase the inventory, but whatever it is, stop it!"

During my first week with ABC Off-Road Supply, I found the outside of the building to have zero marketing appeal. In fact, just the opposite. There were only a few "off-road" vehicles parked in the front of the building, and the rest were employee vehicles that were of no value to the company. All the windows in the front showroom needed to be washed (inside and out). The building also needed a new coat of paint. The lights on the building needed new light bulbs, and the employees should park their vehicles in the back of the south lot. The good news was that this cosmetic change did not take much time to accomplish, and it made a material difference to the facility's appearance.

Jordan chimed in, "Bob, you know that we sell off-road products on the internet, and we buy products to satisfy the demand for internet orders, right?"

"Yes, I understand this, Jordan, but this company has too much inventory, and no one knows the location of each SKU." (SKU stands for "stock keeping unit.")

"Yes, I agree with that," he conceded. "There is a lot of old inventory in warehouse 2 that moves very slowly. We have been trying to get rid of it for years—unfortunately unsuccessfully."

"Okay, Jordan, we are going to move that inventory up on the priority list of what we need to accomplish." Then I said what I had been really wanting to say: "I was saving the best for last, and I am not kidding. Whoever is responsible for letting warehouse 2 get to that current condition should be fired. I would suggest that the company take 100,000 in cash, build a campfire with the dollar bills in the middle of that warehouse, and burn it all up. I don't know if the inventory stored in that warehouse is good, old, or what. But that warehouse needs to be cleaned and organized immediately."

"Bob, can I ask you a question?" Scott said.

"You just did!" I quipped.

"Okay, can I ask you another question?"

"You just asked me another question."

Scott smiled at me but continued, "Yesterday, you intimated you had not decided whether you would accept this turnaround engagement. Have you decided?"

Jordan and Brian looked at me with concern.

"Scott, now I am going to ask you a question. Do you believe that I would get up at 4:30 AM on a Sunday, catch a five-hour flight across the United States to spend three and a half cold days in Utah if I was not going to accept this turnaround engagement? When I left my home early Sunday morning, it was 75 degrees, a bit warmer than Ogden, Utah."

Scott responded, "No, sir, that would be silly to make that trip unless you were going to do the turnaround."

"Scott, you didn't have to ask me that question, right?"

"No, sir."

Brian added, "Bob, we have never worked with a consultant before. Can you share with us the process you go through to improve the financial results of our business here? Also, how should we introduce you and what you are doing for the company?"

Jordan spoke up and said, "Brian, I met with the management team yesterday and told everyone that Bob is the acting CEO of the company. I explained that everyone should be open and honest with him when he asks any questions."

"Bob, are you okay with that?" Brian asked.

"Whatever makes sense with you and Jordan is good with me," I told him.

"So, how do we get started? What do we do first?" Scott asked.

"Do you have regularly scheduled management meetings?" Even as I asked the question, the two owners were already shaking their heads no.

"Well then, we will have a management meeting every Wednesday from noon to one. The meeting will happen whether or not I am here. I will explain more about that meeting later."

Management meetings are costly for companies. If you calculate the payroll expense of all the people attending meetings, the costs could be as much as hundreds and hundreds of dollars. With that in mind, I developed management meeting rules for my clients, which are listed here:

- There will be an agenda for the meeting distributed to everyone at least 24 hours before the meeting. Whoever is chairing the meeting is responsible for creating the itinerary. Everyone should be prepared to participate intelligently with all topics discussed.

- The attendance of the complete management team is mandatory.

- All cell phones must be in silent mode, and only emergency calls answered.

- The meetings will be set for the same time and day weekly. Therefore, the managers can post the meetings on their calendars for the balance of the year. This procedure will ensure that there are no future scheduling conflicts.

- Each meeting will start on time and last a maximum of one hour.

- Someone will be responsible for distributing the recorded minutes immediately after the meeting.

- The first item on each agenda will be the follow-up on any prior unfinished tasks.

- Finally, if anyone is late to the meeting, that person will put a $20 in the dish on the conference room table. The second time a manager is not on time, it will cost that person $100, which will be donated to a local charity.

ABC Off-Road Supply
(SAMPLE) MEETING AGENDA

Meeting Called By: Brian   **Date:** 3/21
Facilitator: Bob   **Time:** 12:00 Noon
Attendees: Brian, Jordan, Ron, Wes, Kurt   **Location:** Conference Room

AGENDA ITEMS

TOPIC	PRESENTER	TIME ALLOTTED
1) Meeting Minutes	Bob	10 Minutes
2) Marketing	Bob	10 Minutes
3) Sales Commission Plan	Kurt	20 Minutes
4) Sales Quota for the Sales Team	Kurt	10 Minutes
5) Future Management Meetings	Bob	10 Minutes

Other Information

SPECIAL NOTES: Task Responsibility worksheets are distributed to every manager attending the meeting. Please review the sheets to prioritize and establish a deadline for each task. Once completed, please provide a copy to Brian, Jordan, and Bob for their review. We will discuss the status of the tasks at each future management meeting until the completion of all items.

Typically, with my clients, we start the day with what I call a "stand-up meeting." I hesitated a little before I explained what a stand-up meeting is. Every one of the guys was looking at me, waiting for an explanation.

"A stand-up meeting is when the owners and managers get together for ten minutes first thing in the morning. Since the retail doors open here to customers at 9:00 AM, the management team should meet every morning from 8:45 to 8:55 AM. The meeting should last only ten minutes. I call this a stand-up meeting because you don't have enough time to sit down and get comfortable. If you did, the meeting would be over by the time you have had your first

ABC Off-Road Supply
TASK RESPONSIBILITY LISTING
Date: _____

Bob Curry			
Priority	**Task Description**	**Deadline**	**Status**

sip of coffee. Everyone attending the ten-minute meeting should set their phone alarm to go off at 8:40 and 8:55 AM. When the first alarm goes off, everyone should be on their way to the meeting. When you hear the second alarm, the stand-up meeting ends. The purpose of this meeting is for every manager to share with the group their goals for that day. Everyone should prepare and always be on time. One of my major pet peeves in life is to have people arrive late for a meeting. Being late to a meeting, in my eyes, is disrespectful to your fellow managers and the owners of the company. Everyone should come well-prepared to all management meetings.

"I think that tomorrow, we should have an all-hands meeting to announce what I am going to be doing here at ABC Off-Road Supply and why. The all-hands meeting means that we meet with every employee (all hands), so there are no false rumors about this consulting engagement or ABC Off-Road Supply. I suggest that we meet tomorrow morning in the shop where there is plenty of room for all the employees at the meeting. Brian, you and Jordan should start the all-hands meeting and give the employees your explanation about the future of the company and why I am here. My suggestion is not to hold anything back. We need 100 percent effort from 100 percent of the employees. To accomplish this turnaround, we need everyone pulling the rope in the same direction. If anyone here is pulling in the other direction, they are out of here . . . quickly. After you finish, I will talk, but only for a maximum of ten to fifteen minutes."

"Bob, I will schedule the meeting for 8:15 AM, which will give us forty-five minutes. We unlock the front doors to let customers in at 9:00 AM."

I responded, "That should give us plenty of time, 8:15 is perfect."

"Tomorrow at noon, we will meet for lunch in the conference room with the three of us, Kurt, the sales manager, Wes, and Ron."

Scott said, "Ron is not a manager right now."

"Scott, I want someone in the meeting who knows the most about the inventory. Who would that be, in your opinion?"

Jordan spoke up and said, "Well, that would be Ron."

I asked, "Brian, does Kurt have a daily or weekly sales meeting?"

"No, I don't think that he does, but I can check."

"No, not necessary. We will talk about the sales team tomorrow at the manager's meeting. Normally, I only like meetings that last a maximum of one hour, but the initial meeting tomorrow will probably last a little longer, so plan for it, gentlemen."

"Do we need to prepare for this meeting?" Scott asked.

"Not for this meeting, but all future meetings, you will."

Brian inquired if there was anything else we needed to discuss before we broke up our meeting.

"Yes, Brian, there is one last thing, and it is crucial. I have been doing turnarounds for the past twenty-five years. I have worked with over seventy-five distressed companies in all different industries. During my career, I have been successful in accomplishing the turnarounds for every engagement I started. I have never been fired, quit, or not finished the consulting job. The reason I am telling you this is because, while I am here, we follow my rules. I have been doing turnarounds for a long time. I know what works and what doesn't work. You gentlemen have tried to make this company successful and failed. Now, if you do hire me, from now on, we follow my rules, and that is absolute."

"Bob, Jordan, and I hear what you are saying, and we are both committed to following your direction. If you have any problem with what we are doing in the future, pull us into your office, and let's meet. It is our commitment to you that we hired you to do a job. The last thing we are going to do is interfere while you are turning this company around."

"Well, thank you, gentlemen, and let's get to work. We have a lot to do. Go with confidence!"

* * *

Brian and Jordan got up and left the room. Scott stayed behind and said, "I am so glad you are here. Thank you again for accepting this turnaround."

"Let me ask you an important question, I said. "And please do not take this the wrong way because I don't mean to insult you or anything."

"What, Bob?" He looked concerned.

"What is your specific role with this company? So far, it is not clear to me what I need to assign you to accomplish. Can you please help me out here?"

"I am so glad you asked. I started with the company in a consulting role with Brian and Jordan because they needed help. I have tried to come up with a mission and vision statement for ABC Off-Road Supply. I have been trying to help them in any weak areas of the company. Can I close the door? I would like to spend a few minutes with you to explain my problem."

"Sure, Scott, that is not a problem."

Scott closed the door and sat back down at the table. "Bob, I was hired here four months ago to help with cleaning up this company, much like you described in our meeting five minutes ago. Unfortunately, I don't have the turnaround experience over the years like you do. Some evening, we should have dinner together, and I can share with you everything I have done, which is much like your career. Here is the problem: I agreed to join the company at a 40,000 annual salary. Bob, I have never made less than 150,000 per year for the last twenty years of my career. I accepted the salary, first because the company could not afford to pay me what I am worth. Second, I knew that I could earn and get paid a much higher salary soon. I knew that if I started here at a lesser salary, in a few months, they would see my true value and increase my compensation. Do you see my problem here?"

"I sure do! You accepted a lower paycheck here, and it is probably going to be a long time before this organization is going to afford to pay you an additional 110,000 dollars. It is going to be a real challenge for the company to pay you the salary you are looking to earn. Why did you ever agree to accept forty thousand if you wanted a salary of a buck and a half a year?"

"Well, I knew that I could make some changes here and get this place extremely profitable soon. Then I wanted to open ABC

Off-Road Supply franchise stores around the nation and manage the franchisees for the company."

"Scott, attempting to sell franchises for ABC Off-Road Supply is years off . . . many years in the future. This company is not doing the simple 'blocking and tackling' for a straightforward business yet. I think this is going to be a problematic turnaround because there are no financial statements or an accountant to manage the finances. There is no control over purchasing and inventory. This company needs to get control of its on-hand inventory and input the information on the accounting software. Those are substantial projects to accomplish here, especially while the company has no cash or a bank line of credit. A big part of this engagement's plan is teaching Brian and Jordan how to manage this business. Right now, two off-road supply guys are leading this company rather than two businesspeople operating an off-road supply company. Scott, increasing your salary that much would be impossible to do *and* keep the business out of bankruptcy."

Scott looked stressed and said, "How about if I take control of internet sales for the company? That area of the business has a huge upside. If I take control and double or triple the sales, what do you think about that? Would that help me earn the kind of money I need to support my family?"

I asked Scott, "What experience do you have with selling products over the internet?"

"None, but how hard can that be?"

I answered, "Well, right now, I don't know, but I am going to find out soon."

"Bob, this is going to be perfect. I can take over that area of the business and generate enough cash to pay my salary. How does that sound?"

"I am not going to make any commitments on my second day here, but if you manage and grow the internet sales, that sure would make it easier on me."

"We are going to be a great team here," Scott said with great enthusiasm. "I am so excited."

"But, Scott, I want to make this 100 percent clear. This turn-around is my responsibility, so you, Brian, and Jordan are going to have to follow my direction, period. Do you understand?"

"Yes, of course, I am going to be a great asset to you during this turnaround process!"

"Okay, Scott, let's get to work."

Scott got up and stuck out his hand for a shake. I shook his hand, and then Scott gave me another "man hug." I did not know if Scott was going to be an asset or a liability for this engagement. But if he was not going to follow my direction, I was going to have to make him disappear. I sincerely hoped he was going to help and did not get in the way of the success of this turnaround.

* * *

After Scott left, I went to see Brian, who was standing behind his computer terminal at the sales counter in the main showroom.

"I know that we do not have financial statements, but I am assuming you can give me monthly sales by sales category," I said.

Brian nodded.

"Good, please print me a copy of the sales report for the last thirteen months, from the beginning of January last year to the last day of January this year."

"Do you want it printed month by month or the total for the thirteen months?" he asked.

"Month by month, please."

"Sure, give me a minute, and I will print the reports."

Brian pointed to the printer under the middle of the front sales counter. A minute later, my sales reports were sitting on top of the machine. I thanked Brian for his help and went back to my office.

I sat and my desk and built an Excel spreadsheet that showed the monthly sales by salesperson and the totals for internet sales. When I completed the worksheet, I found the numbers fascinating. Brian was the top salesperson by a wide margin, followed by Joshua. Joshua averaged close to $100,000 each month. The rest of the sales team were all selling between 50 and 60 percent of Joshua's monthly sales totals. I wondered how that could be. They were all standing side by side at the same sales counter selling the same products. I opened a new Microsoft Word document after I set up folders for sales, financial, inventory, operations, and policies/procedures. I filed the newly created sales analysis in the sales folder. I then recorded all my notes about sales from my meeting with Brian, Jordan, and Scott that morning. They were:

✓ There are no daily or weekly sales meetings.

✓ Kurt, the sales manager, sells next to nothing, which makes no sense to me. He should be a working manager and lead by example.

✓ The sales team makes ordering mistakes that end up on the "return to vendor" racks in the warehouse.

✓ There are no monthly/quarterly sales quotas.

✓ There are no sales contests for the sales team.

✓ There is no sales training offered to the sales team.

✓ The salespeople are not paying attention to the customer pick-up racks in the warehouse.

✓ The sales team needs to be groomed and dressed better when waiting on customers.

✓ Kurt doesn't post the daily/weekly/monthly sales totals for the sales team to see. I believe the more you put the sales team's daily sales figures in front of them for all to see, the more they are motivated. A good salesman always wants to be the number-one salesman on the list.

✓ Joshua, second only to Brian, is the top salesman, with the others selling 50 to 60 percent of Joshua's monthly totals. I have identified that this is a significant opportunity to grow the company's sales. I plan to motivate Kurt and the other four salespeople to improve their sales totals to match Joshua's and Brian's.

* * *

At noon, I looked up, and Jordan was standing in front of me. It shocked me because I did not hear or see him walk into the office. (This happens to me regularly because when I am concentrating on work, I am oblivious to the environment around me. When I am focused, I usually don't hear or see anything in the room other than the computer screen.)

Jordan said, "Lunch, Bob?"

"Sure, Jordan, what's the plan?"

He said, "Follow me. You, Brian, and I are going out to get a sandwich together. Is there anything you don't like?"

"Hmm, not on this planet," I said. "I have never met a menu item that I did not like!"

Jordan smiled, and we headed off to lunch together. I was looking forward to this meal because lunch was when Brian and Jordan could relax and share with me their true feelings.

I got into Jordan's blue, very jacked-up pickup truck, and he took us to the best burger place five miles from the office.

When we sat down at the booth, and the waitress came to our table, Brian asked, "Do you have Fireball?"

I honestly had no idea what he was asking the waitress. Fireball was new to me.

The waitress said, "Yes, of course!"

Brian looked at me and asked, "Fireball and Diet Coke?"

I laughed and said, "Yes, of course!" I had no idea what I had just agreed to drink at this lunch. *It does not get any better than this!* I thought.

When the waitress returned with our "beverages," it dawned on me that Fireball was an alcoholic beverage. I could not remember a time when I had an alcoholic drink during lunch—especially when visiting a client! I had never had Fireball in my life, but I was sure going to sample it that day!

Brian picked up his glass for a toast: "To a successful turnaround!"

With laughter on my lips, I picked up my drink and said, "This is a safe bet! We are going to have a very successful company in four to six months!"

We all clinked glasses and said, "Salute!"

I took a sip of my drink. If you have never had Fireball, which is whiskey, it tastes like cinnamon, cinnamon with a kick. The lunch was excellent, and so was the Fireball and Diet Coke. We were starting to build a relationship that would last a lifetime, during, and after this turnaround.

When we arrived back at the office, I spent the whole afternoon organizing my thoughts about what area of the business I would attack first, second, and so on. I planned to go after the "low-hanging fruit" first to generate as much cash flow as possible. That was just common sense because the company needed cash to pay my fee, so it was necessary to get rid of the "profit killers." Profit killers are usually unproductive people who should not be on the payroll.

Payroll often is the most significant expense category on the income statement. I always review the payroll expense first. I examine 24 months, looking for trends such as increased payroll dollars, or payroll expense as a percent of sales. I also review the headcount by the department to see if any department is growing faster than sales. If any department headcounts were increasing more quickly than sales, I need to understand why. I discuss the situation with the department manager or the CFO to understand the issue. I also compare the actual year-to-date payroll expense versus the operating budget. Payroll expense is usually the first expense area where I make cuts to reduce the outflow of cash.

As I have mentioned, I always keep a tablet next to me so that I can record handwritten notes to transfer to my computer later. The following morning, I would be speaking to the whole company at the all-hands meeting. I prepared my thoughts about what I planned to say. As I thought of the topics I wanted to discuss, I wrote down my ideas in bullet points. I didn't want to forget any of the issues I wanted to cover during that meeting.

My first task was to interview the managers. I planned to evaluate each manager's skills and abilities to manage their area of the company. According to the sales reports that Brian printed for me, the sales last year were $6.3 million. The sales team generated $4.6 million, and the website and internet stores (eBay and Amazon) sold $1.7 million. Both numbers surprised me. I thought that the internet-related sales numbers would have been much higher, especially from the internet stores. I wrote myself a note to review the internet stores that evening back at the hotel. I wanted to understand the source of the problem. Was it the operations of the stores, the products, the marketing efforts, or ABC Off-Road Supply's internal processes?

I could see the sales from the sales team growing by 20 to 33 percent the following year, and internet sales could quickly increase by 50 percent. If this company were to grow as much as I thought it could, it needed a reliable management team. If the sales increase and a weak set of managers were supervising the business, the company would implode. It was my responsibility not to let that happen. That was why interviewing the management team was the first task on my list.

Brian and Jordan walked into my office and asked me what time I was planning to finish up today. I looked at my watch, and it was already 6:15 PM. I was shocked that the afternoon had gone by so quickly.

Brian said, "We close the retail store at six, and usually, we are out of here by six-fifteen."

"Well, then, I better get my laptop packed up and get out of here quickly. I don't want to be left behind and have to sleep on my desk."

Five minutes later, I was in my cold car, warming it up to melt the snow before I traveled back to my hotel.

In my room, I sat on my bed under the covers and rested my computer on my lap, reviewing everything I had done during the day. Next I reviewed my notes for my all-hands meeting talk in the morning. I also reread my notes to prepare for the noon management meeting. I closed my computer, put it on the bedside table, and dozed off to sleep.

Chapter 4

START THE TURNAROUND PROCESS

"To achieve goals you've never achieved before, you need to start doing things you've never done before."

—STEPHEN COVEY, AMERICAN EDUCATOR, AUTHOR, AND BUSINESSMAN

WEDNESDAY MORNING, I WOKE UP AT 6:30 AM WHEN MY alarm went off. I slept much better than I had the night before, mostly because I was exhausted from the long day the day before. Plus, I usually adjust better to the change in time zones after a day or two because I go to sleep earlier when I am staying in a hotel.

I took my time in the hot shower; it felt so good. After I finished, I got dressed and headed to breakfast. When I got out to the breakfast area, Brian and Jordan were there waiting for me. I was a little surprised to see them, especially because both guys had a big blueberry waffle drowned in maple syrup on their plates. Each had a cup of coffee and was munching away on their syrup-filled waffles.

I walked up to their table and said, "Good morning, gentlemen."

Brian swallowed his bite and wiped his mouth. "We decided to come and meet you for breakfast!"

"Great, I am glad that you did! Did the waitress bring you a Fireball and Coke?"

Brian laughed. "No, we asked, but she looked at us a little strange.

She told us that they don't serve alcoholic beverages at breakfast. She said they don't even have Bloody Marys."

"So, does that mean if we come here for lunch, we can get your favorite drink?" I asked.

"No, Bob, I don't think that is the case here," Brian said and took a swig of his coffee.

I put down my backpack and went to get a bowl of fruit and a tall glass of orange juice. When I returned, Jordan said that he hoped I didn't mind that they had joined me for breakfast.

"Absolutely not," I assured him. "It was a great idea. The more the three of us spend time together, the better this turnaround will go. Meeting for breakfast is a nice opportunity for quality time together."

Brian, Jordan, and I needed to spend quality time together while I was visiting ABC Off-Road Supply during the turnaround. The only way the turnaround was going to be successful was if I could get the two owners to start thinking like business people who were managing their company rather than two auto mechanics who were working for their company. Having breakfast together was an excellent opportunity for us to plan the day and talk about our accomplishments the day before.

I added, "And a free breakfast is never a bad thing."

"Bob, I am very pleased with how this turnaround has started," Brian said. "Jordan and I agree with your direction. Now, all we have to do is implement everything on our list to change."

"As I am sure you can imagine," I said, "making the changes is the hardest part of the whole turnaround."

"Where do we start first with the changes?" Jordan asked.

"I always start with the low-hanging fruit first because that will generate the most significant increase in positive cash flow," I explained.

"Should we divide up the areas and attack each to get this turn-around done quicker?" he asked.

"Yes, the more the two of you can accomplish, the faster this company can become profitable and improve the cash flow. My thoughts are that, Brian, you should work with Kurt and grow the sales with the sales team. I believe that Jason, Taylor, Warren, and Michael can increase their monthly sales to close to 100,000 dollars each, which would improve the total sales by close to 200,000 or 2.4 million dollars annually. They should all have monthly sales quotas between 80,000 and 100,000 dollars. We should put an incentive plan in place to reward them for every month they hit their quota in sales."

Brian looked concerned. "Can we afford to reward the sales team more money when our bank account is currently upside down?" he asked.

"Brian, it is all about the numbers. Think about it: let's say we put a reward program in place, and sales increase by 100,000 dollars. The gross profit on your sales in the past, according to the last financial statement published by Carole, was 37 percent. Therefore, the 100,000-dollar increase in sales will generate a gross profit of 37,000 dollars. If we pay the salesperson 500 dollars for reaching his sales quota, we end up with 36,500 dollars extra to pay our bills. Money motivates people, at least it should if the salespeople are any good. Competition within the sales team also drives them to sell more. I believe that in the room next to the sales counter, on the whiteboard, we should list the month-to-date sales by the salesperson on that board and update it daily. The salesmen are in that room a hundred times a day. If their sales total is fourth or fifth on the list, I believe that it will motivate them to do whatever they can do to get off the bottom half of the list. Posting those daily totals will take someone five minutes each day but will motivate five guys every minute they are standing at the sales counter to increase their sales.

Brian said, "I love the idea, Bob. I will have it implemented starting today."

"Guys, there are many little things we can do at your company that will produce better daily sales results. All we must do is get them done. My son, Bobby, has a phrase that he uses for his business: *The Difference Is Doing It*. I believe that phrase certainly works here at ABC Off-Road Supply. Posting the daily sales totals does not cost us one dollar of expense but will generate cash from the additional sales."

"What do you want me to do, Bob?" Jordan asked.

In working with distressed companies, I have always believed there is never one issue that represents 100 percent of the company's problems. Rather, there are 100 problems, and each is one percent wrong. As you fix all the "one-percenters," then the business will be profitable. Each day, the management team must work on fixing those "one-percenters." Then shortly after, the company will be generating excess cash and profits for the business to get caught up with the vendor payables."

"Jordan, your business's most significant problem is the amount of money the company had tied up in the inventory. We need to get the on-hand inventory balances and current costs on the computer. We need to stop stock-replenishment purchases and only buy against customer orders. This buying strategy is going to be more work for your purchasing department, but by buying for only customer orders, it will reduce the on-hand inventory. If the company has the on-hand inventory to fill customer orders, fill the order with stock inventory. The more we lower the total inventory, the more cash we are going to have in the bank. Also, all the stock in warehouse 2 needs to be organized. We need to know what is in that warehouse so we can focus our salespeople on selling it. Once we have a list of parts, we can market those parts on our website to sell them to our internet customers."

"There is a lot of old inventory in that warehouse to sell," Jordan said.

"I know, but inventory is not like wine; it does *not* get better with age. Selling products out of warehouse 2 is like found cash. As we sell that inventory, we will never replenish it, so all it does is generate funds to run the business. By the way, I saw a jeep hardtop in the warehouse. Where did that come from, and why is it in that warehouse?"

Brian explained, "Warren ordered that for a customer, and he ordered the wrong top. After we discovered the error, the vendor would not approve the return, so we are stuck with it."

"Why is it in the warehouse rather than displayed in the showroom or listed on the internet to sell?"

"Hmm . . . good question, Bob."

Both Brian and Jordan had their phones out and were putting notes into their notes app. These guys could input information into their phones almost as fast as I could talk. Both owners were knowledgeable and extremely focused on improving the finances, sales, and operations of their company. I slowed down to let them get caught up with their notes. The short break allowed me to take a few bites of my bowl of fruit.

Once they caught up with me, they sat their phones down and took a few more big bites of their blueberry waffles. We ate and talked until it was time to get to work; we would all be speaking at the all-hands meeting soon. We finished our breakfast and headed to our cars. My Lexus was not as cold or frosted that morning as it had been on the previous two mornings. I turned the defrosters on high, and in a few minutes, the windshield wipers cleared off the snow and ice for me to see well enough to drive safely to work.

* * *

When I arrived at the facility and walked into the shop, thirty-five employees, along with Brian and Jordan were present. They were talking and standing around while they all waited for the all-hands meeting to start. Brian and Jordan stood in front of the group, waiting for me. I put my backpack down and went to stand beside them.

Brian started, "Thank you, everyone, for getting here early so we could have this all-hands meeting. Is everyone here?"

Wes, the service manager, said his whole team was there. Kurt nodded, indicating that the sales team was also present. Ron confirmed that his team was there, including the part-timers who didn't officially report to work until the afternoon. The only ones left were the ladies in purchasing, Carole, and Matt. (Matt was the guy who had created the operating reports for the shop activity. He was a little on the crazy side, and Brian jokingly referred to him as "Rain Man.")

Scott came through the shop door at the very last minute. He walked up to me and handed me a Starbucks latte and said, "I would have been here earlier, but it seemed like it took an hour for the barista to make your latte."

Scott handed me the coffee cup, and I almost blushed as if I were a prima donna who had Scott fetch me coffee each morning.

I was impressed that 100 percent of the employees were here on time to attend the meeting.

Brian started by saying, "The purpose of this meeting is to let every employee in the company know what Jordan and I are trying to achieve at ABC Off-Road Supply. I don't think anyone would be surprised to know that the company is struggling to make a profit. Jordan and I have worked very hard to grow this company, but it always seems like we run into roadblocks that set us back. We are tired of trying to get through those problems using a trial-and-error method of decision-making."

Jordan took a step forward and said, "We decided that we have struggled enough and need to do something different this time. Scott had read two business books recently and suggested that Brian and I also read them. The names of the books are *From Red to Black* and *The Turnaround*. The author of those books is standing next to me. We called him two weeks ago and had a conversation on the phone about him coming to Ogden, Utah, to help us make this company profitable. He agreed to come, and we hired him to turn this company around to be cash-flow positive. He flew here on Sunday from sunny Fort Lauderdale to be with us. Monday and Tuesday,

Brian and I met with Bob about what his mission would be with our company."

Brian continued, "I have been very impressed with our conversations about what he wants to accomplish, even though he has been here for just two short days. The reason that we called this meeting today is: Number one, we want each of you to know that we hired Mr. Curry. You are going to be seeing him around here for at least four to six months helping us. Number two, we also want to let everyone be aware that whatever he asks you to do, it will be with the same authority as if either Jordan or I asked you. And number three, this turnaround is going to require hard work and cooperation from every employee who works for this company. It is going to take some time to change everything we currently are doing that is not *best practices* and convert this company to be profitable soon. So, now I am going to ask Bob to say a few words and share his thoughts about ABC Off-Road Supply. After he finishes sharing his thoughts with the group, feel free to ask him any questions you may have."

Brian looked at me and took a small step back.

"Thank you, Brian, and Jordan, for inviting me to Utah to work with ABC Off-Road Supply. I must say, Utah may be the most beautiful state I have ever been in, and also the coldest so far. When I left Fort Lauderdale, it was 75 degrees.

"I want to share with everyone here a few things that I see at ABC Off-Road Supply that must change for this company to be profitable in the future. I also want you all to know that you all have to participate in this turnaround or it is not going to happen.

We need to improve the appearance of the facilities and staff to our customers. I believe that when customers come to this facility to purchase our products and services, they should see an organized parking lot and a great looking building with an easy to read sign on the roof over the front showroom. The showrooms should be clean and marketing many of our products and services. Our sales team should be well-groomed and very professional. Every customer should feel like our sales team appreciates them coming to our showrooms. The shop must always be clean and safe. Our techs appearance must be professional much like our sales team. These changes really are easy to accomplish and they do not require a lot of money or time to make these changes.

Clean up the warehouses and reduce the dollar value of the parts inventory. We have a cash problem at this company because we have too much inventory stored in warehouses. Much of the inventory moves too slow which causes more problems. We will talk more about solving this inventory problems. The bottom line is that we need to reduce the investment in inventory by at least 50%.

Currently, our sales team acts like a bunch of "order-takers" rather than a group of aggressive, hungry salesmen. For this company to be profitable in the future, we need to grow our sales aggressively. In order for this company to increase our sales volume, the sales team must go out and get the sales rather than waiting for our customers to walk through the front door. The sales growth is never going to happen with five salesmen and a sales manager sitting on stools all day long behind the sales counter.

We also need to upgrade our website, so it is quicker and much easier for our customers to find the products that they are looking to purchase. We currently have approximately 10,000 products listed on our website for sale. We should have ten times that number of products for sale.

Our financial and operational reporting must be timely and accurate for our management team to make good business decisions to manage this business profitable.

Since I have been here a few days to observe the operations of this company, I have learned that this is a great company with a wonderful opportunity to be very profitable in the future. There are a lot of incredibly talented people working for this organization who are currently underachieving. All the changes that I am and will be suggesting are not difficult to accomplish. We all need to focus our time and energy to upgrade the areas that I have noted, and this company will hit its potential quickly and be profitable very soon.

We will need the combined help of every employee in this room to work as one big team. We need to treat every customer who walks through the front door like he or she is the best customer in the world. Everyone who works here is going to treat our customers the same, with a great deal of care and respect. We need our salespeople to treat our customers as if the customer is your mother. When our customers bring their vehicles here, they expect the work to be done professionally and on time. When any vehicle leaves this shop, our customers expect their jeep or truck to be perfect. That is what we are going to do, without exception.

"Right now, this business seems like it is about to file bankruptcy and close its doors soon. We all need to treat this company with respect. Everyone should act like this is your company and work like you own the business. You all should work like this the best company in the USA, and we are all lucky to be employed here. We all need to work hard and work smart.

"My role here is to suggest the changes to the business that are going to improve the image, management, production, sales, customer service, reporting, communication, hiring practices, and financial results of this company. I do not have a lot of time here to be successful. You all can depend on me being very aggressive about making the changes that are needed to make this business successful. I try to communicate what needs to be improved, upgraded, or stopped, and then we get the work done. This group of employees needs to work as a team every minute of every day. We need to help each other to be successful. When the company is successful, the employees are successful. I am not going to leave here until we accomplish all these goals. I have worked with more than seventy-five other companies in the past twenty years, and I know what needs to change here. I am going to assume that all of you are ready, willing, and able to turn this company around. Now, if any of you have any questions, I will try to answer them at this time."

One of the technicians raised his hand and asked, "Mr. Curry, my name is Joshua, and I work in the shop. I have a few questions for you. What do you know about running a company like ABC Off-Road Supply? Have you ever turned around a company in this off-road supply industry? What do you know about off-road vehicles?"

"Thank you for your questions, Joshua. No, I have never worked with a company like ABC Off-Road Supply, and I know nothing about this business other than what I have just noted here in the last five minutes." I stopped talking and kept my eyes on Joshua. "Well, please finish your answer," he said after he hesitated a few seconds. "You have to have a better answer than that!" "You are right, Joshua, I do. Over the past twenty years, I have worked with companies in every different industry you can think of, including retail, wholesale, distributors, healthcare, service, and manufacturing. I have worked with companies that have had less than half the annual sales of this company as well as companies in excess of one billion dollars in sales. Like ABC Off-Road Supply, I knew nothing about those companies before I started the engagements, nor had I ever managed such a company. But, Joshua, I will share with you what I have learned as a turnaround specialist. A successful company does not depend the location of the company, or the type of service or the products they sell. The quality of the management team is what determines the success or lack of success of the business. If you have a quality management team, your company will be profitable. If you have a weak management team or even a weak manager, the company is going to lose money. "So, Joshua, when I choose to accept a consulting engagement like ABC Off-Road Supply, much of my work is with the management team to help them manage the business using best business practices. My major goal is to coach each manager to run their department successfully. When I finish this engagement and walk away, I will be able to look back at the organization and say, 'ABC Off-Road Supply has a strong management team, and the business is generating huge sales and profits!'"

"Mr. Curry, what if you make all those changes that you stated earlier and the company is still not profitable, then what do you do?" Joshua asked.

"Well, Joshua, I don't know. In the past twenty years of my career in this turnaround business, that has never happened to me. Each company that I worked with in a turnaround situation have resulted in great success because the client was very profitable with a great management team when the engagement ended. So, I really don't have an answer to your question."

"Joshua, I will share with you and this group some of my personal beliefs that will help everyone here understand what I believe that makes all businesses successful.

Henry Ford once said, "If you think you can or if you think you can't, you are right." I believe if we are all positive, positive things will happen. If you ever want to be successful in life or business, you have to be hungry and want it more than anything. That is what I believe about ABC Off-Road Supply. That is why I am here right now, because I am hungry to make this company successful and I want it more than anything. I am committed to the success of ABC Off-Road Supply. But, the only way that this company is going to turnaround to be successful and profitable, every person in this room must believe and want it to happen more than anything.

Jordan said, "Joshua, do you have any other questions, or are you going to shut up now?"

I was a little shocked by Jordan's comment, and I said, " Joshua's questions were fine. I probably have been asked those same questions thirty times, but usually, it was not by one of the shop techs. It's normally the owner of the company who asks that question."

Ron, the young man who was responsible for the warehouses and inventory, stepped forward, and asked, "Mr. Curry, how are all of us going to learn all the things in the company that you want to change or improve?"

"That is an easy question," I said. "Thank you for asking it, Ron. First, I would like you all to call me Bob. Mr. Curry was my father, and he passed away in 1980. I will be meeting with the management team daily to discuss all these issues. The managers and I will discuss the problems that I am looking forward to improving. Then the managers will have these issues to work on so they may commit to a deadline to accomplish. I will follow up with each manager to see if they are achieving the goals we all agreed to focus on and accomplish.

"I have learned during my career that it is not one thing that is 100 percent wrong at ABC Off-Road Supply, it is 100 things that are all one percent wrong. As we, this group of employees in the room, resolve each of the 'one percenters,' one by one, ABC Off-Road Supply will become successful—in fact, very profitable. If we all commit to making this company successful, it will be successful, I guarantee it!

"So, with the show of hands, who here is committed to joining the management team to make ABC Off-Road Supply the most successful off-road supply company in the United States?"

I looked around, and every hand was in the air.

"Thank you, everyone. Let's get to work and make some money! But before I let you go, Joshua, do you have any more questions you would like to ask?"

"No, Bob," Joshua replied, "but I will be watching you because I want to be a turnaround consultant someday."

I gave him a big smile. "If that happens, you will love it because you get to meet all kinds of great people, just like this group at ABC Off-Road Supply. Thank you again, everyone, for your time. Also, please feel free to see me if you think there is something in the company that needs my attention. And, finally, Go with confidence!"

Suddenly, everyone in the room started to applaud. I did not expect that, but I did believe it was a very positive sign concerning the turnaround. A few moments later, they all started to disperse.

I looked at my watch, and it read 8:40 AM. I was pleased. Both Brian and Jordan reached out their hands for a shake.

Jordan said, "Nice job, Bob."

"That was the easy part," I told him. "Now, we must do what we say, which is not as simple."

"Okay, let's get on with it," Brian chimed in. "I am not getting any younger."

"Hmm . . . neither am I!" I agreed.

"Are we going to have our stand-up meeting now?" Jordan asked.

"Yes, sir," I responded. "Let's meet in the conference room."

"Who should all attend?"

"You, Brian, Kurt, Ron, Wes, and Scott, unless you think someone else should join us," I told him.

"No, that sounds good!"

"Everyone should be there in five minutes, and the meeting should last a maximum of ten minutes!"

* * *

Kurt was the last one to enter the conference room, but he was the only one who had a notepad to take notes. The rest of the managers had their phones out to punch in notes on the notes app. I set the alarm on my phone for 8:55 AM.

"Okay, group, this is our first stand-up meeting. I named it that because, by the time you sit down and get comfortable, the meeting should be over. The goal is to ensure that we all know what we need to accomplish during this workday. First, Kurt, the showrooms are dirty, dusty, unorganized, and need cleaning. I would suggest that when your salespeople are not busy with a customer today, they start cleaning up the inventory shelves to be more presentable with our customers. Do you have any questions about that?"

"No, Bob, that is pretty straightforward, and I agree that we need to make the sales area more presentable to our customers."

"Then, I want you to come up with a plan on how each one of the salesmen is going to sell at least 100,000 dollars per month."

I looked at Kurt, and he was taking notes.

"Bob, can you give me a couple of ideas on how I can accomplish that?"

"Yes, Kurt, I can, but I am not going to do that right now at this stand-up meeting. We will meet later to develop that plan."

"Yes, sir!"

"Brian, I would like you and Kurt to meet sometime soon to develop the sales-growth plan together."

Brian said, "Yes, sir, I can do that."

"Ron and Jordan, we need the inventory in both warehouses to be organized. We are going to take a physical inventory soon, so this place needs a lot of work before we can even think about counting our inventory. Do you have any questions about what needs to get done?"

Jordan said, "No, Bob, we know what needs to happen to make this place more organized. Ron and I will put together a plan. Once we complete the game plan, do you want us to share it with you?"

"Yes, that would be a good idea. . . . Wes, the shop is a dump. These guys don't care if their work areas are a mess. Many of the techs look like they are homeless. The shop is unsafe. There is a ton of work to do to clean this place up. But I want to make this clear. I do not want to slow down the shop production even a little, but at the end of the day, every day, this shop should look like it is a brand-new garage ready to work on the vehicles. Fixing any problems that affect employee safety is the top priority. Wes, you, Brian, Jordan, and I should walk the shop after this meeting and identify any unsafe situations. Then I will depend on you putting together a plan to fix the issues. Is everyone okay with this plan?"

Everyone nodded as they were putting notes into their phones.

"Gentlemen, this business is going to be better every day from now on. We need to require everyone who works for this company to make a better effort. Every day when each of us leaves at the end of the day to get into our cars to go home, I want you to look back at this building and say to yourself, 'That company is much better today than it was yesterday!' For this business to be profitable in the future, we all need to make our employees work harder and smarter than they did yesterday. I tend not to be very patient with getting this business cleaned up. I am warning you right now, I expect to see everyone doing their job, and when business is slow, we work harder to make the appearance of this company to our customers materially better. Please don't ever stand around during the day. If you have some spare time, find something to clean up in this facility. If any of your employees are standing around, assign them something to do to accomplish our goals.

"What we talked about in this meeting is a rough plan of what we need to accomplish. We will soon have a detailed plan to document what needs completed week by week. Does anyone have any questions?"

No one said a word. Right then, my alarm went off. I hit the button to silence it.

"Let's make this happen, and let's do it quickly! We need to raise the bar here with every employee to do a better job. It depends 100 percent on this group in this meeting. Let's make this business profitable, starting with February. Thank you for your time!" Then I looked at each member of the team and said, "Go with confidence!"

* * *

My goal of the all-hands and stand-up meetings was to get everyone in the company working together as a team. I wanted to make sure that everyone knew the future mission of ABC Off-Road Supply and that a lot of change would be happening soon. I wanted everyone to know that they all must participate in the turnaround for it to be successful.

It was 9:00 AM, and our first stand-up meeting had ended. That meeting was not how I wanted future meetings handled. My goal was to set the tone with this group immediately. As Brian, Jordan, Kurt, Ron, and Wes were leaving the room, I stopped Brian, Jordan, and Wes to remind them that we were going to walk the shop right now to develop a plan to get it cleaned up and safe.

Right then, someone standing behind me tapped me on my shoulder. I turned around, and Scott was standing there with his typical smile. I immediately realized that I had not assigned Scott anything to do. I decided right then that I needed to develop a "Scott plan" to make this guy productive while he was working for this company.

"Bob, what do you want me to do today?"

"Scott, what do you think that you should do to help this company turn around?"

"I am not sure because there is so much wrong with this

company," he said. "I don't know where to start. Ever since I joined the company,, I have been asking Brian and Jordan how I could help. They have a hard time giving me any direction at all."

"Hmm . . . Scott," I said. "Have you noticed that I have not asked Brian or Jordan for their advice on where I should start the turnaround? I am here to make better business decisions than have been made here in the past. I suggest you start analyzing internet sales."

"If you were going to do the analysis, how would you start?" Scott asked.

At this point, Scott was alarming me. He had no confidence to decide anything other than which Starbucks to go to each morning. I had about as much faith in Scott as Scott had in Scott, which was almost zero.

"I suggest you first analyze the sales. Pull the sales reports by month for the past twelve months to understand the trends. I suggest you meet with the local marketing company that is placing the AdWords to understand what is driving the people to our website and internet stores. I think you should figure out the strengths and weaknesses of each internet sales outlet. I understand that Brian hired a new company to upgrade the website for the company. That is a project you can take charge of and make happen. Let's have you dig into all the internet sales, and we will meet at the end of each day to see what you have learned and accomplished. Then we can discuss the next step to grow the sales. Make sure you thoroughly understand the whole system from the time the customer places the order, the purchase of the product to fill the order, and the receipt of the order to shipping that product to the customer. We need to understand how effective our investment in the marketing firm is. I am guessing that ABC Off-Road Supply is getting taken advantage of because of how naive management is about internet marketing."

"I could not be any happier about this assignment," Scott said enthusiastically. "I am very excited. Thank you very much. You know I want to have a big role in this turnaround. I would love to do what you do for a living."

"Well, Scott, let's do what is necessary to make this turnaround successful first," I cautioned him. "Okay, I am on my way to do some interviews with the management team. If you need anything, I will be with Kurt first."

"Enjoy your time with him," Scott said, as he headed out. "I am going to my office to write up my plan of attack for the website and internet sales. Then I will set up a meeting with David, the owner of the marketing company."

"Please make sure I am here for that meeting. I want to meet that guy."

"Sure, Bob, no problem."

* * *

Brian, Jordan, Wes, and I walked the shop to review the area to check on safety issues that needed to be corrected. It was clear that all three of these guys were embarrassed about how bad the place looked. They had all neglected to enforce rules for the techs to keep their bay area clean and safe. I suggested that each evening before the techs go home, they should take a few minutes to do the following:

✦ Get rid of any cardboard boxes from all the parts installed on customer vehicles.

✦ Put all their tools away in their toolbox.

✦ Sweep up the area.

✦ If there was any oil spilled during the day, they must clean it up before they leave to go home. Oil on the floor is an extreme safety hazard.

As the three of us were walking and identifying these problem areas, Wes was making notes so that he could discuss the issues with the techs sometime soon.

* * *

After we finished reviewing the shop area, I found Kurt in the sales area standing behind his desk. "Kurt, do you have some time to spend together and chat?"

"Sure, Bob, where do you want to meet?"

"How about we go to my office? It is nice and quiet back there."

"Could you give me five minutes, Bob, and I will meet you there?"

In my office, I had a tablet and started writing down the safety issues in the shop area. Then I created a list of questions I wanted to ask the sales manager.

Kurt showed up at my office door and gently knocked to get my attention. "Are you ready for me, sir?"

"Kurt, yes, and it is okay to call me Bob. Calling me, *sir*, is not necessary, plus it makes me feel old. I am just a regular guy, just like you!"

"I would hardly call you just like me. I have not written two books and turned around many companies all over the USA," he said.

"Well, Kurt, regardless of all that, I am just a normal guy like you and every other employee in this company."

"Okay, I will take your word for it. So, what do you want to talk about?"

"Kurt, first, tell me about yourself and talk about your sales team."

"I hate to tell you, but they are not *my* sales team. They are Brian's sales staff."

"Why do you say that?" I asked.

"Because I did not hire any of those five guys. I was not even consulted or given a chance to interview them before Brian hired them."

"Hmm . . . why not? When did you start in your current position?"

"I worked in the shop for eight years and on the sales floor for the last four years."

I made some notes while Kurt was talking. I was a little bit shocked that Brian had not included Kurt in the hiring process for new sales associates. This problem was a classic situation of an "off-road" guy running a business rather than a businessman managing an off-road company. I turned the page on my tablet and titled the page "Issues I need to talk to Brian about." The hiring process was number one on the page. Kurt stopped talking as I took notes. When I was done and looked up at him, he started talking again.

"I do not think of myself as a sales manager, Bob. I am more like sales support for these five guys. Because of my time in the shop working on off-road vehicles, I help most of the salesmen with writing up their orders. They make a lot of mistakes that I catch when I review the customer orders. The off-road supply business is very detailed, and it is easy to make mistakes on the sales orders. The issue is that there are many different types of vehicles. Because the manufacturers continuously change the cars and trucks, the parts needed for the repairs change, too. The orders require that each salesperson be careful with the parts they order.

"Recently, Warren ordered a hardtop for a customer's jeep. When the part came in, the hardtop did not fit the vehicle. Warren thought the customer's Jeep Wrangler was a 2010, but he was wrong. It was manufactured in 2011, which required a different top. The hardtop cost us 2,000 dollars, and the vendor would not let us return the part. So now it is sitting back in warehouse 2. The customer got mad at Warren because he ordered the wrong part. We reordered the correct part number and had it flown in because the customer needed the top immediately. He was going on a cross-country trip and was leaving in two days. We spent 4,400 dollars on the order, and the retail sale was 2,500 dollars. Now we have a 2,000-dollar part in our warehouse that is very difficult to sell. That thing will probably be in the warehouse for five years before we sell it. Plus, it is going to get all dirty, dusty, and maybe even damaged, which will make it unsalable."

I took some notes and asked Kurt, "Did Warren's commission check get dinged for the 2,000-dollar mistake?"

"I am not sure, but probably not."

"Okay, when we finish this meeting, I would like you to have that part pulled out of the warehouse, clean it up, and put it in the front showroom with a price tag to get rid of it. That hardtop is not going to become more valuable sitting in the warehouse—in fact, just the opposite."

Kurt asked me for a sheet of paper from my tablet to take notes. I gave him a second tablet that I had sitting next to me.

"Am I going to be taking *a lot* of notes?" he asked.

"From all the issues I have seen with the sales team, yes."

Kurt smiled and asked me for a pen also. Then he made a note about the jeep hardtop in the warehouse.

"Tell me about all the tires and wheels in the front showroom," I requested.

"What do you want to know?"

"I guess, why are they all in the showroom? We are wasting this valuable space. The front showroom should have four or five off-road vehicles such as jeeps, pickup trucks, or SUVs."

"I agree with you completely, Bob. It would be great to have those vehicles in the front showroom so that we could show our customers what all our products look like on a vehicle that we sell every day."

"By the time I get back here in about ten days, I want all those tires out of there, and off-road vehicles parked in that area. Got it?"

"But do I have the authority to make these changes? Should we ask Brian and Jordan to sit in this meeting?"

I hesitated for a moment before answering his question. I understood why he had asked. Kurt did not even have the authority to interview a candidate for a sales position, let alone make significant changes to the showrooms. "The answer is yes, Kurt, you have the authority to make these changes because I just gave you the authority. Brian and Jordan hired me to turn this company's financial results around. To accomplish that goal, we need to make some changes to this business. I am not planning to get approvals for any of the changes I will make. As of this past Monday, I am making the decisions here. I must do the job Brian and Jordan hired me to do, and I am going to be successful. So, if you have any more questions, let's get them on the table right now and get them all answered, and then move on, okay?"

"I have no more questions," he said. "But I must tell you that I love it that you are here. I have been afraid for years that some Monday morning, I would show up to work and find the front door padlocked with an out-of-business sign plastered to it. If you can turn this company around, I will be your biggest fan!"

"At six-foot-three and 300-plus pounds, you would be my biggest fan for sure!"

Kurt laughed, and we continued the conversation. We talked for another two hours, discussing what I needed to know to jump-start the sales of this company, including internet sales. Kurt's information and suggestions were valuable. We both had several pages of notes. Finally, Kurt asked me if he could just keep the whole tablet. He said he would take it home that evening to clean up his notes. "Then I will break down each issue into tasks that I can assign to some the sales staff," he concluded.

I said, "Of course!" After all, I had plenty of tablets for notetaking, and I was glad he was taking the initiative. I planned to clean up my notes and add them to my computer files for this client on my plane trip home Wednesday evening.

Kurt and I also had a detailed conversation about each of the salesmen, including their strengths and weaknesses. Having met them earlier, I was not surprised by anything Kurt had to say about their different personalities. The sales associates were easy to read.

There was a slight tap on the door, and Jordan poked his head in my office. "Lunch?" he asked.

I looked at my watch, and I could not believe that it was already 12:30. Kurt and I had been talking for three hours. My guess would have been that we had only been together for an hour. Time does fly when you are having fun! I looked up at Jordan and said, "Yes, it just so happens that I *am* hungry."

Jordan said that he and Brian would pick me up outside in five minutes, and I assured him I would be there.

Kurt stood up and put his hand out for a shake. "Bob, you cannot imagine how much I am looking forward to working with you over the next several months," he said. "I read your two books, and your personality is exactly like I thought it would be—no-nonsense, just get the work done."

"Hmm . . . I hope that is a compliment!" I exclaimed as I began putting on my nice warm parka.

"Yes, it is. You being here is very exciting for me. I can't wait to get home and tell my wife all about you. Initially, I was a little intimidated about meeting you because of what you do for a living. But now I feel just the opposite."

I was glad to hear that. "Kurt, please do me one favor," I said. "After you clean up your notes, please copy and paste them on an email and send them to me. I want to compare them to mine to make sure I did not miss anything. I will do the same and send you mine after I merge our lists."

Kurt agreed to my request and shook my hand again. I went out to the showroom front door and hopped into the passenger seat of Jordan's very blue pickup truck.

From the backseat, Brian asked, "How did your meeting go with Kurt?"

"Excellent, he gave me a ton of valuable information. We both have a significant follow-up list of to-do's with three pages of notes."

"What all did you talk about?" Brian asked.

"Sales. We talked about growing the sales in the retail store, the shop, and the internet stores. We are going to accomplish this turn-around by improving the appearance of the facility, parking lot, and retail store. The sales will grow when we put off-road vehicles in the front showroom and out in front of the parking lot. We need to clean up the appearance of the sales staff. We must clean up the main showroom, so the products on the shelves look salable to the customers. We need topflight managers on the management team to manage the shop, supervise the sales team, and oversee the financial department. We need a reliable manager to run the purchasing and warehouse departments."

"Bob," Jordan chimed in. "I am responsible for the purchasing and warehouse departments."

"Yes, I know. Jordan, I want the warehouse area protected, organized, and in perfect condition. I want the dollar value of the inventory down at least a 250,000 dollars in the next two or three months. I want the warehouse cleaned up and looking like we know what we are doing as a management team. Jordan, are you proud of how the warehouses look right now, including warehouse 2, the customer pick-up, and vendor return area?"

"No, sir, I am not."

"We need those areas cleaned up quickly to the point that you can come to me and say: *I am very proud of how we cleaned up the warehouse area. I am pleased with the new security over our total inventory area. We now have all our on-hand inventory balances entered in the computer software, and the counts are accurate. Our inventory balance is down by 300,000 dollars in the past two months. I am happy because I can now tell you the exact dollar amount of inventory we have in our warehouse. Each part in our inventory has current vendor pricing. We have 'minimum and maximum automatic order points' assigned to all the parts with high inventory turns. We have everything we received today inputted into the computer and stored in the proper location. We shipped every order received today, without exception. Our vendor returns area is 100 percent clean. We sent all the parts to the vendors timely for credit. The customer pick-up rack is empty because our sales team called our customers to come to the store to pick up their parts. Each customer showed up today and picked up their orders. We are paid current with 100 percent of our vendors. Our inventory turns have doubled in the past three months. At our last physical inventory, we had zero dollars shrinkage.* Until we can make all those statements accurate, I will not be happy!"

Jordan looked in the rearview mirror at Brian and said, "This guy is tough!"

"I know, that is why we hired him," Brian replied with a chuckle.

At lunch, after we sat down and the waitress took our orders, Jordan asked me what I had planned for that afternoon.

"I am going to interview Carole and Wes," I replied.

Jordan looked at Brian and said that he hoped I wouldn't make them cry. I told Jordan that I want to make it crystal clear to every employee and manager in the company that we are not going to fool around and "tippy-toe" through this turnaround. We are all going to make material changes to the operations of this company and make them quickly.

"You sure have a lot of the people talking," Brian said between bites of his lunch, "and they are liking what you are doing so far. Jordan and I have endorsed your changes to every person in the company. If you have any problems, please let us know, and we will fix them."

"I don't need help with anyone who is pulling the rope in the opposite direction," I told him. "If that happens, I will terminate that person and ask them to leave immediately. In all my other turn-arounds during the past twenty years, that has rarely happened."

"Why do you think that is? Why don't you get any pushback from the employees who want everything to stay the same with no changes?" he asked.

I thought about that for a moment while I took a sip of my beverage. "I believe there is an air about me that shows I have great confidence in what I am trying to accomplish. Employees see that I let nothing get in my way. I think people are a little afraid of me initially. But when they see that I know what I am doing and the result of my work will be of great benefit to them, they all line up and work hard to help me."

Jordan looked over at Brian and said, "Okay, I am completely convinced that hiring Bob was the right decision. He has been with us for only three days, and I believe he knows more about the company than I do."

Brian laughed, and I said, "That is my job, Jordan. I need to know all the details so I can fix the problems and put policies and procedures in place. Once I fix a problem, I never want it to reoccur. And, by the way, I have only been here for *two and a half days*—not three."

＊ ＊ ＊

Once we finished our lunch, we headed back to the office. I had two more interviews to accomplish before my flight back to Fort Lauderdale at 5:45, which was the only direct flight from Salt Lake City to Fort Lauderdale. Brian told me he would drive me to the airport and that we should be ready to leave at 4:00 PM. I agreed.

Back at the office, I hunted for Wes for our interview. Since my talk with Kurt took three hours, I wanted to get with Wes immediately because I was out of there at 4:00. I found the service manager in the shop chatting with some techs. I asked him if we could spend some time together so he could give me information about the shop operations.

We decided to meet in the conference room at the south end of the shop. As it turned out, the conference room was a poor choice for a meeting. The noise from the shop was loud, even though the conference room was enclosed. During the interview, Wes first told me that he did not think that he was doing a good job managing the shop operations. He said that the responsibilities were too much for him, and he could not keep up with the amount of work.

Wes was showing up in the mornings at 7:00 AM and working until 6:00 PM plus taking home paperwork with him each evening to get caught up. Wes said that he promised Brian he would stay on the job for one year, but it did not look like he was going to be able to keep his promise. I could see right away that this interview was not going to last very long at all.

Wes said, "Bob, I am going to be sixty-five soon. I don't want to work this hard anymore. When Brian said he was hiring you to turn this company around, I decided to schedule a meeting with you as soon as possible. My health is not good. My wife is getting cranky about the time I am putting into working here each week."

"So, if I read the tea leaves correctly, you want me to find a new service manager as soon as possible?" I asked.

"Yes, sir, that would be accurate."

"Okay, Wes, thank you for giving me a heads-up rather than a big surprise. I will promise you that we will begin the search for your replacement starting today and make it a priority. Sir, will you commit to me that you will stay until we find your replacement?"

"Yes, Bob, I think I can talk my wife into those terms and conditions."

"Thank you for being so honest; it is appreciated. Have a great day and kick some butt out there while you are still here."

Wes gave me a hearty laugh. "I will give the job 100 percent effort as long as I am receiving a paycheck from this company."

When Wes left the conference room, I pulled out my tablet to record some of my thoughts about the service manager position. I did not want to forget anything discussed in this meeting.

I went to find Brian and Jordan to give them the news about Wes. Neither was surprised. They commented that Wes was not long for this company because of how he had been managing the shop.

"By the time you get back here for your next visit, we will have a new service manager working for ABC Off-Road Supply," Jordan promised.

I breathed a sigh of relief. "That is good news because Wes has one foot out the door and the other one on a banana peel. Do you have a candidate in the 'on-deck circle' ready to start?"

"Yes, we do, he is an ex-military officer who was responsible for the fleet of cars on the local military base about ten miles from here."

"Guys, are you sure that your current group of techs can work for a military type? I noticed that most of your techs are millennials who will not react well to someone barking orders at them."

Jordan and Brian exchanged worried looks.

"Hmm . . . that could be a problem," Jordan said. "What should we do?"

"My suggestion is to use your best judgment when hiring a new manager over the largest group of employees who work for this company. The last thing you need is to have another turnover of a service manager after Wes leaves. I would love to interview the guy before you make a decision, but I guess that is not possible with me flying out of here this afternoon."

"I am semi-confident that this guy will be okay," Brian assured me. "He worked for the company a couple of years ago. He handled the setup of the stores for our internet sites."

"You like bringing ex-employees back, huh?" I commented.

"Well, I normally stay in touch with the employees who leave the company for a valid reason. It is a relationship thing!"

"I understand," I said. "My advice is if you hire this guy, you need to read him the rules before he starts. He needs to understand that this isn't a military facility. Don't get me wrong: I have the ultimate respect for the military, and I strongly recommend hiring them once they reenter the civilian world. But I also want this company to be profitable, so whomever you hire, that person needs to be a good fit. The constant turnover of management positions is a problem that gets in the way of this company being profitable."

Brian said, "I understand."

By now, it was just about time to leave for the airport. I packed up my computer, and soon Brian and I were on our way to the airport. During the twenty-five-minute ride, Brian talked about how thrilled he was to be working with me. Brian shared his positive feelings about how this story would end. This co-owner of ABC Off-Road Supply told me he believed it would not take long to get his company cleaned up and profitable. I simply sat in the passenger's seat and listened.

Brian pulled up to the Delta Airlines terminal and put the truck in park. He got out, pulled my suitcase out of the backseat, and put it on the sidewalk. Then Brian turned and hugged me. "Travel safely," he said. "I look forward to seeing you in ten days."

"This trip was a pleasure, Brian, and I look forward to the challenge. As soon as I return home, I will send you an email with a list of everything I would like you and Jordan to work on while I am away."

"Okay, I look forward to receiving it! I'm excited to get the process started."

We shook hands, and Brian got back into his jeep and headed back to Ogden.

My flight was five hours from Salt Lake City back to Fort Lauderdale. While on the plane, I had plenty of time to organize my thoughts and develop the email I had promised Brian I would send him that evening.

When I first toured the ABC Off-Road Supply facility, the condition of the place stressed me out. I had the impression this company was too far gone, plus most of the management team was either going to leave or be terminated. At the end of the third day, I felt better because I had faith in Brian and Jordan. I believed they wanted their business to be successful, perhaps even more than they wanted air to breathe!

* * *

The email that I sent to Brian and Jordan later that night listed the following items for them to focus on before my second visit.

✓ Clean up the shop and make it safe for the techs to work on vehicles.

✓ Take 99 percent of the tires out of the front showroom and replace them with four to five off-road vehicles.

✓ Create a company policy to have all employees park their off-road vehicles along the front of the parking lot to display them to every car that drives past the ABC Off-Road Supply facility.

✓ Develop a company policy about how the salespeople should be groomed and dressed appropriately.

✓ Create a company policy on the operating procedures for the customer pick-up area in the warehouse.

✓ Develop a company policy for the RTV ("return to vendor") inventory, stating who is responsible for keeping that area at a minimal level of stock.

✓ Start advertising and recruiting an accounting manager to handle the financial department of the company.

✓ *Schedule a meeting with the gentleman who handles the marketing for the company. (Please send me the Google Analytics reports for the past three months for my review.)*

✓ *Have the inventory and shelving in the retail showroom cleaned up, and then get rid of all the cardboard. Please review the pricing of all the stock for accuracy.*

✓ *Please send me a recap of the payroll (headcount and dollars) for the trailing 12 months using the following categories: management, sales and marketing, technician staff in the shop, inventory and warehouse employees, and administrative.*

✓ *Please send me the internet sales by internet store for the prior 12 months.*

I knew that this was a great deal of work for them to accomplish in ten days. I wanted to push the management team to see what they could achieve between my visits. Since the company did not have current financial statements, I planned to get as much financial information about sales and payroll so I could start measuring the company's weekly/monthly progress.

Chapter 5

COMMON SENSE
IS NOT THAT COMMON!

"There are no secrets to success. It is the result of preparation, hard work and learning from failure."

—COLIN POWELL, AMERICAN POLITICIAN

MY NEXT FLIGHT TO SALT LAKE CITY WAS UNEVENTFUL, which was perfect for me. I like five-hour flights when, fifteen minutes after the plane takes off, I am fast asleep until ten minutes before the plane lands. On this flight, I had a wonderful four-hour nap. Some naps are better than others. This nap was a great one!

When I got off the plane, I texted Brian that I would be in the passenger pickup area #7 at terminal 2 in 10 minutes.

He texted me back immediately: "I will be there in five minutes, and I got you coffee."

I did not check my bags this time, so getting out of the airport was much quicker than my first trip to Utah. Brian was sitting in his ABC Off-Road Supply–logoed gray Jeep Gladiator when I got to the pickup area. When he saw me, he jumped out of the vehicle and grabbed my carry-on suitcase. He loaded it in the backseat and then hopped back into the Gladiator.

It was a bright, sunny day with not a cloud in the sky, but once again, the air was frigid, and the ground was covered in snow. Since it was only the second week in February, I guess I should have expected it to be like this. Being that I live in Fort Lauderdale, cold to me is different than it is for the people who live in Utah. I looked around at the beautiful snow-capped mountains surrounding the airport. Utah is a beautiful state—worth putting up with the cold for a short while.

When I hopped into the passenger seat, Brian had a big smile on his face. I asked him my standard question, "How is everything at ABC Off-Road Supply?"

"You are going to be pleased," he told me.

"Why is that? What happened?"

"I am not going to spoil the surprise. You are going to have to wait and see. And, Bob—" He pointed to the center console. "There's your hot coffee."

"Thank you, Brian! A hot cup of coffee in this cold weather for a Fort Lauderdale guy makes all the difference!" I took a sip, and then I asked Brian if he hired the guy we had talked about to replace Wes to manage the shop.

He nodded. "Yes, he started last Monday. Jordan and I called him the Thursday morning after you left. That afternoon, we interviewed him and offered him the job. Because he worked for us before, we knew Jayson well. His responsibilities were to work on our internet parts sales. He just sat in his office all day and added parts to be sold on our website. He required very little supervision. He was able to start immediately because he was unemployed. He did not have to give a two-week notice to an existing employer."

"Why was he unemployed?" I asked.

"Hmm . . . I don't know. We didn't ask."

"Did you do a background check and have him do a drug test?"

"No, we did not."

"How was his first week on the job?"

Never, and I mean never, should a candidate be hired without a proper background check and drug test. There are too many possible problems that can occur when hiring an employee without doing the appropriate investigation in the candidate's background history. If the employee's position requires a degree or license (doctor, dentist, CPA, college instructor, etc.), these requirements must be checked with the third party (university, AICPA, state medical board, etc.) to verify that the person possesses the legal requirements for the position.

Hiring an employee is an easy thing to do if you don't do it right. All you need to do is put a mirror under the individual's nose to determine if he is breathing. There are no shortcuts that should be taken when recruiting and hiring an employee. All companies should do the proper background checks and drug tests 100 percent of the time when going through the hiring process.

The employee Brian and Jordan hired to work at ABC Off-Road Supply had been unemployed, which should have been a red flag when they offered him the job. It would have been nice to know why he had been jobless.

It is crystal clear to me that a big challenge with my turnaround engagement at ABC Off-Road Supply was the owners' hiring practices. Neither had any idea of the best practices when it comes to hiring new employees.

"Well, Bob, your intuition that he would be a 'drill sergeant' type of manager was a good guess. He is a screamer. I am afraid our new service manager may not connect well with our current group of techs."

I sighed. "If that is the case, we need to put our screamer on ninety-day probation and watch Jayson closely."

"Bob, what do you mean by ninety-day probation policy?" Brian asked.

When hiring a new employee, you should always notify the employee in the job offer letter that he or she is on a ninety-day probationary period with the company. The ninety days allows you and the company to carefully evaluate the employee's performance and determine if that person is a good fit for the position. The probationary period gives you the chance to terminate the employee with minimal exposure to a wrongful termination lawsuit initiated by the employee. This policy has two benefits: It helps the company get rid of a "bad hire," and you can do it with minimal risk of having to pay legal fees.

I didn't answer his question. Instead, I asked, "Do you have an employee manual?"

Brian said he didn't, and I pulled my cellphone from my pocket and dictated a note to my voice-memo app reminding myself to develop an employee manual for ABC Off-Road Supply. I had four or five sample employee manuals in my computer files from past turnaround clients. It would be easy to modify one of them for this client. I also made a memo about developing a "90-day new-hire probation policy."

Regardless of size, every company should have an employee manual. A well-written employee manual is a company's tool that establishes the rules of conduct for your organization. It should document the policies and procedures to guarantee a safe, healthy work environment for every employee. Solving problems for your employees are much easier to resolve if your company has a clear and concise employee manual.

The manual should include information about company paydays, employee benefits, personal leave and sick time, vacation policy, and paid holidays. The clearer the document is on company policies, the better. Moreover, the employee manual should be a "working document." In other words, the HR department should update the manual every time a relevant issue occurs in the company that the employees should be aware of.

I thanked Brian for sending me the sales and payroll information I had requested in my email from ten days earlier. That data had been vital for me to develop my action plan for the first three months of this turnaround engagement. One thing I learned when I analyzed the sales is that the off-road supply business seems to be seasonal. The highest sales totals for the previous 12 months had been from March through June and October through December.

When I did the analysis, I created a long list of questions I wanted to ask Brian and Jordan on this trip. My goal was to understand the sales information and payroll costs better. I wanted to learn as much as I could early on in this turnaround engagement. I knew I had no room for any mistakes because this company's available cash was incredibly tight.

* * *

When Brian pulled into the ABC Off-Road Supply parking lot, the first thing I noticed was the two dozen pickup trucks, jeeps, and SUVs all lined up, perfectly spaced in the front of the facility. Four of the vehicles were parked up on ramps, tilting the jeeps toward the street. Whoever had arranged the cars and trucks had done a fantastic job.

"This looks great, very professional," I told Brian. "What an upgrade in the appearance of your company. People driving past the facility are going to notice this. This location is excellent, right on Main Street. Now the business looks successful to all the thousands of cars driving up and down this street daily."

"I now know what you meant during your first visit," Brian said after exiting the Gladiator and grabbing my suitcase. "The traffic in the store has dramatically increased since we paid attention to the appearance of our parking lot. We had a great week of sales. Your direction on your first visit has already impacted the health of the company. I believe this little change in arranging the vehicles in the parking lot made a big difference."

"This is not a little change, Brian. You are marketing your business to the driver of every automobile that drives past your company daily. Dressing up this parking lot full of vehicles is a big change. I have a feeling you are going to have several weeks of improved sales compared to the prior year."

As we walked toward the entrance, Brian said that they had also changed every light bulb and fixed all the broken light fixtures on the building. He said they had done the same in the front showroom so that the showroom vehicles would have spotlights on them after dark and until 1:00 AM. People who drive past the facility would now know what ABC Off-Road Supply is selling!

Brian and I walked into the retail showroom. Jordan and Scott were waiting at the door to greet me. I shook their hands.

Scott was wearing his big "Scott smile" and said, "Bob, welcome to the *new* ABC Off-Road Supply."

"Scott, whoever took charge of the outside of this building, did a great job."

Jordan said, "Thank you, Bob. The funny thing is, making the outside look so much better only took us an hour."

"What a difference. Great job!" I told him. "Now, we have to keep it that way every day from now on!"

The improvements in the retail showroom were more noticeable than the parking lot. I looked at Brian and said, "Wow, are we in the same showroom I visited two weeks ago?"

Now I understood why Brian had such a glowing smile on this face when he picked me up from the airport. The place looked terrific! Someone had taken charge of this retail area and kicked butt. The floor was clean and shiny. The products on the shelves were well-organized. There was not a spot of dust anywhere.

"Come see the front showroom," Brian said with excitement, and I eagerly followed him.

Five vehicles were parked on the showroom floor: three different types of jeeps, one pickup truck, and a blue SUV they called "Blueberry" (it had obviously gotten its name because it was the exact color of a blueberry). All the tires had been removed from the area, and the fancy wheels were mounted on the wall. The front windows were clear (no streaks or residue from the cleaner), and the newly polished floor glistened in the light. Above the wheels on the back wall, Brian and his team had installed three television monitors. The TVs played continuous loops of videos with off-road vehicles showing off their abilities to go where no other vehicle could go. Jordan said that Michael, one of the sales guys, contacted five or six off-road product vendors, and they had supplied the videos. Brian noted that buying and installing the eight television monitors took one day and cost less than $3,000.

"Eight televisions?" I asked. "I only see three."

"Follow me!" Brian said.

The four of us walked back into the retail showroom to the sales counter in the back of the room. Five more TV monitors were mounted up high on the wall behind the sales counter. They had done an excellent job with this project. The monitors lit up the room. I could not believe all the changes this management team was able to make to this business in ten days. I was impressed.

"Guys, you have performed an absolute miracle in this sales area! I cannot believe this is the same retail showroom from ten days ago."

"Bob, we are not done with our tour yet. We have a lot more to show you."

Before we left the sales area, I shook hands with all the sales guys and said hello to each one. The sales staff were all wearing new light-blue ABC shirts with a new pair of khakis. Warren was beardless; he referred to his face as "clean-shaved." I could not believe the improvement in this place in a week and a half.

Three whiteboards were mounted on the walls of the small room right off the sales area. The service manager was using two of the boards for scheduling the customers' vehicles in the shop. The third whiteboard listed each salesperson's month-to-date sales with their monthly sales quota and the balance they needed to sell to hit their quota. Whoever had laid out the whiteboard to post the sales had done an outstanding job. It looked professional and well-organized.

Brian wanted to go out to the shop to show me what else they had accomplished while I was away. I wanted to stop here to see what they had done with this room. It was clean, organized, and a good motivator for the sales team.

So far, all the improvements painted a clear picture that these two owners had listened to every word I said during my first visit. It also showed me that they were not lazy. They had both rolled up their sleeves and gotten the work done!

* * *

As we were walking out, Jayson, the new service manager, was entering the room. Brian introduced me.

Brian looked at Jayson and said, "Jayson, this is Bob Curry, the guy that I was telling you about who is helping us to improve our company and make it successful."

Jayson reached out his hand, and we shook hands. "Mr. Curry, do you mind, could you show me your big stick?"

I looked at him like he was crazy. "Big stick, Jayson?"

"Yes, sir. The way these guys have been working their tails off since your last visit, I assumed you had a big stick that you were going to beat them with if they did not get this place cleaned up." Jayson's attempt at humor did not make me laugh.

Jayson was over six feet tall with a muscular build. He looked to be in his late thirties or early forties with his head shaved bald. He indeed looked like a stern guy with a grim look on his face. Brian had told me earlier that Jayson was a "screamer." I could see that in his eyes. He looked like a drill sergeant, even without the uniform.

"I do not have a big stick, Jayson. All I use to motivate my clients is confidence and common sense."

Jayson asked, "Confidence and common sense? How is that, sir?"

I had a feeling Jayson was going to call me "sir" the whole time, so I did not ask him to call me "Bob" because I knew it probably would not change anything. "Yes, Jayson, confidence, and common sense. I have a lot of confidence that I can turn this place around to be profitable. I believe we can very quickly grow sales, reduce expenses, and clean this place up. I think that if we reduce the inventory level, it will improve the company's cash situation. Then I am planning a few more changes to improve cash flow, besides aggressively growing the sales. Very quickly, life is going to be different for every employee who works for this company. Once that occurs, ABC Off-Road Supply is going to be a very successful business."

Then Jayson asked, "And the common sense? How does that fit?"

"None of the changes we are making are magic," I replied. "The decisions I am making to turn this company around come from my past experiences with other turnaround clients and common sense. My goal is to teach this management team how to run this business to take care of their customers, employees, and vendors. If they do that, then all they need is common sense, and everything will be okay. But, unfortunately, I have found in my past experiences, the problem with common sense is that it's not that common."

Jayson just nodded and said, "Good to meet you, sir. I am sure that I will see a lot of you around here, right?"

"Yes, I will be here three to four days a week, every other week."

"It is a pleasure, sir, to meet you!"

"Thank you, Jayson."

He immediately went off to help a tech with a vehicle problem.

* * *

I followed Brian, Jordan, and Scott out to the shop. Scott walked beside me, and I sensed that he had something on his mind he wanted to share with me. In fact, it was showing all over his face, as if his head was about to explode. Finally, he asked, "Bob, what did you think of Jayson? You have to know he was not my first choice."

"He seemed okay to me," I replied. "But, to be honest, my opinion does not matter. What matters is whether he performs his job well or not. If he gets the shop productive and making money, I will be a big fan. I have straightforward rules about managers and employees. If they are productive, show up at work on time to do their job, and get along with everyone in the company, I love them. If they don't, I am not in their fan club."

Scott shook his head in acknowledgment, and I went on,

"Business is about making money. The employees are *tools* for the company to make a profit. If the employee is not a useful tool for the company to be successful, I either train them to do their job better or find a new employee."

Again, Scott nodded to indicate that he understood what I was saying, but then he grew quiet. Perhaps what I had said intimidated him. Scott did not have a lot of confidence about his contribution to ABC Off-Road Supply so far.

Once we all got out in the shop area, material changes to this area of the business also became apparent. Over the weekend, Brian, Jordan, and their team had pulled everything out of the shop, scrubbed the concrete floor, and then painted it gray. They had all stayed late Sunday night to put everything back in place to avoid any unproductive time on Monday morning. The shop area looked great. I mean, it looked as good as a shop could look for this type of work. I was impressed.

Sometimes, much like in ABC Off-Road Supply's situation, it does not take a lot of sweat and payroll hours to clean up the environment of a company's facility. All it requires is "fresh eyes" and discipline to clean the place and then keep it clean. Business owners and senior managers should always have fresh eyes and question everything that goes on because it is the right thing to do. My turnaround career has involved fixing issues for company owners who had walked past their problems for years. They had walked past, or ignored, the troubling issues for so long that they were no longer able to see their challenges.

Brian said, "I have one more area to show you, Bob!"

We walked over to the inventory area. There were security cameras installed.

Jordan said, "Follow me, Bob, I want to show you our new security system."

We walked into his office, which was inside the purchasing department. There was a big TV monitor next to his desk on the wall showing the views of the sixteen different cameras they had installed. The cameras were mounted high up on the walls all over the company.

Their amazing progress proved to me that this turnaround was going to happen. These guys had worked their tails off for the past ten days. If they continued to make this much steady progress, this business would be successful quickly. These positive changes proved to me that almost any business could go "from red to black" if the managers work this hard daily to improve their business.

I suggested to Brian, Jordan, and Scott that we schedule time now to talk about what we needed to accomplish during this visit.

Scott said, "How about we all meet in the conference room in ten minutes?"

"Sounds like a plan," I responded.

All four of us headed to our respective offices to get ready for the meeting. I had a list of stuff I wanted to talk about with Brian and Jordan, but the tour had interrupted that conversation. However, it had been a positive interruption—these guys had made great progress! I unpacked my backpack and found my notes. I then headed to the conference room with the coffee Brian had picked up for me. It was a little cold, so I stopped by the break room to "nuke" it for thirty seconds.

* * *

When I arrived at the conference room, Scott and the two owners were already there. Scott and Jordan had their computers open to take notes, and Brian had a white tablet in front of him to write on.

"Well, gentlemen, you have done an amazing job cleaning up this business, my congratulations. I am so impressed with the dramatic progress you have made in such a short time."

"This progress has been very tough on all of us," Brian commented. "We worked long hours until exhaustion set in. I bet we all slept well last night. I know I did!"

"I believe it. You have accomplished a lot! What do you have next on your task list?"

"We all wanted to talk to you before we started our next project," Jordan said.

"Okay, here are my thoughts. I know that you spent some money to make all these changes happen. So, my suggestion is for our next project to generate some cash to replenish that money. Brian, do you have the sales team's commission plan in writing?"

"I have it written down in my head," he responded.

I smiled. "Okay, then take what you have in your head and write it down on a sheet of paper so that I may read it."

Brian wrote down on his tablet to email Bob the sales commission plan.

I explained, "I am going to review it and see if I can come up with some adjustments to the plan to get the salespeople excited and motivated to sell more and make larger commissions. Next, Jordan, please remind me, what is your current labor billing rate in the shop?"

Jordan said, "It is 92.50 per hour."

"Okay, effective at noon today, let's raise the rate to 125 dollars for all new orders."

Brian and Jordan looked at each other like I was kidding.

Scott said, "Bob, are you serious? You are going to increase the labor rate by 32.50 all in one day?"

"Hmm . . . you know, Scott, let me think about that before I decide. Okay, I have thought enough about this issue to make the decision. Yes, raise the labor rate at noon today."

All three guys started making notes about our second topic because, for the most part, they did not know what to say about my decision.

"Gentlemen, while I was home, I did some research on labor billing rates in the specialty automotive shops. The minimum rate that I found was 135 dollars, and the highest rate was 150 dollars. Based on my research, we are materially underbilling for our work in the shop. If all goes well this week, we will make another rate increase soon. How do we make this happen?"

Brian said, "I will tell Kurt after the meeting."

"Brian, instead, why don't we ask Kurt to join us now since we are making some decisions that are going to affect his sales team?"

Scott said, "I will go get Kurt and ask him to join us."

I commented, "Great, Scott!"

When Kurt and Scott returned, Kurt was prepared with a white tablet and pen to take notes.

"Good morning, Kurt. We were discussing some issues in the sales area of the company that will affect your salespeople. We wanted you to participate in the discussion."

"Thank you, Bob. I appreciate that!"

"First, I am going to take a good hard look at the sales commission plan and probably make some adjustments to generate some excitement with the sales team. And, Kurt, you are more than welcome to review and approve any adjustments to the plan. Once I look at it and make some comments, I will forward it to everyone in the room for your comments." Then I announced to all present, "Just as a general comment, when I or anyone on this management team circulates information, please make it a priority and respond as quickly as possible. We do not have the luxury of a lot of time to make decisions. We do not need an act of Congress to change policies and procedures to improve the profitability of this business. Unfortunately, I have not seen the financial statements yet because they are not available. So, since I cannot make good business decisions using current financial statements (that do not exist right now), I am going to assume the worst and hope for the best. Is everyone clear about this issue?"

All the guys looked up from writing their notes and nodded.

"Okay, then, let's move on. Kurt, we are going to change the hourly labor rate your salespeople are charging our customers on sales quotes from 92.50 to 125 dollars per hour for retail orders and 60 to 65 dollars for the wholesale orders. This change is valid for orders that are written immediately after this meeting. Kurt, are you okay with that decision?"

"Yes, sir, and the sales team will be as well. I believe we have been undercharging our customers for our labor. I have felt this way for years."

Kurt's comment made me think about another general point I wanted to discuss with this team. "Gentlemen, I want to make this clear. This turnaround of ABC Off-Road Supply business is your responsibility, not mine. My role here is to help, support, coordinate, and add my years of experience while I am here. ABC Off-Road Supply is your company, and you are going to be here when I am long gone. If you see something you believe should be changed, improved, stopped, started, or whatever, say something! I am new to this business, but I have already spotted many things that should be changed. The key to the success of this turnaround is to be aware of all the problems and then fix them. I cannot fix anything if I don't know there is a problem. Please, if you see something that needs our attention, write it down. Share it with me anytime, in a meeting, by email, text, smoke signals, or pony express. The faster we fix all these issues, the faster that you will not have to deal with my being around here, disrupting your life."

"Bob, you are not disrupting anything," Brian said. "I love it that you are here. I am looking forward to continuing our work together and learning from you."

Jordan added, "As am I."

Scott chimed in, "Me too!"

If nothing else, I now had the management team's loyalty. "Okay, let's move on."

They all put their pens back to paper.

"Every Wednesday at noon, we will hold the formal manager's meeting. Let's order in lunch for these meetings so that we can use the hour efficiently. At the manager's meeting, we will review accomplishments made during the first half of the week and plan which actions must get done over the next two and a half days. The meeting will last for no longer than one hour. We need to manage our employees—and if we are in meetings all the time behind closed doors, we are not adequately supervising our staff."

They all agreed to this, and I excused Kurt from the meeting since we had already covered what he needed to know.

Brian glanced at his watch. "Bob, I asked our marketing guy,

David, to come in this morning to meet with you. He should be here by now."

"Great!" I said. "I am looking forward to this meeting. Do you want to bring him here so we can meet in the conference room?"

Brian replied, "Sure, I will go check to see if he is in the show-room. I will be right back."

Jordan and Scott stayed in the conference room because, as they told me, they wanted to watch me in action with this vendor. I was not sure what they meant. Five minutes later, Brian returned with David. I stood up and shook David's hand and introduced myself.

David was a big guy, probably six-foot-five and in his mid-forties. He weighed at least 250 pounds but looked a lot heavier because he was wearing a thick winter coat. He did not look like the "computer nerd" or "marketing geek" I was expecting.

He took off his coat and put it on the back of one of the chairs. After he sat down, he asked, "So, Mr. Curry, how can I help you?"

"You can help me by explaining what you do for ABC Off-Road Supply and what you charge for your services?" I told him.

"I do marketing services to drive business on the internet to the company. I purchase AdWords for ABC Off-Road Supply. I make the phones ring here. My work sends people to ABC Off-Road Supply website, so the company sells more of its products to customers all over the world."

"Well, David, that is all wonderful. What do you charge the company for your services?"

"Mr. Curry, the company spends approximately 5,000 dollars a week for me to purchase the AdWords."

I wrote that down and asked, "How is the 260,000 dollars broken down between the AdWords cost and what you keep as your fees?"

He shifted in his chair. "I don't have those exact figures with me."

"I don't need the exact figures. Just give me the ballpark amount that this company spends on buying AdWords and how much they pay you to purchase the AdWords."

"Sir, I will not share that information with you. That information is confidential."

"Well, I am going to have to disagree with you. We are going to need the breakdown of the cost of your fees and the total dollar amount paid to Google for the AdWords. Do we have a contract with your agency?"

"No, not a written one."

"Brian, do we have a verbal contract with David's agency?"

Brian answered, "I am not aware of any contract."

"David, do you have a written or verbal contract with this company?"

"No, sir, I guess not."

"Well, then, before we get too involved with your fees, can you please share with me the most effective AdWords that drive business to my client's website?"

"Mr. Curry, I definitely cannot tell you the exact AdWords we use! That is part of our secret sauce! Would you like to review the Google Analytics reports? These reports document the quality of our marketing services."

"I am afraid that you do not understand what I am asking, David. You need to understand how important it is for you to answer my questions honestly. I need to know this: If Brian and Jordan's company is paying you 260,000 dollars per year to purchase AdWords, how much do you pay the vendor and how much do you keep for payment of your services?"

David looked glum and annoyed as he opened his laptop to find the answer to my question. His expression quickly turned furious as he searched his records. "We have paid 187,200 dollars in the past twelve months for the AdWords."

I used the calculator app on my phone and then looked up at David. "That means that you kept 72,800 dollars for the year as your fee, correct?"

"Yes, sir."

"So, you are charging ABC Off-Road Supply a 28 percent fee to purchase the AdWords, correct?" I looked at Brian and Jordan and said, "My other clients are paying their marketing firms between 10 and 12 percent fees for the same work that you are paying this gentleman 28 percent. Okay, David, thank you for your time. This meeting is over."

"Mr. Curry, what is wrong? I have been doing a great job for this company. I am getting the feeling you don't like me or respect the job that I have done for this company."

"No, sir, there is no problem, no problem at all. Your services are appreciated. But the issue is that I need to make sound business decisions for this company to grow their sales and be profitable. What I hear from you is that your services, which you refer to as your *secret sauce,* are top secret. Well, sir, if those are the terms and conditions for your services, your business with this company ends immediately after this meeting."

"Wow, what did I do to deserve this treatment?" he asked in a fluster.

"Sir, you materially overcharged this company by 133 percent for your fees. If you had changed the market rate for your services, an additional 42,000 to 47,000 dollars could have been used for ABC's marketing. I am sure that your Google Analytics reports would have looked a lot better with the additional AdWords rather than the money going into your firm's checking account. How many employees work at your firm, David?"

"I do not have any employees; I only have 1099 people I hire for special projects."

"How many 1099 people work on the ABC account to find and purchase the most effective AdWords?"

"I do all the work myself for this account."

"Okay, thank you for your time and the great job you have done for this company, but your services will no longer be needed."

"Mr. Curry, is there any way I can save this account? I love working with Brian and Jordan."

"Well, sir, if that is the case, please go back to your office and bring the file with all the paid invoices for ABC. I want to review the information before I make that decision."

"If I show you that information," David said, "you will know all my confidential information, and then you will not need me to do your marketing. You are going to cause this company to have a huge dip in their internet sales. Do you realize that?"

"I promise you that will not happen. Five minutes after you leave this conference room, I will have a national advertising firm on the phone and hire them to do the same services you have done that will cost this company about 50,000 dollars less per year. I am confident we will not experience a dip in sales. In fact, I am guessing we will see a 20 to 25 percent growth in internet sales within the first sixty days. Again, thank you for your time, your expensive services, and have a great day."

David gave Jordan and Brian an incredulous stare. "Are you okay with what this gentleman is doing here?" he asked.

ABC Off-Road Supply was using a one-person marketing firm that was charging the company outrageous rates for its services. The sole proprietor of this firm was charging ABC a fee of 28 percent of the cost of the amount spent on AdWords. Two of my current clients were paying a fee equal to 12 percent and 10 percent of the total amount paid. Unfortunately, some companies out there have no idea of the market rates for this type of marketing service, ABC Off-Road Supply being one.

Jordan looked at Brian and said, "I will answer David's question." Brian nodded, and Jordan turned his attention to David. "Yes, I am pleased with Bob's decision. He has exposed how much you have been overcharging us for marketing. Now we will hire a professional firm to do our marketing services. We will pay a fair market price to the new firm. As Bob said, David, thank you for your time and have a great day."

David stood, put his laptop in his backpack, pulled his coat off the back of the chair, and stormed from the room.

I picked up my phone and called the marketing firm that I used for several other of my clients. The firm's name is XYZ Marketing, located in Hollywood, Florida. I turned on the speaker on my phone so that everyone in the room could hear the conversation. I got the owner of the firm on the phone (Anthony Smith) and first asked him about his golf game.

He said, "Bob, my game is getting better from tee to the lakes or tee to deep in the woods. The last time I played eighteen holes, I only lost fifteen balls. I am now keeping the 'balls lost' statistic on the second line of the scorecard right below my scores. A good round for me is losing less than a dozen balls per eighteen holes. Did I tell you that I talked to the pro shop about making larger scorecards?"

I knew I should not ask, but I did anyway, "No, why do you need a larger scorecard?"

"Bob, when you score double digits on back-to-back holes, it is hard to write your scores in those small spaces on the scorecard!"

"Anthony, enough about your wonderful golf game. The reason I called is to see if you would like a new client for your firm. Are you interested?"

He said that he would love to have a new client. I told him that they spend $5,000 per week on AdWords, email blasts, and social media. I told him that he would have to waive the first month's fees, and all the funds would purchase leads in the next 30 days to drive sales. I added that he could charge a 10 percent monthly fee starting on month two of his services.

He responded, "Bob, I will draw up a contract and send it to you as soon as you provide me the contact information of my new client."

I looked at Brian and Jordan, and they were both nodding their heads. I told Anthony that I would email him all the information he needed within the next half an hour, and we ended the call.

Brian, Jordan, and Scott were all staring at me.

"Gentlemen, what's up?" I asked.

"Bob, how did you know that David was overcharging ABC Off-Road Supply so much with his fees?" Scott asked.

"I didn't know. I was investigating and asking questions. I could tell from the look on David's face that he was hiding something, so I went after what he was trying to hide. As soon as he told me the information was confidential, I knew that I had him."

Jordan said, "If I am calculating this correctly, you just saved the company 44,200 dollars, which includes not paying a marketing fee for the first month of services."

"Plus, I am seriously projecting a 20 percent growth in internet sales during the next year. That should be an increase in sales between 400,000 and 450,000 dollars. The firm I called to replace David is very good at what it does. The problem with David was that he had figured out that the management team here was not very knowledgeable about marketing and took advantage of you with his fees. When he raised his prices, and you did not know about it or say anything, he raised them some more. I hate people who make a living by taking advantage of their clients."

To manage a business successfully, the management team must have access to data and information about the company to make sound business decisions. The same is also true about the marketing function, as described. Just having a daily bank balance does not accomplish that goal. Information and reports from the balance sheet, income statement, budgets, cash flow forecasts, inventory turns, Google Analytics, and shop productivity reporting provide the required information to make daily decisions to manage the business. Without this information, the managers are shooting from the hip and guessing what to do next. This type of decision-making does not translate into a profitable business.

Now that we were all on the same page, I said, "Okay, I will forward all the information to the new marketing agency. As soon as we get the new contract, we will all sit down and review the terms and conditions together. Then we need to talk further about how we allocate the funds to the different categories: emails, digital media, pay-per-click, and social media."

"How do we do that?" Jordan asked. "I have no idea how to spend our money to get the most effective value for our market dollars."

I replied, "First, we put together a plan on how to spend the money. Next, a month or two later, I review the results from Google Analytics. Then I adjust the spending by category and review the results again. I keep changing the spending per category until I find what works best. It is a trial-and-error method, but it is better than trusting someone like David to make those decisions and pay royally for his guesses. My advice is, if you are going to spend 260,000 dollars on marketing, you need to pay close attention to how you are spending that money. I think this company should be doing a whole lot more posting on social media than it is currently doing to increase internet sales."

"How do you suggest we do that?" Brian asked.

"That issue is relatively easy to solve. I am guessing that every one of your employees has Facebook, Instagram, and other social media accounts. I suggest we start a monthly competition among your employees. The employee who has the best posts to the ABC Off-Road Supply social-media accounts gets a prize. The prize may be dinner at a nice restaurant, a twenty-five-dollar gift card, or something special. The award is not as critical as the employee getting acknowledged for making social media posts. By making a game out of posting to social media sites with the employees, the company receives excellent marketing at a minimal cost. Also, the employees get excited about winning the competition. What a great win-win situation!"

Scott was smiling ear to ear. "I love the idea, Bob! I will take charge of this project and get it started immediately."

"The videos I have seen from Moab are a lot of fun to watch," I told him. "They would draw a lot of attention to our website. The more pictures and videos posted to Facebook and Instagram; the more people will visit our website. When more and more people are visiting our website, more internet sales occur."

"I will make this happen! Trust me!" said Scott.

Unfortunately, to date, I had nothing to go on to be able to trust Scott.

The alarm on my phone went off, indicating that I had a meeting with Carole, the bookkeeper, in five minutes. I wished I had more time to meet with Brian and Jordan because I had more issues on my "Brian and Jordan list." I quickly finished all my follow-up notes from this meeting and headed over to Carole's office.

Bill asked before I left the meeting to go visit Carol, "Bob, I have to ask you a question before you go. Is your marketing friend as bad of a golfer as he indicated when you were talking to him on the phone?"

I responded, "No, he is not that bad. He was making up those comments to get you guys laughing. He is a very friendly and funny guy. On the golf course, I am laughing my butt off for 18 holes because he is so funny."

Bill responded, "I did not want to comment while you were on the speaker phone with him, but my first thought was *Wow, he must be really a bad golfer!*"

* * *

When I walked into Carole's office, I could feel the stress pouring off her. I guessed she was about seventy years old. She looked more like a grandmother than a bookkeeper. I do not mean that grandmothers cannot be bookkeepers; it was more her mannerism and the way she dressed that did not quite fit in this environment. I introduced myself.

"I know who you are, Mr. Curry," Carole said. "I have one question for you. How soon can you get me out of here?"

Hmm . . . Carole's question was not a good foundation for a strong accounting department. This poor woman basically felt like she was in jail and was asking for my help to her get out. I felt terrible, and I immediately wanted to help her.

I answered, "Carole, I will do everything that I can to help you get out of here as quickly as possible. We will start recruiting for an accounting manager immediately. I promise you that I will give it my maximum effort to hire your replacement."

"Mr. Curry, I cannot wait to retire. Even though I am here only three mornings a week, it is too stressful for me."

I stared at her, thinking about what to say next. I could not think of anything to say to her right then. I decided to get out of her office to avoid adding stress to her situation. Poor Carole, she looked like her head was ready to explode from the pressure.

I headed back to my office to review my notes from my early meetings and clean them up. I had an interview scheduled with Ron, but first, I wanted to start the process of recruiting an accounting manager.

I found Scott in the sales area and asked him to join me in my office. We walked back to my office together. On the way, Scott asked me if I was upset about what went down with the marketing guy. "I did not think he was doing a good job here," Scott told me. "I felt that we needed to hire another marketing firm a long time ago. He was charging us too much for doing a mediocre marketing job."

"If you think there is a problem in this company, you need to tell me immediately and not wait until I find this stuff out myself," I said. (Scott made me laugh: He knew there was a problem with David *after* I fired the guy.) When we got to my office, I said, "Okay, let's move on to a new topic. We need to recruit and hire an accounting manager to replace Carole. We need to find someone as quickly as possible. But I am not going to sacrifice hiring the right person to get her replacement fast. I will not settle for someone who is not qualified or a good fit for the position. It is more critical to find the right person than to find someone who can start soon. Scott, does the company have a job description for an accounting manager?"

"No, sir, but I can use Google and find one."

"Never mind about that, I think that I have four or five on my computer from other recent turnarounds. I will find one and send it to you. Where can we advertise to find a finance person?"

"Don't worry about that, Bob. I will deal with it. I will try to get some candidates in here before you leave for Fort Lauderdale on Thursday evening."

I thought that maybe I had accidentally found something that Scott could do to help me. I sat down at my desk to find a couple of job descriptions on my computer for an accounting manager. I found three, reviewed them, and emailed the best one to Scott. I made several notes on my tablet. I did not want to forget anything important that I needed to accomplish, especially with the Carole issue. Scott left my office and was off to start advertising and recruiting for an accounting manager.

I had planned to interview Carole, but immediately upon entering her office, I knew that asking her any questions would be fruitless. Hopefully, Scott would do a great job of finding candidates for this position. A good candidate would be an accounting manager level employee to fulfill all this client's financial needs.

* * *

I went to find Ron for our scheduled one-to-one, a little late because I first had to deal with the Carole issue. I found Ron in the warehouse, packing parts for customer orders. After we shook hands, we decided to go back to my office for some privacy during our conversation.

I asked Ron to tell me all about his job with ABC Off-Road Supply.

Ron took a long pause like he did not know where to start. "Mr. Curry, I'm not sure what to tell you first. We start each morning putting away all the parts we received the day before that we didn't get to during the previous day. Then we finish shipping any open customer orders that we did not have time to do yesterday. This place is so difficult to keep organized because the parts inventory is not in the accounting software. Sometimes I have no idea where to put the inventory because stuff is spread all over the warehouse. We always have a tough time finding parts for the customer orders. Unfortunately, we are not very efficient here."

Ron and I talked for more than an hour about all the problems with the warehouse and inventory. I took seven pages of notes. There were many problems in the warehouse that needed attention immediately. We then decided that Ron would give me a detailed tour of both warehouses.

To get to the first warehouse, we had to walk through the front and retail showrooms. I was pleasantly surprised. There were several customers in the retail showroom. Brian was waiting on a customer and looked up as Ron, and I passed by. He smiled and gave me a wink that seemed to suggest it would be another great sales day. Rather than rush through the sales area to get to the warehouse, I stopped to take this all in—a crowded room of customers.

When I am doing a turnaround engagement, there are many stressful times, mostly because change creates stress for the company. But there are also times when I need to stop and smell the roses. This moment was one of those times.

Ron and I got to the first warehouse. We were walking through the racks when I asked Ron, "What are your fastest-moving products, and which are your slowest-moving parts?"

"I have no idea. I do not have any reporting since the inventory is not on the computer," Ron answered.

For a business that had sold $6.3 million the previous year, there were very few critical issues more important than knowing their inventory turns. We needed to fix a lot of problems with the company. There were three significant problems with ABC Off-Road Supply: Number one was the management team, number two was no financial reporting, and number three was not having an inventory software system on the computer with operational reporting. Inventory valued at $750,000 is such a material asset for this company. This amount of stock was causing a cash flow issue. I knew we needed to focus on the inventory problems and get the financial reporting current. I was following Ron around, but my mind was on fixing the company's problems.

I followed Ron to warehouse 2. When we entered, Jayson, the new service manager, was standing behind Alec, one of the young techs, who was working on a big Ford pickup truck. He was installing new tires and wheels on the vehicle. Alec did not seem to notice Jayson standing immediately behind him.

Suddenly, Jayson screamed in a booming voice, "Alec, where are your protective safety glasses?!"

Alec almost jumped a foot in the air. Jayson was right, and Alec should have been wearing his protective eyewear. I felt sorry for Alec. My first thought was that no one should treat another employee like that—and I mean never. Twenty-one-year-old Alec was a rookie tech. He had made a mistake and would probably make more mistakes in the future. Yelling at him as Jayson did was wrong. I knew that Alec was extremely bothered by the transaction with Jayson, and rightfully so. Alec reached into his toolbox for his glasses and put them on.

I was so glad I had seen this happen because it spoke volumes about Jayson's management style and ability. I am not the kind of individual who makes snap judgments about people, but I was not comfortable that Jayson was going to be the service manager for this company very long. That was bad. It was now my responsibility to make sure that another transaction like that never happened again in the four walls at ABC Off-Road Supply.

I knew that Ron had a lot more to show and tell me about the two warehouses and the inventory, but I ended our tour immediately. "Ron, please go back and finish shipping your orders, we will continue this tour later!"

Ron saw the angry look on my face. "Yes, sir!" he said and then quickly disappeared back to his shipping area in warehouse 1.

I asked Jayson to follow me back to my office. I told him I needed to have a chat with him in private. He had a stern look on his face because he knew I did not like how he had behaved with Alec. I did not want to talk with Jayson about the screaming event in front of other employees.

When we got back to my office, I closed the door. I turned and looked at the service manager and asked, "Jayson, how would you react if someone screamed at you as you did with Alec?"

Jayson's eyes were glued to the floor. I am sure he thought that screaming at Alec in front of me was going to cost him his job. Jayson started to talk, and I interrupted him.

"Never mind, I don't need to know your answer. Jayson, I have a strong recommendation for you. Don't ever do that again at ABC Off-Road Supply while I am visiting this company. If you do, it will be your last fifteen minutes working for this company. That type of management style is *not* acceptable at this company."

"Do you have the authority to fire me?" Jayson asked.

That was a risky question to ask me in this circumstance. I hesitated for a few seconds and then said, "Do you want to test me? Would you like to see if I have the authority to get rid of a poor service manager working for this company? My suggestion, sir, is for you to go back to your shop and work with each of the service techs to make them more efficient at their job. After you stood behind Alec and screamed at him, I am sure that he needed to go to the men's room to change his underwear. Your management style creates very costly employee turnover. A word of advice, sir, don't ever speak to another employee with that tone of voice again. Thank you for your time. But before you go, I have one last question for you. How do you think Alec feels about you right now? Before you answer that question, let me ask you another. What if, instead of standing behind Alec and screaming at him to scare him to death, you treated him with respect? How do you think he would have reacted if you had reached over, picked up his protective glasses, and handed them to him? Then you could have said something like, 'Here you go, Alec. Put these on to protect your eyes while you are working on the pickup truck!' By handling the transaction like that, he probably would not hate you right now."

Jayson did not say a word. He turned around, opened my office door, and went back to the warehouse.

The situation with Jayson and Alec had really gotten to me. I could feel my blood pressure rising. Right then, I decided I would not let that situation bother me and make the rest of my day unproductive.

Rather than stress, I decided to fix the problem so that no one else would stress over this guy's inappropriate behavior.

I did not scream at Jayson during our conversation, but I am sure that he felt just as bad as Alec had on his walk back to the warehouse. If you are a manager and must scream at your employees to get them to do something, you are not a manager! You are a screamer who does not have any self-control or any management skills.

I sat at my desk and wrote up the incident on my computer. I decided that Jayson needed a formal reprimand for his mismanagement of the situation. At the bottom of the document, I put two lines for both Jayson and me to sign and date the write-up. I would then place it in his personnel file. I walked backed to the shop and found him. I asked him to join me in the conference room to read my write-up about the transaction with Alec. After he read it, I asked him to sign and date the document. Jayson did what I asked and then walked back to the shop. I gave the write-up to Carole on my way back to my office and asked her to file the report in Jayson's personnel file. I planned to talk with Brian and Jordan about the incident when I had a chance so that they were fully aware of what had happened.

* * *

Later, Jordan walked into the office and said, "Lunch? Are you hungry, Bob?"

I looked up and asked, "Are you planning on ordering in, or are we going out?"

"The three of us are going to get one of the best burgers in Utah."

I closed my laptop and asked without a hint of humor, "Do they serve Fireball at that burger restaurant?"

Jordan gave me a puzzled expression. "What happened? Are you upset about something?"

"No, sir, I am hungry," I said, getting up and grabbing my parka. "Let's go find Brian and get those burgers."

"He will not be hard to find," Jordan said with a smile. "He is sitting in his pickup right outside the front door, waiting for us."

At lunch, Brian and Jordan asked me what was going on. They said I looked stressed, which was not like me. I told them about my frustration over the situation with Jayson and how much it had bothered me. I also told them about my conversation with Jayson afterward in my office. Neither Brian nor Jordan was surprised because they had witnessed Jayson's screaming act firsthand. When I heard that, I made a strong recommendation to find his replacement and do it soon. My concern was that every technician in the shop would quit and find new jobs to get away from Jayson's poor management style. Jordan asked me if we should give Jayson another chance to change.

"Jordan, are you kidding?" I asked. "This guy obviously does not have any self-control. You cannot have a manager on your team who acts like that."

They agreed with me and committed to start looking for his replacement. I suggested that they write up the situation they had previously witnessed, have Jayson sign and date it, and then put it in this personnel file. I assured them that my write-up was already in his personnel file.

After this discussion, I began to relax. Brian asked me if I wanted a Fireball and Diet Coke. I turned down the offer. If I had an alcoholic drink with lunch, I would be napping in my office all afternoon. I ordered a cheeseburger and a salad per Jordan's recommendation. The burger was great, but it was too big for one meal.

* * *

That afternoon, I spent the balance of the day with Ron. Together, we analyzed the problems with the warehouses and all the inventory. As I listened to Ron's comments about his recommendations on how to fix the situation, my confidence in the young man grew. I learned a lot during my time with him. He clearly understood his job but did not have the tools to accomplish his goals with the inventory. Every day, he tried to keep his head above water. At the end of the afternoon, I had another six pages of notes about ABC Off-Road Supply's hundreds of thousands of dollars of unorganized off-road inventory. Unfortunately, my afternoon with Ron resulted in a bigger backlog for him. The good news, however, was that I was going to help him get the inventory organized. He and his staff's productivity would be materially better, as would the shop technicians. Since the warehouse was unorganized, the shop staff was continually waiting for the parts to complete their job with the vehicles. While the techs were waiting for the parts they needed to do the work on their assigned vehicles, their labor time was being wasted. The company was losing money on those tech's labor for every hour they were idle.

Later, I had transcribed my written notes into my work files on my computer and organized them from the top priority to the lowest. As you can imagine, the screaming service manager was at the top of my list. Then getting the replacement for Carole was number two. I designated both of those issues as "material" problems.

At six o'clock, I packed up my backpack, put on my nice warm parka, and headed to the front door to go to my hotel room as quickly as possible to relax for the evening. On my way through the retail showroom, Brian was standing behind the sales counter with a big smile.

"What are you so happy about?" I asked him.

"Bob, this was our best sales day for as long as I can remember. You, sir, must be our lucky charm!"

"Brian, my father once told me an old Irish blessing that has stuck with me since the day he shared it with me: *May good luck be your friend in whatever you do and may trouble be always a stranger to you.* I will also share with you what I learned about luck in my business: *The harder you work, the more luck you will have.* With that wise piece of advice, good day, and I hope that you have even a more magnificent evening. I will see you in the morning!"

I opened the front door and headed to my car as a cold burst of wind and snow hit me in the face.

* * *

During the rest of the week, my focus was on finding qualified candidates for the management positions (accounting manager, service manager, and sales manager). I developed job descriptions for each position and reviewed them with Brian and Jordan. I wanted to make sure I covered all the responsibilities and duties of each job. Cleaning up the facility, shop, two showrooms, and warehouses was a great start to turning this company around. However, these successes were not nearly as important as having a strong management team to run the business.

After spending more time with Kurt, I was not sure I needed to replace him as the sales manager. He had excellent product knowledge about off-road products, which was very hard to replace. I knew Brian had not given Kurt a chance to manage the sales department and be successful. I believed we needed to give Kurt a chance to prove himself to be a qualified sales manager for ABC Off-Road Supply. Brian had never given Kurt the responsibility to recruit, interview, and hire new salespeople. Kurt had not even gotten a chance to interview any candidates before they were on the payroll. The first time he met them was when the new employee showed up on their first day at work and stood at the sales counter.

I knew that my self-esteem would take a nosedive if I were a sales manager whose boss would not let me participate in the hiring process. If I am managing a sales team, I want to at least share in the responsibility of picking my team players. I gave Kurt a "black mark" for letting Brian step all over him and doing nothing about it. However, I decided to empower Kurt to handle all the responsibilities of the sales department and support him in being successful. I needed to meet with Brian to share with him my plan to help Kurt to grow as a manager. I didn't *need* Brian's authorization and support, but I wanted him to get behind Kurt's and my efforts. The task of finding replacements for the service and accounting managers was enough of a disruption for this company, let alone recruiting and hiring a new sales manager.

I created a list of changes I wanted Kurt to work on between now and my next visit. His accomplishments during that period would help me decide whether or not he would remain in the sales manager position for this company long term. My list included the following:

✓ Create a new sales commission plan for the sales team to incentivize them to sell the older inventory in warehouse 2. Also, I want a "tier" commission plan, so the more the salesperson sells, the higher the commission rate. The first tier should start at $65,000 and below. After the salesman reaches between $65,001 to $80,000 in sales, his commission rate is increased by one point. The next tier starts at $80,001 and goes to $100,000. My goal is to get every sales associate who stands at the sales counter to fight hard to get his monthly sales above a total of $100,000.

✓ Create a list of monthly sales contests to motivate the salespeople to compete and increase sales.

✓ Schedule a daily stand-up meeting with the sales staff each morning to get them pumped up and excited about having a great sales day.

✓ Create a daily procedure for checking customer pick-up inventory in the warehouse and call customers immediately the day the products are received.

✓ Develop a list of topics the sales team needs training in to grow their sales skills. Determine how to train the group such as 1) Hire an outside sales trainer or, 2) Task each sales associate to research different sales topics, and then take turns training the rest of the team. Once each salesperson has done their research and is ready to teach the group what he learned, develop a schedule for the training sessions.

✓ Schedule weekly sales meetings after work, possibly a dinner meeting with the sales team. At the meeting, discuss the overall performance of the team and future sales goals.

I met with Kurt and went over the list in detail to answer all his questions. He knew that I was testing him with this challenge. When I talked with him, he had a serious-minded attitude. My gut told me that Kurt thought that his job was on the line based upon his results for the next ten days. I looked Kurt in the eye and told him I depended on him to be successful with these tasks.

We shook hands, and Kurt responded, "Bob, I promise you that I will not let you, Brian, and the sales team down. I am going to kick butt and get all this work done, plus more." Then Kurt asked if he should email me the results as he finishes each item on the list.

"Kurt, that is a good idea," I said. "I will review your work and redline it if necessary."

"Bob, I sincerely want to thank you for giving me a chance to be a real sales manager for this company. I have always wanted to prove myself, but I never had the chance before now." With that, Kurt gave me a quick "man hug" and left my office.

I felt surprisingly good after getting Kurt started on managing his sales team. Kurt's assignment allowed me to concentrate on getting qualified managers in the shop and the accounting department. Those two positions were now my emergencies at this company to fix quickly. The number-one priority was to find a replacement for Carole because I needed current financial statements.

It was 4:00 PM on Thursday, and Jordan showed up at my door. I looked up, and he had a big smile on his face and said, "Bob, I am your Lyft driver to transport you to the airport."

I packed up and followed Jordan to his big blue pickup truck. On the trip to the airport, Jordan talked with enthusiasm about what a great professional learning experience it had been for him and Brian to work with me so far. I always love hearing when a client is pleased with how the turnaround engagement is progressing.

Chapter 6

SEARCHING FOR QUALIFIED MANAGERS

"The worst crime against working people
is a company which fails to operate at a profit."

—SAMUEL GOMPERS, LABOR UNION LEADER

DURING MY FIRST TWO VISITS AT ABC OFF-ROAD SUPPLY, the company had made significant progress from the start of the turnaround. ABC's appearance was much better. The shop, show-rooms, the sign, and the building had truly improved. That progress was a good start, but there was much more to accomplish. The most significant issues we needed to get done was 1) to hire a replacement for Carole, 2) have a quality service manager to oversee the shop operations, and 3) possibly a sales manager who effectively directs and motivates the sales team. I needed to see current financial state-ments as soon as possible to determine exactly how bad the financial situation of the company was at this point. Working a turnaround without having accurate and timely financial statements is like driv-ing your car blindfolded.

* * *

When I arrived at the Salt Lake City International Airport for my third visit, Scott was there to pick me up. While he was driving me to the client's office, he told me that he had three candidates for me to interview for the accounting manager position. I was pleased because I needed accurate financial statements as soon as possible. Unfortunately, the existing bookkeeper, Carole, was never going to be able to do the job. Not only did she want to retire, but she also did not have the skills, motivation, education, or experience. Plus, she was only working twelve to fifteen hours a week for a job that requires at least a forty-hour workweek.

Scott handed me a file with the three résumés for the accounting position. I read all three résumés. Unfortunately, none of them had the education or experience I was expecting from a candidate to fill the position. For some reason, I did not think that a librarian, bus driver, or assistant manager at a Denney's restaurant would be five-star candidates for Carole's position. None of these résumés would have jumped out of the pile if I were reviewing them. At that exact moment, I realized I could not depend on anyone else to recruit an accounting or service manager. Jordan and Brian had crashed and burned when they hired Jayson as the service manager.

Scott told me that each of the candidates fit into the salary range we had discussed for the position, but none of them had an accounting degree. Our conversation was so depressing. I asked Scott where he had advertised to find the applicants.

He hesitantly answered, "I put an ad in our church bulletin and on their website."

My depression increased. Scott told me that the candidates would be in today at 11:00 AM, 12:30, and 2:00 PM. The good news was that I could interview these three individuals and then start a new "real" search for a valid candidate immediately after my last interview.

* * *

We arrived at ABC Off-Road Supply at 9:30 AM. Once I was in the retail showroom, I found Brian and Jordan and asked if they had a few minutes to meet and update me about what had happened since my last visit. The three of us went to my office, and Scott followed us there even though I did not invite him. I had a list of items I wanted to discuss with the owners. The first issue on my list was sales for the two weeks and year-to-date compared to the prior year. My priorities on this visit were to make progress with replacing Carole, determining the future of Jayson (the screaming service manager), and how Kurt had done with our sales department list. Kurt's progress or lack of progress was going to decide on Kurt's fate. Getting these management positions resolved was critical, and the inventory problem was next.

When we got to my office, the four of us sat down at the conference table after I took off my parka and got my computer out of my backpack. Scott, in his "Smiling Scott" way, started telling Brian and Jordan that he had three great candidates lined up for interviews for Carole's accounting manager position.

I just shook my head no and said, "Scott, those people are not qualified for the job. I am looking for someone with five to ten years managing an accounting department for a company with at least 10 million dollars in sales. The ideal candidate would be an executive who has supervised the finance department for a car dealership in the area. I want a career professional who possibly has a CPA certificate, and either has or is studying for their MBA. Those résumés you gave me this morning are for a butcher, baker, and candlestick maker. These people are not the candidate I am looking to hire for ABC Off-Road Supply accounting department. I suggest that you call those people this morning and cancel those interviews."

With sad eyes, Scott said, "What reason should I give for canceling the interviews?"

"I suggest you tell them the truth: I reviewed their résumés, and they do not have the qualifications for the position. You can make me the bad guy, so you don't get a bad reputation in your church."

Brian gave me a funny look and asked, "Bob, what does this have to do with Scott's church?"

"These candidates all go to Scott's church. That is the only place he advertised for the position."

By now, Scott's head was down.

"Scott, I thought that we already talked to you about this issue," Jordan said.

I looked at Jordan because I did not understand his comment.

Jordan looked at me and said, "Every time we have an opening here to fill, Scott tries to fill the position with a person from his church."

Scott still refused to look up, so I said, "Scott, why don't you go call those people right now and cancel the interviews. When you finish, come back to the meeting."

"Okay," he said, finally looking up. "I will call them, but I think you are making a mistake by not interviewing them."

I raised my eyebrow, but he had already left my office.

Jordan looked at me. "It irritates the crap out of me that he did that. I told him not to do that again, and now he tries to get you to hire his church people."

"They simply weren't qualified," I said. "Let's move on. We have a lot of important stuff to discuss."

Unfortunately, I now had another task on my list: to recruit and hire a new accounting manager. I knew that I had to interview and hire a candidate. But it would have been a lot easier if Scott had done a valid search to find three to five candidates and saved me the time. Scott was so excited about those candidates that I thought he had done something right.

"Bob, since you mentioned it, how long do you think Scott is going to be working at this company?" asked Jordan.

I hesitated before I answered Jordan's question.

After a short pause, Brian said, "To be honest, Bob, unfortunately, as I think about it, I cannot name one thing I am aware of that he has accomplished since he started working here five months ago."

"Guys, I have bad news for you. Before I left and went home from my last visit, Scott shared with me that he wants a very significant pay increase soon."

Brian said, "You have to be kidding, right?"

I shook my head, no.

Brian took a deep breath and said, "If you are okay with my decision, I am going to plan on Scott's exit soon. Do you agree?"

"I do because I do not have anything I can assign to him with confidence that he will get the task done and done right. Giving me those résumés for unqualified people was a complete letdown."

Jordan spoke up. "Good—decision made. Brian and I would normally hesitate to decide this issue, but it is clearer to us now that a tough decision like this needs to be made now that you have joined the company. Bob, I love your style. You act with strength and confidence. That's a great combination."

"Gentlemen, let's review our respective lists and get to work. Your employees are probably wondering what we are doing here."

With a big smile, Jordan said, "We are making ABC Off-Road Supply profitable!"

Right then, Scott walked back into the office. "Okay, I canceled the three interviews. What did I miss while I was gone?" he asked.

Brian announced, "Meeting adjourned!" and he and Jordan got up and left the office.

Scott asked, "Bob, what happened?"

"Nothing. What are you planning to work on next, Scott?"

"Before I answer your question, do you think that I screwed up with Brian and Jordan by inviting those people from my church to interview for the accounting manager position?"

"The short answer is yes. And I am pretty sure that you knew it was a mistake before you asked me. Let's get to work. We have a lot to accomplish!"

I got up from my chair and walked out to the sales area, and Scott went back to his office, dejected.

* * *

As I was walking, I was thinking. I knew that I wanted to find a qualified replacement for Carole's position quickly. I decided to check out ZipRecruiter and LinkedIn to recruit an accounting manager. LinkedIn's fee to advertise for the job was only $25. I decided to try that immediately, and if I did not get some good candidates in a few days, I would place an ad on ZipRecruiter. I went back to my office, signed on LinkedIn, and placed the ad, using Brian's ABC credit card (which I retrieved from him) to pay the fee. I crossed my fingers, hoping to find a qualified candidate soon.

Next, after returning Brian's card, I went to see what Jayson was doing in the shop. Hopefully, he had learned his lesson from my previous visit. When I found him in the shop, I walked over to shake his hand and say hello. "How are you doing?" I asked, "How is everything going in the shop since my last visit?"

"I have not bit off any technician's heads and spit them out," he replied, and I guessed that meant things were going okay. He scratched his head and gave me a narrow look. "Why do you ask?"

"Jayson, it is my job to ask. It is my job to make sure that everything out here is going smoothly and productive," I explained.

"I know that you don't trust me now, but things have been going very smoothly. These guys are like a bunch of privates in the army with no idea how to do their job."

"Jayson, who are those two guys—are they new employees?"

"Yes, sir, they are new hires. We needed some new blood in the shop."

I felt my alarm growing. "How much experience do these young techs have installing lift kits, shocks, doing alignments, etc.? They look very young!"

"Well, sir, they both just graduated from mechanics school and were looking for a job, so I hired them."

"Did we do background and drug tests on these kids?"

"No, sir, was I supposed to?"

I expected more out of Jayson than just acting naive to the rules. Coming from a military background, he surely knew better, or at least I thought he did. I walked away with a feeling of frustration and went to find Brian and Jordan. I asked them both about the new hires in the shop. They looked at me with a blank stare.

Jordan said, "Bob, Jayson just introduced me to the two new employees and told me that he had just offered them a job. Brian and I were a little dumbfounded by what he did."

"Gentlemen, please do me a favor and start an immediate search to find a new service manager. I cannot handle having this guy working here."

The pair walked away after my comment. The two owners

seemed a little intimidated, witnessing how obvious it was that I did not want Jayson on the payroll for another week.

I went back to my office and wrote up Jayson for hiring two new employees without the proper approval and for not following proper hiring procedures. Even if he had the appropriate authorization to put those two rookies on the payroll, they should have taken a drug test, and the company should have done a background check on each candidate. Later that day, I planned to get with Brian and Jordan to have a meeting with Jayson. I wanted to discuss my write-up with my favorite service manager and then have him sign and date it. This guy was destroying the corporate culture of this company, plus he was not following the hiring rules for the company. Now I had one more significant problem. I was going to have to deal with Jayson, probably before I flew home at the end of this visit.

Brian and Jordan scheduled a manager's meeting during lunch to discuss the status of what was going on in the company. Our earlier meeting had not been very successful since we got sidetracked talking about Scott. Jayson was going to be attending this meeting, so I reviewed my write-up again and brought it to the meeting. That way, after the meeting was over, I could pull out the write-up and go over the problem with Jayson in front of Brian and Jordan. I looked at my watch, and I had five minutes to get to the conference room without being late.

* * *

I was the last one to arrive in the conference room. Everyone (Brian, Jordan, Scott, Ron, Kurt, and Jayson) were seated with either a tablet or their computer in front of them. I felt my phone vibrate in my pocket after I sat down at the table. It was a text message from Jordan letting me know that the meeting was starting in five minutes, and I should not be late! I read the text and told Jordan I had just received his message from five minutes ago.

Brian started the meeting by saying, "I called this meeting because with Bob here this week, I want to make sure this a very productive week. I want everyone here kicking butt and taking names. I have a list that I want to go over, so we are all aligned with what we all need to accomplish this week. Bob, do you have anything to say before I get started?"

"Yes, did you order lunch for this meeting? I am hungry."

Everyone laughed. Just then, Warren walked into the meeting, carrying a big box with lunch for all the meeting attendees.

"Warren, bless you, my son! I am famished, and your timing is perfect! Jordan, what did you order me?"

Jordan stood up and pulled the box of food in front of him, and started handing out sandwiches and drinks to everyone. The order was from Jimmy John's. I was lucky enough to receive a roast beef and cheese sandwich with mayonnaise and a Diet Coke. I immediately unwrapped the sandwich and took a big bite. Everyone else in the meeting did the same, and then we all set aside our lunches so we could get started with the meeting.

Brian stood up and walked over to the wall-mounted whiteboard and picked up a black marker. He grabbed his notes and put them down on the table in front of him. That way, Brian could read his list while writing it on the whiteboard. He listed one of the bullet points on the board to start the discussion. The first item was: *Clean up warehouse 2 and start marketing and selling the older inventory.* Brian said that Jordan and Ron would oversee the cleaning up the warehouse and organizing all the stock on the racks. Then they were to take a physical inventory and distribute the information to the sales team to start selling. Brian suggested that the salespeople begin marketing the products on eBay, Amazon, Facebook, and the local internet store, KSL. Brian told Kurt that we should develop a new commission program incenting the salespeople for the sales of the old, slow-moving inventory.

I looked at Kurt and smiled because he had already created the new commission plan and emailed it to me last week. I told Kurt I had reviewed his suggestions, and we could meet later to discuss it. I told him that, overall, I thought it was well done.

Kurt nodded and said, "Thank you, sir!"

One of my missions at ABC Off-Road Supply was to get Kurt

selling rather than being a sales support to the sales team. Kurt was a valuable support to the salespeople to reduce their ordering mistakes, but he also needed to be selling $100,000 per month.

Brian moved on to the next bullet point. "I want to grow our internet sales by at least 50 percent over the prior year. I want to continue to increase the number of products offered to our customers on our website, eBay, and Amazon stores. Next, I want the warehouse department never to ship a product to our customer later than twenty-four hours after we receive the customer's order. We have Derek adding the products to our stores and Kenny working on the customer service function with our customers. I will be responsible for working with Derek and Kenny to accomplish these goals. Ron, you and your team need to increase your shipping efficiency to get all the orders out to our customers within twenty-four hours." (Derek and Kenny were two employees who worked for the company from their homes. Derek lived in Georgia, and Kenny resided in Arizona.)

Ron nodded, acknowledging he already knew his shipping responsibilities.

Scott looked at Brian and stated, "I am not sure if you are aware of it, but Bob assigned me to take charge of internet sales. I am now responsible for doing all the things you just described. I am very excited about the assignment."

Brian said, "I am okay with that, Scott. You and I can work on accomplishing this goal together, growing our internet sales. Having such an aggressive goal like this probably requires our combined talents and energy to get it accomplished."

"I am afraid that you don't understand, Brian," Scott said, raising his voice an octave. "This assignment is mine, and I want to work on it alone. Kenny, Derek, and I will accomplish this goal. If you are going to be involved, I really don't want to work on the task. Kenny and Derek are going to be on my team and will answer to me. Honestly, I think it is best if you stay out of our sandbox and let us be responsible for internet sales. In fact, if you don't, I am not sure I even want to continue working at ABC Off-Road Supply."

Brian gave Scott a hard stare and said, "Okay, I am okay with that."

Scott looked confused and asked Brian to please explain his response.

Brian said, "I am okay with your resignation, effective immediately. I am confident that with Bob being here and supporting me through the sales growth, we will be successful without you here. You should know better than to threaten me about anything. That does not work with me."

Scott grew pale and asked, "Are you serious? Do you want me to leave?"

"Yes, Scott, yes, I am serious. You can go clean out your desk and leave right now."

I thought that Scott was going to faint. He picked up his laptop and left the conference room. I looked at Jordan and told him to follow Scott to make sure nothing bad happens as Scott exits the company.

Jordan nodded and went to catch up with Scott.

All the managers looked shocked, and I announced, "Meeting adjourned!"

Everyone quickly gathered up their sandwiches, drinks, and computers, and went back to their own offices.

Brian said, "Bob, could you believe him challenging me like that?"

I shook my head and said, "I actually could not believe those words were coming out of Scott's mouth."

"Did he talk to you about this before?" Brian asked.

"No, of course not. I talked to Scott about getting involved with growing internet sales, but I never said he should be doing it independently. If he had said something like that to me, I would have fired him on the spot. Scott's challenging you as he did in front of your management team was a fatal mistake. If you let him get away with that behavior, your whole management team would never respect you as the owner of this company."

Jordan returned to the conference room fifteen minutes later and said that Scott was gone. The three of us sat together and finished our lunch. The conference room was quiet for a while because Brian was feeling very emotional. When we finished our sandwiches, we decided to have the next managers' meeting tomorrow at noon again. Brian gave me his list of issues and asked me to review it and update the list with my suggestions. I took it and went back to my office.

Five minutes later, Brian came to my office and closed the door. He said, "Bob, what am I doing here? Am I screwing up my company?"

"Brian, nothing you did today screwed up your company. That was an excellent decision. You made a bad decision four and a half months ago when you hired Scott. You hired a guy who added no value to your company. You spent about 20,000 dollars on Scott, and he accomplished nothing."

"Have I made any other hiring mistakes, in your opinion?" he asked.

"Well, since you asked, I will not hold back my feelings. Jayson, your service manager, should not be working for ABC Off-Road Supply!"

Brian said, "I knew you were going to say that. But I have good news for you. I interviewed an excellent replacement for Jayson. I can have him come in tomorrow so you can meet him."

"That would be great. I would love to meet the candidate. Do you have his résumé so I can review it before I meet him?"

"Yes, I do, I will go get it now."

Brian left the office and returned in three minutes with the résumé. After handing it to me, he said, "I hate to admit it, but Joshua, my service manager candidate, worked for ABC Off-Road Supply before."

"I am so surprised!" I joked. "Okay, give him a call and get him in here as soon as he is available."

Brian smiled and said, "Okay, consider it done!"

After Brian left my office, I signed on to LinkedIn to check if anyone replied to my ad for the accounting manager position. Five people had responded to the advertisement, and they all lived within ten miles of the company. I printed the résumés and reviewed each.

Three of the candidates had adequate qualifications I wanted for the position.

I found Brian and Jordan to show them the résumés to get their opinions. They both agreed that any of the three candidates looked like a good fit and that I should schedule an interview immediately. Jordan offered to take the responsibility to contact the people and schedule the interviews.

When Jordan asked how soon he should schedule the interviews, I told him, "Hiring an accounting manager is a senior priority, get them in here as soon as possible."

"I am on it right away. Bob, you are here until Thursday afternoon, right?"

"Yes, my flight home is at 5:30 PM, so I will need to leave here between 3:30 and 4:00."

Jordan said, "Okay, great, I will be your Lyft driver to the airport again on Thursday!"

Fifteen minutes later, Jordan came back to my office and gave me the résumés with the interview times marked on each. The three interview times were 9:00, 10:00, and 11:00 AM the following day. Jordan sat down at the table in my office. He had something on his mind that he wanted to discuss. I looked him in the eye and then sat down at the table across from him.

"Bob, this is all very exciting. I had no idea that we could accomplish so much this quick," he said.

"Jordan, we have just started. We have a ton more to get done before we can begin to relax."

"Who's talking about relaxing? I love this pace. . . . And, by the way, one of the young techs in the shop heard that you were looking for a new accounting manager to replace Carole and told me that his mother is looking for a job."

"Hmm . . . did you ask him about his mother's qualifications?"

"No, but I will ask him to get her résumé."

"Okay, do that and let me see it if she as the experience we need for that position."

"Will do!" Jordan got up out of the chair and left the office.

I put the résumés on my desk. I decided to walk out to the shop to see what was going on. By the time I got there, Jordan had already received the young tech's mother's résumé and handed it to me.

I reviewed her education and work experience. She had worked at a large car dealership for seven years as the assistant controller. Recently, the car dealership was sold, and she had lost her job. The buyers had replaced the whole financial department team in the dealership. I handed the résumé back to Jordan and asked him to call this woman to see if she could come in for an interview at 1:00 PM. Five minutes later, Jordan showed up at my office door and handed me her résumé with 1:00 PM written across the top.

I shook his hand and said, "Job well done, my friend! Now let's cross our fingers and hope that one of these four people is perfect for the position and falls into the proper salary range."

"Bob, everything is going to work out well. I have a positive feeling about these four people. It is a little different from the résumés Scott gave you on your trip from the airport."

"Yes, Jordan, none of these candidates listed librarian, bus driver, or an assistant manager at a Denney's restaurant as their most recent work experience."

Jordan laughed and went back to his office.

Kurt tapped the door to my office and asked if I had some time to meet with him about all the items on the list that I assigned him during my last visit.

"Kurt, my door is always open to you, and if I don't have time, I will make the time. Come in and have a seat."

"Bob, here is the list of the items you wanted me to accomplish. Number one: *Create a new sales commission plan for the sales team to incent them for selling the older inventory in warehouse 2.* Bob, you received my email last week about the commissions? I assume you liked the program since I did not get a return email."

"Kurt, you nailed it, that was what I had in my mind when we talked last time. Great job, what is next?"

He read the second item: *"Create a list of monthly sales contests to motivate the salespeople to compete and increase sales.* Okay, Bob, here is the sales team's idea about monthly sales contests. We brainstormed together and came up with eleven different sales contests for the rest of the year, from February through December. We also created a list of prizes for the winners of the monthly contests. I plan to have small slips of paper and put them in a fishbowl. At the last sales meeting each month, one salesperson picks out the new contest for the next month, and another salesperson picks out what the prize is going to be. We are trying to get some excitement in the monthly competitions, so the guys get motivated about the whole idea."

"Kurt, one of the salesmen picking out the contest and another picking out the prize from a fishbowl is a great idea. That is definitely going to create some excitement! Great job!"

Kurt continued, "We have monthly contests for the highest sales of the old inventory in warehouse 2. Another one is for the salesperson with the highest sales total over their monthly quota. Examples of the prizes are dinner for two at a nice local restaurant, two weekends off in a row for the winner, and so on."

"Kurt, I like your ideas, excellent job."

He looked very pleased by my praise, and he went on, "One of the contests we are going to run every month of the year is a special prize for everyone on the sales team. If all five salespeople beat their monthly sales quota, they all win an incredibly special prize. I have not figured out the prize yet, but it is going to be good. I figure if all our people hit their quota, the company is going to be very profitable. Then, another contest will reward the whole sales team for zero mistakes for sales orders. I hope that every salesperson wins this contest because, Bob, the sales errors are costly for the company. I think I told you before about when Warren ordered the wrong part number for a jeep hardtop for a customer, right?"

"Yes, you did, I think that mistake cost the company about 2,000 dollars, and the inventory is still sitting in the warehouse 2."

"No, Bob, we moved the hardtop to the front showroom last week and sold it to a customer the first day!"

"Awesome, Kurt!" I said, getting excited by all this news.

"Yes, I know, that was a happy day for Brian and Jordan. The salesperson got a 10 percent commission on that deal in cash!" Kurt read the next item: *Schedule a daily stand-up meeting and meet with the sales staff each morning to get them pumped up and excited about having a great sales day.* The sales team and I have a stand-up meeting every morning at 8:30 to 8:40 AM. We scheduled the meeting at 8:30 because I have the management team stand-up meeting at 8:45, and I cannot be late for that meeting. So far, these meetings have worked well with the team. Then, every salesperson cleans the showroom until the front doors are unlocked to let the customers in when the store opens."

I nodded as Kurt read the next item: *"Create a daily procedure for checking their customer pick-up inventory in the warehouse and call their customers immediately the day the products are received.* Bob, each salesperson is now required to check the customer pick-up racks before the store opens and at noon each day. They are not allowed to let any product sit on those racks longer than two business days. Brian decided that if there are any customer pick-ups on the racks when it is time to hand out the monthly commission checks, the salesperson does not get his check until he resolves every product on the racks."

"Kurt, it is your job to be all over these guys so that they take care of their responsibilities and never have to receive their commission check late!"

Kurt said, "Bob, I know that. This issue is easy for me to handle. The customer pick-up rack is about fifteen steps from my desk. I promise you that I will be all over these guys about the products on the customer pick-up rack."

"Good job, Kurt! Let's hear the next item."

"Develop a list of topics that the sales team needs training to grow their sales skills. Determine how to train the group such as 1) Hire an outside sales trainer or, 2) Task each sales associate to research different sales topics, and then take turns training the rest of the team. Once each salesperson has done the research and ready to teach the group what he learned, then develop a schedule for when the training sessions. Okay, Bob, here is my sales training plan. I assigned each salesperson a subject for them to research and become an expert on the sales topic. The list includes:

1) How to greet a customer when he or she enters the showroom, 2) How to close a sale, 3) Phone sales techniques."

"Kurt," I interrupted, "it is obvious to me that you have knocked this list out of the park. You do not have to continue. I am confident that you are doing a great job of managing the sales department. My congratulations, my friend. Now get back out there and get that sales team kicking butt!"

"Thank you for your time, Bob!"

"I am the one who needs to thank you. Keep up what you are doing, and we will be a very successful off-road supply company!"

"Bob, just give me one more minute of your time to finish these up because I want to get your opinion. The next item on the list was to *schedule weekly sales meetings after work (maybe a dinner meeting) with the sales team to discuss the overall performance of the team and future sales goals for the future.* Bob, just to cover the last item on the list, the sales team goes to a local restaurant immediately after work for our weekly sales meeting. We had the first meeting last Wednesday, and it went very well."

"Kurt, great job and keep it up. I have high expectations for your successes with the sales department!"

"You know, Bob, I read both of your books. I have a feel for how *high* "high" is with you! I know in a few months that ABC Off-Road Supply is going to be a different company than it was last year. I knew when you gave me those assignments that I needed to kick butt, or I was going to get my butt kicked!"

"Kurt, Kurt, Kurt, you are way too big for me to kick your butt! Besides, you did a wonderful job. My compliments!"

* * *

Five minutes after Kurt left my office, Brian texted me. His message stated that he was sending Joshua back to talk to me. Brian was with a customer, so he said he would come to my office after he finished with them. Since two Joshuas worked for ABC (one salesman and one tech in the shop), I was not sure who Brian was sending to meet me. Shortly after that, Joshua, the candidate for the service manager position, arrived and introduced himself. I asked him to have a seat.

I have a set list of questions I usually ask when interviewing a candidate for a manager position. During the interview process, I first try to get the individual to relax and be comfortable when talking to me. If the person is relaxed, he will usually not give me the "canned" answers to make him sound like he is the perfect candidate for the job. I joke around a little during our initial conversation. After a few minutes, I get the person answering my questions honestly. Once that happens, I can get a more accurate opinion of the candidate.

Joshua was young for a manager-level job in the shop. I am guessing he was in his early thirties and had a young-looking face. He had a friendly smile and an outgoing personality. Since many of the techs working in the shop were millennials, having a younger manager would probably work well.

I told Joshua that we would be doing a background check and a drug test before hiring a candidate to manage the shop. I asked him if that was going to be a problem with him. Joshua commented, "That is new for ABC Off-Road Supply. When did that start?"

"It started the day that I started working here. Joshua, are we going to find any problems in your background, or are you going to have a problem passing a drug test?"

"No, Bob, you will not have any problems with my personal history. I don't do drugs. Drugs make you stupid, so I don't spend my hard-earned money to try and get stupid."

I started laughing. Joshua was funny. I asked him when he would be able to start if hired.

Joshua responded, "Two weeks."

I asked him why he left ABC Off-Road Supply the first time around. He had a valid answer, and I believed him.

"Bob, I am a young guy. I am trying to create a career and a personal life for myself. I have a girlfriend. I would like to marry her someday. I would like to purchase a home when we get married. To afford all that, I needed to make more money than ABC Off-Road

Supply could afford to pay me. I left here on good terms, and I am friendly with Brian and Jordan. I was working in the shop, earning a salary as a technician at ABC. For many weeks, I was working six days a week to increase my paychecks. I have excellent experience with the work that is done here in the shop. I can handle the service manager's job. I believe that Brian and Jordan also think I can manage the shop here, or they would not have called me when the position became available."

The more I talked to Joshua, the more I liked him. But my liking Joshua did not make him a qualified candidate for the job. I do not have the qualifications to determine if Joshua could handle the service manager's responsibilities for this company. I was going to have to depend on Brian and Jordan to make that decision since they knew Joshua and his skill set.

Just then, Brian and Jordan walked into my office and sat down after they both shook Joshua's hand. I told Brian and Jordan that Joshua and I had a friendly conversation. But I had no way to judge Joshua's skills to manage our shop.

Jordan said, "Bob, I believe that Joshua has the skills, talent, and ability to handle the job."

Brian spoke up and said the same thing.

"Well, gentlemen, I will share with you my views about the issue. This company has had three different service managers in less than one year. That is a problem. Management turnover, in my opinion, is the costliest expense for a business. I believe the cause of 90 percent of the turnover is due to hiring the wrong candidates. Many companies have poor hiring policies and procedures. If companies did a better job hiring, there would be much less employee turnover. This company has done a poor job of recruiting, interviewing, checking the background of candidates, hiring, and onboarding new employees. That will change going forward at ABC Off-Road Supply. For this company to be more successful, it's going to start with the hiring process."

The two men nodded their understanding, and I continued, "I don't want you to hire Joshua to be the service manager for this company unless you are sure that he is going to do an excellent job. Joshua, I don't want you to accept the service manager job unless you are absolutely certain beyond a shadow of a doubt that you can commit to being successful and stay with the company for a long time. The last thing this company needs is another turnover of a management position. The shop in this company is a significant source of revenue and profit for ABC. We need a *star* performer managing the shop. We need someone who is going to display leadership skills with this group of young employees.

"Joshua, I can look at you right now and tell you that this is a significant position for this company. You are going to be under a microscope until you have the department productive and profitable. If Brian and Jordan offer you this job, you better treat it with the respect that it deserves. Gentlemen, if you decide to hire Joshua, the two of you cannot let him fail at this job. I know that the two of you could handle this job blindfolded. This young man's success in the position is your success. I want you both to be accountable for Joshua's success at ABC. We cannot have another lousy hire for this company."

When I finished speaking about this hiring transaction, all three men wore serious expressions.

Joshua said, "Bob, I can commit to you that the service manager position will be the strength of this company in the future if I am managing the department."

I stood up, shook all their hands, and thanked them for the time. They all walked out of my office.

Jordan turned around and came back to my office to ask me a question. "Bob, do we hire him or not?"

"Jordan, yes, that is my recommendation. He is a material improvement over your current service manager."

Jordan responded, "That is what I thought you were going to say!"

"If you are going to hire him, get a background check and a drug test done immediately. Also, we have to handle the other little issue related to hiring Joshua."

"What is that?"

"You and Brian need to terminate Jayson. We probably need to talk about that before it happens."

Jordan said, "Okay, Bob, I will go get Brian, and let's talk about it right now."

Five minutes later, Brian and Jordan were sitting at the conference table in my office.

Brian asked, "When do we need to fire Jayson?"

"My suggestion is to terminate him the day before Joshua starts in the position. We do not need a gap between Jayson leaving and Joshua starting."

"We *are* busy right now," Jordan agreed. "The shop is humming with work, which is exciting. I don't want to put a kink in that!"

"Okay, gentlemen, you just made a good decision," I said. "You need to keep your eye on Jayson to be sure he does not do any damage to the shop during the next two weeks."

"Agreed!" the owners said in unison.

"Okay, good! Go with confidence!"

With that, I sent them on their merry way.

Early in my career, I worked for a great company that had excellent hiring practices. At the time, the owners recruited me for the chief financial officer position for the organization. Their old CFO was in a car accident and unfortunately died. I wanted to share this true story because the owners of this business were so amazing that they constantly gave me goosebumps. This company, in my opinion, is a perfect case study on how to manage a successful business!

The two owners of the company told me, "Bob, we have a minimal amount of turnover here because we treat the people with the respect that they deserve. We pay everyone here a fair salary for their position. We bonus everyone in the company out of profits. My partner and I believe that the way we make money in our business is to hire the best people in the area. We treat our employees with respect, give them the tools to do their job, provide them a pleasant work environment, and compensate them appropriately."

They reviewed every employee in the company in January and July. They shared with them what they are doing right and what they were doing wrong. The review times in this organization were easy to deal with because they only hired the best people. Everyone loved working there and respected their job. The owners boasted that they did not have an employee leave the company in two and a half years.

This story is true about a real company. I know because I worked there for eight years. I would still be there if the owners had not sold the company. Even when they sold the company, they were again extremely fair to the employees by sharing half the proceeds of the sale with every employee.

Hiring the right employees and treating them with respect is a significant component of successful companies.

Chapter 7

THE SEARCH
WAS SUCCESSFUL

"Quality is free."

—PHILIP CROSBY, BUSINESSMAN AND AUTHOR

I WOKE UP THE NEXT MORNING IN THE HOTEL FEELING great. I knew that this was a big day for my client, ABC Off-Road Supply. Yesterday, I interviewed a great candidate for the service manager position. Today, I had four scheduled interviews for the accounting manager. Based on the résumés I had reviewed, I believed there was a good chance we were going to find a qualified candidate for the job to replace Carole. This hiring could be a big step forward toward getting this company going in the right direction. Every company, regardless of its size, needs timely, accurate financial, and operational reporting. That still did not exist for this organization. If I could choose the right candidate who was qualified and motivated to do the work necessary, I would have proper reporting soon. That was extremely exciting! I could not wait to get to work and start interviewing the candidates.

* * *

I went out to the lobby to get a little breakfast and a cup of coffee. Jordan and Brian were sitting over in the corner of the breakfast area.

I greeted them, "Good morning, gentlemen!"

They said in unison, "Good morning, Bob!"

Jordan asked me how I slept last night as I was putting down my backpack.

Brian said, "Bob, please hurry up and get your breakfast; we need to talk."

Since Brian was so passionate, I just got a cup of coffee and a blueberry muffin.

I said, "So what is up, Brian? Is there a problem?"

"No, sir, no problem at all. I am so excited that we are making great progress with the company. That it makes me both happy and sad."

"Okay, Brian, you are going to have to explain that statement!"

"I am happy that so much has been accomplished in such a short time. I feel the whole atmosphere of the company changing. I now see the light at the end of the tunnel. You have been here part-time for just two months, and we have had record sales both months. Record sales meaning the company has never hit 700,000 dollars plus in one month since I started this company almost thirteen years ago. You come here twice a month for three or four days for two months, and the company just takes off. How is it that you can travel to a small town in Utah and visit a business that you have never been to before to start a consulting engagement? The engagement is for a company and industry that you know nothing about, and you are so successful? How does that happen? Bob, I was lying in bed last night thinking, *How can he do this?* You have provided us a plethora of stuff on your list to change on the first day and a half that you were here. Every one of the eleven items you listed on your first visit was right on the money. I keep asking myself, *Why didn't Jordan and I notice all the stuff and fix them long ago?* So that explains why I am sad. Between the two of us, we should have found the problems you found and fixed them. You knew nothing about us, the employees, the company, or the industry, and you nailed it with all the problems and issues with ABC Off-Road Supply. If we had fixed these problems, we would not be in the financial situation that we are right now."

"Brian, I suggest that we put a positive spin on this situation.

Think about it this way. Your company is in the process of turning around to be profitable and cash-flow positive. If you did not hire me, your company probably would not be turning around. You would be searching the internet to look for a reasonable bankruptcy attorney. While I am making changes to your company, you are learning how to transition from being an off-road supply guy running a business to a businessman owning and managing a very successful off-road supply company! Think about the value of the training that you are getting for free!"

Jordan added, "Free, Bob? How about the cost of your fees?"

"Jordan, here is what I believe. Your company is probably going to make a profit of 500,000 to 600,000 dollars this year. If we compare that to your loss last year—103,000 dollars—that is an improvement of 600,000 to 700,000 dollars. That does not include the profits in future years. As you know, my fees are going to be substantially less than the benefits of the profits and cash flow. Then, by the end of the turnaround engagement, you and Jordan are going to be very savvy businessmen who own and manage a business and make big profits in years to come. In my view, the two of you are developing into businessmen, which is more important than the profit improvement for ABC."

Jordan said, "I don't know, Bob, improving the profitability of the company by 600,000 to 700,000 dollars is pretty important to us!"

"I agree, but if we had a great year in growing the sales and profits and then the engagement ended, think about it—you may not be able to maintain it."

Brian said, "Bob, I understand what you are saying, and I agree."

We all finished our breakfast and headed to the office to start the day, feeling uplifted and motivated.

* * *

At 8:45, the management team had a ten-minute "stand-up meeting" to plan the day and briefly share our thoughts. At the meeting, I asked Brian and Jordan if they would like to participate in the interviews that morning with each of the accounting manager candidates. They both said no because they would not know what to ask an "accounting type" candidate.

Brian said, "If you pick a winner out of this group and want to hire one of these guys, then Jordan and I would like to talk to that person."

I agreed, and the stand-up meeting ended.

I walked out to the showroom at 9:00. A nerdy-looking guy was standing at the front door looking around like he had no idea what to do. I had the first candidate's résumé in my hand. I asked him if he was here to interview for the accounting manager position. He shook his head yes and stuck out his right hand to shake hands. I shook his hand and asked him to follow me to my office.

I hate to admit this, but when the guy shook hands, he had a handshake like a dead fish. His handshake turned me off, even though I knew that a firm handshake means nothing about being a qualified and experienced accounting manager.

In my office, we sat at the conference table and chatted about his background and work experience. His experience was okay for this position, but I did not think that he had the personality to be able to deal with Brian and Jordan. It was my opinion that I need a "leader type of person" to replace Carole. This guy was not the one. If anything, he was a "follower" with minimal self-confidence. Also, I needed the accounting manager to be highly qualified because he or she could not depend on either Brian or Jordan to add value to the accounting department. After all, neither of them knew anything about accounting or financial statements.

The interview did not last long because I did not want to waste his time or mine. I walked him to the front door, shook his dead-fish hand, and sent him on his way.

I thought to myself, *Oh well, one down and three interviews to go.*

When I was standing at the front door as he was leaving, I looked back at Brian, who was standing at the sales counter. He gave me a "thumbs up or thumbs down" hand signal. I returned the sign with my thumb pointing toward the floor.

Fifteen minutes later, another candidate was standing at the front door, holding a big leather briefcase. I went over to him, introduced myself, and asked him to follow me to my office. This guy was much more professional than the first candidate, possibly too professional. He was wearing a three-piece suit. I guessed that his price tag was going to be too high for the accounting manager job with ABC Off-Road Supply. I immediately asked him about his expected compensation level. He was looking for a $100,000 salary plus bonus. That ended our conversation. When I told him the salary range we were offering, he stood up to shake my hand and left. Now I was getting a little worried that I may not meet a valid candidate for the job today. I had hope, but I was still nervous.

The third candidate showed up fifteen minutes early for the 11:00 scheduled interview. That was fine because the last interview had only taken twenty minutes. This candidate was in his mid-fifties. He had work clothes on but more casual than the previous guy with the three-piece suit. I was only guessing, but I thought that this guy would fit in with the ABC employees, which is essential. I believe that the senior financial person in any company should have an outgoing personality and leadership qualities to do his job well. The accounting manager or controller of a company needs to get along with the management team and the employees. Employees need to feel comfortable going to the accounting manager to share information so that he could do his job better.

We talked for over an hour about him, the position, and ABC Off-Road Supply. When we talked about salary, he was at the very top end of our budget for the job. If the fourth candidate was not a "keeper" for the position, I decided I would bring this guy back for a second interview and introduce him to Brian and Jordan. I would like to get a second and third opinion about him before I pulled the trigger and hired him. I was lukewarm with him, but I was not sure why. After I thought about it for a while, I decided that I was not going to "settle."

There was a tap on my door. I got up to answer the door. It was Jordan seeing if I was interested in going to lunch. I told him yes and that I would meet him out front in five minutes. He asked me how the search was going for the accounting manager to replace Carole. I gave him the same thumbs down signal I had given Brian earlier. The candidate's back was to me, so I wasn't concerned he had seen the gesture.

I ended the meeting with this candidate in the next five minutes. He told me that he was interested in the position and asked when he could expect to hear back from me. I told him that if he did not get a call from me by Thursday at noon, I would not be deciding for probably two more weeks. We shook hands, and he left.

I put on my coat, then went out to the showroom to meet Brian and Jordan. They both were in Jordan's blue pickup truck waiting for me. When I got in, Brian asked me if any of the candidates were keepers.

I told him that the last one was a "C" or "C+." I said that I would probably bring him back for a second interview unless the final candidate of the day was the "keeper." I added, "I am not going to settle on a person for this job. I will keep searching for the perfect candidate until I find the right person. In my mind, this position is the third most important person in the company next to the two of you. Since neither of you understand financial statements or accounting, we need a strong player in the job."

"Bob, who told you that I don't understand financial statements?" Jordan asked.

I just looked at him and laughed. "Where are we going for lunch?" I asked.

Jordan said that Joshua had called early that morning and asked if the four of us could meet for lunch. He had some questions to ask after yesterday's interview. "Bob, I think that you intimidated him a little," Jordan told me.

"No, I didn't," I responded. "I just asked some questions to see if Joshua was serious about the job and if he had the confidence to kick butt out in the shop."

"Well, Mr. Curry, you did ask some questions, but you also intimidated him. Do you know how I know that? Because you intimidated me."

Again, I broke up in laughter, but I got his point.

We were meeting Joshua at the sushi restaurant across the street from my hotel, which was one of Jordan's favorite places to eat. The food was excellent and priced right, and the restaurant was quiet enough to talk while we ate. When we went in, Joshua was sitting alone at the corner table. He stood up when he saw us, and we all shook hands.

The waitress came over to take our order. She looked at Jordan and said, "The usual? For four?" He said yes, and she went to place the order.

"Jordan, they know you pretty well here, huh?" Joshua commented.

"I am here three of four times a week between lunch and dinner," Jordan replied.

Brian added, "It is that 'Taiwanese thing' with Jordan—you understand, right?"

"I get it!" Joshua responded, and then he added, "Thank you, guys, for meeting me for lunch today. I want you to know that I am very interested in accepting the job. I also want you to know that I will probably be available to start this Monday if that is okay with you. A guy in the shop gave his two-week notice last night, and they had him pack up his tools and sent him on his way."

"Did we give you an offer letter yet, Joshua?" I asked.

"No, sir, I have not received anything in writing about the job."

I made a note on my phone to develop a job offer letter and email it to Joshua. I asked again, "We did agree to a starting salary for this position, right?"

"Yes, Bob, I am starting at 65,000 dollars to be reviewed ninety days after I start."

"Okay, we will email you a job offer with all the terms and conditions of the job. I did tell you that you were going to go through a background check and have a drug test, right?"

Joshua's eyes narrowed. "Can we wait for six months for the drug test?"

I gave him a serious-minded stare.

A smile came to his mouth. "I am just kidding. Just let me know where to go, and I will get it done in the next twenty-four hours."

I relaxed and smiled back. "We will email you the job offer, a consent form you will need to sign permitting ABC to do a background check on you. There will also be a form to take with you when you get the drug test. When you get the email, sign and date the job offer and consent form and email it back. ABC does have your email address, right?"

"Yes, Carole will have it in my old personnel file."

"You need to know that this job offer is contingent upon your coming out clean on the background check and passing the drug screening," I told him.

"I understand that, Bob!"

"Also, you will be on ninety-day probation when you start. You need to kick butt when you start your job, my friend!"

Joshua leaned back in his seat. "No problem. I am confident you will be enormously proud of yourself that you agreed to hire me."

"I love confidence!" I said, and I meant it.

Just then, the waitresses brought our lunch. There were five dishes of different kinds of sushi, none of which I was familiar with until the waitress explained what each one was. She had a Taiwanese accent and spoke so quickly that I did not understand a word she said. I was okay with that because Jordan, my interpreter, was sitting next to me to answer my questions.

Jordan grabbed dish after dish and shoveled pieces of sushi on his plate, and then he started passing the dishes around. "Come on, guys, get eating, we do not have all day!" he urged. "And let me know if you want to order more. We should get our order it right now."

I was thinking that there was enough food on our table if three more guys were sitting with us. We did not need to order any more sushi. I was surprised: when we were all done eating, there was not a piece of sushi left on the table. Jordan paid the check for the whole group with his credit card, and we got ready to head back to the office.

We all stood up and shook hands. Brian and Jordan welcomed Joshua back to the company. I shook Joshua's hand and told him that we need to get the paperwork done quickly if he wanted to start working at ABC that Monday.

Joshua responded, "Bob, as soon as I receive your email, I will jump on it and get this stuff done, I promise."

On the ride back to the office, Jordan suggested that we terminate Jayson at the end of the day, and Brian echoed that sentiment. I advised them that we should wait until Joshua gets the drug test, and we have the background check completed. "I am as anxious as you are to get rid of Jayson," I told them, "but I don't want it done before we have the paperwork completed for Joshua."

"Okay, since you are the *acting CEO*, we will play by your rules," Jordan agreed.

"You are the man!" I exclaimed. "I take back all the terrible things I was thinking about you. You are okay!"

He looked over at me. "Are you serious, Bob?"

"No, of course not, I *don't* take them back!"

Brian chuckled, and Jordan just smiled.

* * *

Back at the office, my next interviewee was waiting for me as soon as I stepped through the front door.

She stuck out her hand and said, "Hello, Bob, I am Denise. I am here to interview for the accounting manager position."

"Very nice to meet you, Denise," I said. "Would you like to follow me back to my office to sit and talk?"

Back in my office, I hung up my parka, and then I pulled out Denise's résumé from my in-basket.

Denise was in her mid-forties and married with two children. Her son was currently working for ABC Off-Road Supply as a technician in the shop. For the past seven years of her career, she worked at a car dealership as an assistant controller. When the owners sold the business, she lost her job a week after the settlement. The buyers wanted to put their people in to manage the financial department. I wrote myself a note to validate her story with Brian. Brian seemed to know everything about all the dealerships in the area. Denise had only been out of work for two weeks, per her résumé.

"Please tell me all about yourself, Denise, including both your personal life and professional experience."

She started talking and did not stop for twenty minutes. She answered all the questions I had listed on my tablet for this interview. Denise was sitting at the conference table, showing no stress at all. I asked her about her role in the monthly closes at the dealership.

"Bob, I handled 100 percent of the work for the month ends. My boss, the controller, was responsible for the financial activity at four dealerships in the area. Since our company was so successful and under control, he spent very little time at our location. He was at our store only two or three days per month. He would stop in once I had the books closed and review the details. Then he would have a management meeting with the whole senior staff. If there were no problems that he needed to deal with, he was out of there for the next thirty days."

I asked, "Please explain your process for doing the month-end. You don't have to get into the minor details, but I would like to hear about your system." My goal in asking this question was to find out if she did all the work or was just making it sound like she did everything.

"I thought that you might ask me that question, so I brought my month-end checklist with me," Denise said. She opened her binder, undid the clips, and removed the checklist. She handed it to me for my review.

"Okay, Denise, please go through the first five items on the checklist and explain what you did for each."

She squared her shoulders in confidence. "First, I reconcile the cash accounts for each bank account, tying it to the general ledger. If there are any required adjustments, I make the journal entry and post it immediately. Next, I—"

I interrupted her before she moved on to the next item on the checklist. It was clear to me that she did the month-end closing work and understood each step. "You do not have to go through the rest. Instead, please tell me a little about your personal life . . . if that is okay with you."

"Sure, I have been married to my husband for eighteen years. He is a nurse. You know my son because he works here. I have an eleven-year-old daughter who is going on eighteen next year. My son was ten times easier to raise than my daughter is proving to be."

A gave her an understanding smile as she went on. "Professionally, I love to work. I love working in an accounting department for a successful business."

"Denise, I need to warn you, ABC Off-Road Supply has a long way to go before anyone would call it *successful*. That is why I am here—to turn the company around."

"Well, Bob, if you hire me, you have found the right person to help you accomplish your turnaround," she stated.

I hoped she was right. "Let me tell you about some of the issues that I am dealing with, so you have the full story about this company," I said. "The last financial statement issued by the bookkeeper was June of last year. I have not seen June's financial reports yet. There has never been a budget developed for this company. There is a cash-flow problem because they spend too much money on acquiring inventory. They probably have twice the amount of stock that they need to take care of the daily work in the shop, as well as the internet sales to customers all over the world. There is no inventory software right now to show the correct amounts of on-hand inventory or the value on the balance sheet. There are probably another hundred issues I am not aware of, but eventually, I will find them and fix each one. I must warn you that if we offer you this job, and you accept it, initially, you are going to be working a ton of hours until you get this place cleaned up."

"Bob, I am not afraid of hard work," she assured me. "You should have seen the condition of the accounting records when I started with the dealership. They were a royal mess."

"I am assuming you can provide me a list of professional references."

Denise opened her binder again and removed a sheet of paper, and handed it to me. It listed eight people who would provide her with a professional reference, including their names, employers, positions, addresses, phone numbers, and email addresses. I reviewed it. Denise had come prepared for this interview!

Next, I told her, "Do you realize that for ABC Off-Road Supply to offer you a job, you must take and pass a drug test and come up clean for a background check?"

"That will not be a problem, Bob!"

So far, I would rate Denise an A-plus candidate for the position. I decided to ask her several more questions, both personal and professional, to see if I could find something wrong with her. But after speaking with her for over two hours, I found nothing.

I decided to ask Brian and Jordan to meet with Denise today and interview her for the accounting manager position with me in attendance. I was lucky; they both had the time. Unfortunately, neither of them had any idea what to ask her. For most of the interview, they just told her about the company and its current issues and problems. As it turned out, it was good for Denise to meet with the owners because she was able to learn about them and hear their views on the company and the accounting department. When they finished, I spent ten more minutes with her talking about the budget we had for the salary for the position. We also discussed the benefits and a start date. Her start date would begin after she passed the drug test and the background check.

We shook hands, and she left the building. I wanted to jump for joy. I believed I had found Carole's replacement.

I sat down at my desk and immediately created two offer letters, one for Joshua and one for Denise. Once I finished both, I walked out to the showroom to find Brian and Jordan to review and sign both offer letters. I then went to see Carole, who was going to schedule the drug test and the background check for both candidates. I told Carole that Denise was going to be the new accounting manager if she passed the paperwork issues. Carole came out from behind her desk to hug me; it was a big hug! Then she kissed me on the cheek and thanked me five times for finding her replacement. I was so happy for her and, just as important, delighted for ABC Off-Road Supply. It appeared that we now had an accounting manager who could adequately do the job and get the financial statements current.

I took the list of Denise's references and gave it to Jordan. I asked him to call everyone on the list and discuss Denise's professional character. I wanted to ensure that she had an excellent professional reputation as well as a good personal reputation.

Doing the reference checks, drug tests, and so on are all necessary steps when hiring a new employee, especially one who will be handling the finances for the company daily. I also wanted to get these two new hires buttoned down before I flew home on Thursday. This company needed these two strong managers in the two critical management positions as soon as possible. Jayson and Carole were not the answers to make this company successful. No company can be profitable with these examples of very weak managers.

Chapter 8

EVERY CONTACT WITH A CUSTOMER IS A MARKETING OPPORTUNITY!

"Hiring the best is your most important task."

—STEVE JOBS, AMERICAN BUSINESS MAGNATE

WHEN I ARRIVED AT MY OFFICE THE NEXT MORNING, THERE neatly placed on my desk was a pile of paperwork. The documents were the results of the two drug tests, the background checks, and the signed job offer letters for Joshua and Denise. I reviewed the drug tests. Both candidates' tests were negative. There were no problems with either of the background checks. Then, finally, there were two signed job offers letters, one from Denise and the other from Joshua. There was a note on the pile from Jordan indicating that he had called all of Denise's references. Everyone complimented Denise for her work ethics, honesty, accounting skills, hard work, and the long hours she put in to get her job done. They all rated her as a "five-star" employee.

After I finished reviewing the information about the two employees, I felt very fortunate that both people came out of the investigation spotless. It was evident to me that Carole had stayed after work last night and followed up on the paperwork for these two people. She did an excellent job. I decided I must give her a personal thank you for making such an effort to get this work done when I saw her next. I knew part of her motivation was personal because she wanted to retire from this company soon. The sooner Denise was sitting at Carole's desk, the sooner Carole could retire.

I now had everything I needed to call Joshua and Denise to congratulate them both for being the new service and accounting managers for ABC Off-Road Supply. I expect that Joshua would give his notice today with his current employer. He anticipated that he would probably be cut loose today at 5:00 PM. If that did come true, he would be available to start that Monday morning in our shop, which was perfect: the sooner, the better!

Denise was free to start right away since she was currently unemployed. I decided that today, I would ask Denise to start work immediately. Then she could sit with Carole to exchange the accounting department information that Carole has saved only in her head. I was hoping that Carole would stay at least a week or two to download everything to Denise. I needed Denise to get a good start at her new job. She was absolutely going to need to spend time with Carole to get a good understanding of everything before Carole disappeared. Then I wanted Denise to start working on getting the financial statements current. I didn't think it would take her very long to get everything current. Life would be good when she handed me an income statement and balance sheet for March!

ABC Off-Road Supply had only three female employees, and one would be leaving soon. I wanted to make sure that we handled the onboarding process for Denise well. I was less concerned about Joshua because he had worked at ABC before and knew the people and the corporate culture of this organization. He also had a comfort level with the two owners. They obviously liked him or they would not have recruited him to return as the company's service manager.

I wanted Denise to get an excellent start at ABC. I planned to send her an email with pictures of the two owners, Kurt, Ron, and the two women in accounting, Rachel and Hillary. Under each of the photographs would be a brief bio of each person. This email would help Denise when she was introduced to everyone in the company. I asked Rachel to please take the pictures and write the bios for the email. Rachel had been with the company for a long time and knew everyone well enough that she could easily write the bios. As soon as Rachel completed all the content for the email, I immediately sent it to Denise. This email was a simple onboarding task, but I was sure it would make a positive impact on Denise before she walked through the ABC doors for her first day of work.

I would be returning to Fort Lauderdale tomorrow late afternoon. Since I would not be here, I asked Jordan to act as Denise's mentor for the first couple of weeks until I returned.

Jordan said, "Bob, no problem! What do you want me to do once she gets here?"

"Jordan, just be there to make her feel welcome. You and Brian take her to lunch a couple of times next week. Be available to answer her questions when she needs help. Sit with her from time to time to make sure that everything is going well. Speak to Carole and ask her to do the same. We want Denise to feel at home here because we need her to be productive and get the work up to date in the accounting department."

"Okay, I understand, I will take care of those responsibilities! Bob, will Denise be allowed to call you if she has accounting questions or needs an answer to a question I can't answer?"

"Yes, Jordan, of course. You, Brian, or Denise can call me anytime when you need me. I will always be available for this company."

"Thank you, Bob. I was not sure if it was okay to call you when you are not here. I thought that if you were with another client, you might not want to take calls from us."

"No, Jordan, if I am in a meeting with another client, I will let the call go to my voicemail and call back immediately when I am available."

"Thank you, Bob, and I will share that information with Brian."

Now it was time to put together a plan to terminate Jayson to make room for Joshua. I decided that Brian, Jordan, and I should develop a termination plan today. My down-and-dirty strategy would be to make him disappear on Friday afternoon. We would have his last paycheck ready and cut him loose at noon.

* * *

The alarm went off on my phone. I had it set to go off five minutes before the start of this morning's stand-up meeting. I headed to the conference room immediately so I would not be late. When I got there, everyone was there standing around the table, ready to start. It was funny because no one was sitting at the conference room table. I am guessing that everyone was taking the term "stand-up meeting" seriously.

Brian started the meeting by asking me if I had anything that I needed to report to the team.

I said, "Brian, I do. I will be brief. This morning, the paperwork is complete for the hiring of the company's new full-time accounting manager. Her name is Denise. Denise's son works for us in the shop doing alignments. I will be speaking to her this morning to schedule when she will be showing up here for her first day of work. Right now, she is not working, so I am thinking that she will be starting tomorrow. Her job experience is excellent. She worked for seven years as the assistant controller for a large car dealership in the area. I am confident she is the exact type of person we need to upgrade the company's accounting department. I would like everyone to stop in and introduce yourself once she gets here. I want her to believe that this company has the friendliest people in Utah working here. We need her to feel welcome the minute she gets here. Denise will initially be working long hours because of the enormous backlog of work to be done in the accounting department. She will be sitting in Carole's office, and Carole will be retiring soon." Then a thought struck me, and I said to Brian and Jordan, "What would you like to do for Carole to celebrate her retirement after all her years of service at ABC Off-Road Supply?"

"Carole is sort of the shy type," Brian told me. "I am sure she would not want any big party for her retirement."

"Well, that is fine, but I would like to get her something acknowledging all her years of loyal service to the company. I also want all our employees to witness that this company is good to its employees, while they are here and when they retire. I think that we should get her a big ole bottle of Fireball. That should start her retirement with a bang! I am kidding. I will leave what to do for her up to the two of you."

"Kurt, do you have anything to report?" Brian asked.

"Yes, sir. We are having a great sales month. I want to keep up the momentum and have a record month. Yesterday, I announced to the sales group that we have a special sales incentive this month for the salesperson who sells the most of our older inventory out of warehouse 2. I will be handing out the incentive plan later today. Our goal is to get rid of all the old inventory in warehouse 2 by June of this year. We will be reporting how each salesperson is doing month-to-date on the whiteboard in the room next to Carole's office."

Brian thanked Kurt and moved on to Jayson to see if he had anything to report this morning.

"Yes, I fired those two young knuckleheads I hired last week. They both were idiots, and I got rid of them fast before they destroyed the production in the whole shop."

All I could think of after Jayson spoke was that hiring Joshua as the new service manager was a great decision!

"Ron, it's your turn," said Jordan.

"Boss, I have nothing to report right now."

My alarm went off on my phone. I ended the meeting right then. I felt like this was a good stand-up meeting and an excellent method of communicating with the management team every morning.

Everyone started to leave the conference room, and Brian said, "Everyone can go, but I want Bob, Jordan, and Jayson to stay behind."

The four of us sat down at the table and waited until everyone else had left the room to find out what Brian wanted to discuss.

Brian said, "Jayson, I am going to have to let you go today. I want you to gather up any of your personal items and leave immediately. I will have your paycheck ready for you in a few minutes. I am sorry that this had to happen, but I do not have a choice. Unfortunately, this just did not work out for either of us. I wish you the best. We will not interfere with you getting a new job. If you want, you can use me as a professional reference. I promise that I will give you a positive recommendation for a new potential employer. Thank you for everything that you have done here."

By the time Brian finished speaking, Jayson's face was as red as a stop sign.

Jayson asked, "What did I do to deserve this?"

Brian answered, "I do not want to discuss this any further. I am going to get your final paycheck now. I will be back in a few minutes. Jordan, please stay with Jayson until he leaves the building."

I stood up, went over to Jayson, and said, "I wish you the best." I shook his hand, left the room, and went back to my office. I did not want to stay in the conference room to hear Jayson's complaints about being fired.

I was surprised that Brian had pulled the trigger on Jayson without the three of us discussing it first. I figured that Jayson's comment about firing the two young "knuckleheads" was the straw that had broken the camel's back. Jayson's comment had made me cringe, and Brian's head had looked ready to explode. I had to give Brian credit; he had handled the termination well. It was short and sweet, with no time for any drama from Jayson.

Brian held a meeting with the techs and tire busters in the shop to make them aware that Jayson was no longer the service manager. Brian told me later in the day that not one tech had questioned the reason for the termination. No one was surprised. Brian shared with them that he had hired Joshua to start as the new service manager, and he would be starting the following Monday morning. Jordan did get several positive comments about hiring Joshua. Almost every tech knew Joshua, and they all liked and respected him.

This change in management was great news because I had been genuinely concerned that all those technicians were searching for new jobs, probably at one of ABC Off-Road Supply's competitors!

Brian handled Jayson's termination well. He did it behind closed doors with only two other people (Jordan and me) witnessing the transaction. Jayson was written up several times in the short time that he was with the company, documenting that he was not a good fit for the department or the company's corporate culture.

It was the right procedure that Jordan stayed with Jayson as he collected his personal stuff, received his final paycheck, and was out the door. There was no drama or arguing with Jayson. The two owners did everything in a very professional manner.

It was also a good decision to call a meeting with all Jayson's direct reports (the technicians) and let them know about the termination. Because Jayson was a terrible manager, getting rid of him probably improved the morale of the whole department. All the technicians knew Joshua and were pleased that the company decided to replace Jayson with Joshua.

Many owners of companies resist dealing with problems. They tend to stick their head in the sand and pretend that there is not a problem. Brian faced the problem that Jayson was a bad hire. Brian made the decision quickly. He was not going to let the problem continue in the future and hurt the company any further.

* * *

I went to my office to call Joshua and Denise. My phone calls went well with the two new employees. Denise would be at the office the next day at 9:00 AM. Joshua's first day would be Monday, as planned. I wanted to have a shot of Fireball with Brian and Jordan to celebrate how well the hiring process *and* the termination of Jayson had gone. Of course, I would *never* have a shot of alcohol at a client's office, but it is nice to think about celebrating "wins." Also, it was not yet 9:00 AM. Apart from a Bloody Mary from time to time, I had never had an alcoholic drink touch my lips before noon—at least not until it was noon somewhere! Because I felt like

I needed to celebrate, I knew something had gone very well with this turnaround engagement!

A few hours later, Jordan walked into my office and said, "Ready for lunch?"

"Yes!" I responded immediately. "I slept in today for the first time in FOREVER. I did not have time for breakfast this morning. When I don't eat breakfast on the road, I am famished by noon. What time is it?"

"It's noon, Bob!"

Well, the empty feeling in my stomach made sense. "Okay, let's go!"

While Jordan, Brian, and I were at the restaurant waiting for our food, I pulled out my list of questions for them concerning marketing. "Since we are sitting here doing nothing," I said, "may I ask you both a few questions."

Brian said, "Absolutely!"

"Okay, the topic is marketing. Other than spending 5,000 dollars a week with 'David, the marketing man,' what other marketing does the company do to either drive business to our showrooms or our website for internet sales?"

Jordan immediately spoke up and said, "Good question, Bob, I am going to assign Brian the responsibility of answering your question."

I looked at Jordan and laughed. "Were you nipping at the Fireball this morning?"

Jordan just smiled and let Brian answer my first question. "I handle all the marketing for the company—not my goofy partner. The answer to your question is no. We don't. What did you have in mind? What kind of marketing?"

"Brian, when we take an order from a customer in our showroom, do we ask the customers for their email addresses?"

"Yes, sir."

"When we get an order from a customer on the internet, do we capture their contact information, including their email addresses?"

"Yes, we do."

"If you had to guess, how many email addresses do we have from customers that have spent money to purchase products and services from your company?"

Brian said, "Just a rough guess, somewhere around 20,000."

I was amazed, and my head was ready to explode. Brian just told me that they had 20,000 email addresses of customers who had purchased a product from ABC. Currently, the company was doing nothing with this customer information to drive sales. "Brian, I have great news for the two of you. We are going to organize all our customer information and start to market to those past customers to sell more products to them. We have such an excellent opportunity to grow our sales by using those emails to announce promotions of our products. Email blasts, when you already own the email addresses, cost next to nothing to contact and market our products to those customers."

I wrote down a few notes to myself so that I could start following up on utilizing the email addresses.

ABC Off-Road Supply had a "gold mine" of 20,000 customers' email addresses that they had not taken advantage of to generate sales. Because nobody at ABC Off-Road Supply had design or marketing expertise to prepare professional-looking email blasts, I hired the outside marketing firm (XYZ Marketing) to design the emails and send them out to the current and prior customers. The cost of the service from the ad agency would be minimal compared to the sales the emails would generate.

My next question was for Jordan. "When we finish a customer's pickup truck in the shop, what is the procedure to give the vehicle back to the customer?"

"I will answer your question, but I'm curious to know what it has to do with marketing," he said.

I explained, "Every time we are in contact with a customer, we have a marketing opportunity. We could put a 'thank you for your business' card in the vehicle when we hand the keys back to the customer. The salesman could also just hand the envelope to the customer when he pays the balance of the invoice. I think we could also give the customer a coupon for 10 percent off on their next purchase in the envelope along with the thank-you card. I also believe we could put in the package a 'request for a customer referral, pre-stamped postcard.' We could offer a reward if the referred customer comes into ABC Off-Road Supply to purchase products or services. Do you like any or all of these ideas?"

"I like them all!" Brian replied, and Jordan agreed.

"Think about this: we will market to every one of our customers to entice them to come back to the company for further services and products *and* refer a friend to ABC Off-Road Supply."

By this time, both Brian and Jordan had their phones out to take notes.

Jordan looked up to say, "I love our lunches together, Bob. We get so many golden nuggets from you to grow the company. I love it!"

Lunch was delivered to the table, but we continued our marketing conversation. "Guys, our goal is to get as many people as possible to come to the ABC showroom to purchase products and services. When we have customers who have visited our showroom purchasing our products and services, don't you think it might be easy to get them to come back? It should be simple for us to do some marketing and get those customers to return to our showroom to buy more stuff from us. The cost of a thank-you card, a referral postcard, and a discount on their next visit will probably cost us only a dollar or two. That would not be very expensive to get that customer to come back to our showroom with his credit card out to give us more money!"

Jordan asked, "Who will be responsible for making sure our customers are getting these thank-you cards, and so on?"

"That is a pretty easy question to answer!" I told him. "Who benefits when the customer comes back to our showroom or refers a friend to do the same? I will answer that question for you: the salesmen. It will be the salesman's responsibility to turn his customers into a returning 'lifetime customer' of ABC."

Jordan and Brian nodded their understanding, and I went on, "When the customer comes to pick up his vehicle, he meets with the salesman to pay the balance of the invoice. At that time, the salesman can hand him the envelope with the marketing information plus his professional card. The salesman can then point out to the customer everything in the envelope and explain the benefit of each. It is at that time the salesman can start building a relationship with the customer. The better the relationship the salesman has with the customer, the more he can sell that customer. The more he sells the customer, the more money he makes. The more he sells the customer, the more profits for ABC."

We took a few moments to take a few bites of our food, and then I said, "Guys, I have another marketing idea. Do we currently do anything like a 500-mile checkup with our customers' vehicles?"

Brian answered, "No, sir, we don't."

"This is another opportunity to get our customers to come back into the showroom so we can sell them more products and services. When the salesman meets with the customer to give them their keys back after their vehicle has been through the shop, he will ask the customer to bring the truck back in thirty days or 500 miles, whichever happens first. Our shop will give the vehicle a thorough checkup to ensure that everything is in good working order. The estimated cost to the company for this free visit is roughly twenty-five dollars, the cost of one hour for a technician. But the opportunity to sell the customer more products and services has much more value."

They agreed that sounded like a good trade.

Next, I mentioned that I had seen information on the internet about "4x4 Off-Road Clubs." "Does ABC Off-Road Supply belong to any of the local groups?" I asked. "Do any of our sales team or shop people belong to an off-road club? Do we offer our second-floor conference room to any of the clubs to use for their meetings?"

Jordan answered, "No, no, and no!"

"Then my next question is: Does it make sense to get our sales-people and shop guys involved with any of the local clubs? Do you think that having relationships with these clubs will generate sales? If so, should we offer our people incentives to belong to these clubs to encourage them to participate and market our company to the members?"

Brian answered, "Yes, yes, and yes, Bob! What a great idea!"

Brian and Jordan were busy taking notes between bites of their lunch. I felt good about our lunch today. I had given the owners several great ways to grow their business without spending very much of the company's funds.

I had one last issue to share with them before we returned to the office. "Do we take a survey from our customers asking how we did concerning delivering our products and services?"

Jordan responded, "We do not. Should we?"

"Yes, we should! It is another opportunity for our salespeople to generate another contact with our customers. It also gives you the ability to see if your customers are happy with how our sales team and shop techs are treating our customers. We should place a preprinted survey form in a stamped envelope on the dashboard of every vehicle that leaves the shop when the technician finishes his work. The survey should have the customer's name and the date of the service already recorded on the form. The pre-addressed ABC Off-Road Supply envelope should go directly to Brian, or you, Jordan. The customer should only have to open the envelope, answer the six questions, and mail their questionnaire to our office. I believe you are going to receive some very interesting surveys! Another real benefit of this survey procedure is that you are going to find that the techs will be more conscientious about their work on the customer's vehicle. When the techs know their customers are going to send surveys to the owners rating their work, the quality of their work will improve. You are also going to find that the salespeople treat their customers better. The salesmen will know that each customer can easily tell management about their level of treatment during the sales transaction. When people see that they

ABC Off-Road Supply
650 Main Street • Ogden, Utah 84201

Current Date
Mr. Satisfied Customer
Street Address
City, State Zipcode

Dear Mr. Customer,

SUBJECT: HOW DID WE DO?

We would like to thank you for purchasing our products and services. In order to improve the quality of our products and the delivery of our services, I would like to ask you to grade us. Our employees and management team are measured and compensated for the quality of their work. We, the owners of ABC Off-Road Supply, use this valuable information to understand better how we are servicing our customers. Thank you in advance for your time and effort in answering these questions and mailing this survey back to us in the envelope provided.

5 = EXCELLENT   4 = GOOD   3 = SATISFACTORY   2 = FAIR   1 = POOR

How would you rate the quality of our work on your vehicle? _____

How would you rate the salesperson as being courteous and friendly? _____

How would you rate the responsiveness of the salesperson? _____

How would you rate the professionalism of the salesperson? _____

How would you rate the service team regarding the delivery
of your vehicle? _____

How would you rate the salesperson: did he answer all your
questions concerning your vehicle? _____

Comments: _____

_____

Respectfully,
Brian and Jordan

Salesman: _____

Service Manager: _____

Technician: _____

192 ◆ The Turnaround 2

are being audited, they are more careful about their work. Just like the IRS, people filing their tax returns are more cautious with the accuracy of the tax return, knowing that the IRS may audit them. The survey form is very simple for the customer to complete. It will take the customer less than five minutes to answer the questions."

Jordan remarked, "Bob, I love the idea. We do need to improve the quality of the work in our shop! This questionnaire will be a brand-new policy for our company. It sounds very simple to implement. All we need to do is order some pre-stamped ABC Off-Road Supply pre-addressed envelopes, and then design a survey questionnaire and make some copies. That is not going to be hard at all, and it is going to have a ton of benefits."

"Okay, my next question for the two of you is: If a customer calls the ABC phone line at 8:00 AM, what message does the customer hear?"

Brian answered, "The message tells the caller that our office hours are 9:00 AM to 6:00 PM from Monday through Friday and from 10:00 to 4:00 on Saturdays."

"We need to do better than that," I said. "We have an opportunity to speak to a customer or potential customer, even before the doors are open."

"What are you suggesting the message say?"

"First, I would like them to be able to leave a voicemail stating their name and phone number so that we can return the call at or before 9:00 AM. I would ask them who they are trying to contact. Brian, does the phone system have the ability to send an email from the call?"

"Yes, it does. Who should get the emails?"

"I think you should create a generic sales department email address such as salesdept@ABC.com and send the emails there. If I were on your sales team, I would love to get those emails to return the calls. Those voicemails and emails could easily turn into an effortless sale. If I were a salesman, I would enjoy responding to those voicemails."

* * *

Once we finished the marketing discussion and ate our lunch, we headed back to the office. Jordan parked his truck on the south side of the building, and the three of us walked into the showroom. The place was packed with customers, more than I had seen since I started working with this company. Every salesperson had at least two people standing in front of him. A dozen customers were walking around the two showrooms.

With a surprised look on his face, Brian asked, "What is going on here? It is Wednesday afternoon, and the place is full of customers. Having this many customers in our showroom midweek in the early afternoon has never happened before. What are we doing to cause this explosion of customers recently?"

Just then, two customers approached Brian with questions. He walked back to his station behind the back counter and took sales orders just like the other five salesmen and Kurt, the sales manager.

With a big smile, Jordan thanked me for being here. He said, "Bob, I never thought that it would be so exciting to work here. Your efforts so far have changed this business around from being depressing to exciting. I am not sure what caused the drastic increase in business, but whatever it was, let's keep it up!"

"Jordan, I can tell you what it is: the hard work that you and Brian have been putting in has made people want to visit the showroom. And I have some good news for you. We are only about 25 or 30 percent done with the improvements to this business. Think about what this showroom is going to look like in two or three months!"

"March starts the beginning of our season. In season, our sales are 15 to 20 percent greater than the rest of the year. The season lasts from March until the end of June."

"Jordan, when we are done with the turnaround, our season will be from the first of January and go through to the end of December."

Jordan said, "Bob, from your lips to God's ears!"

Jordan and I walked behind the sales counter to see if we could help with anything. Each of the salesmen turned to shake my hand as we walked past them. They all had big smiles on their faces. It appeared that this sales team loved being busy with customers on a Wednesday afternoon. When they were working with customers, they were making money. When there were no customers in the showroom, they were making zero compensation. This number of customers in the showroom did not happen very often. Therefore, it was a very good thing that it was happening now!

Normally, the salespeople were looking for something to do in the middle of the week. They were trying to kill time when they had no customers to wait on. Unfortunately, the sales team had been acting like "order takers" instead of salespeople who were aggressively selling to the customers.

I decided that Brian, Kurt, and I had to develop new policies, procedures, and systems. We needed a system that motivated our "order-taking" sales force to be a bunch of hungry salesmen who know how to go out and get the business. We needed our salespeople to get the customers when they were not walking through the front door. Salespeople should *never* have idle time during the day. When there are no customers in the showroom looking for help, the salespeople should be very busy doing stuff to get the customers. As it turned out, our conversations about marketing ideas at lunch was very timely.

* * *

I went to my office to write an email to Brian and Jordan. I wanted to have documentation of everything we talked about and agreed on at lunch. I also wanted to share with them my ideas about a new job description for our sales team. I want our salespeople to be just as busy when there were no customers in the showroom as they were when the showroom is full of off-road vehicle owners. I created a list of all the tasks for marketing to our customers. We need someone to be responsible for making this stuff happen soon. I believe that it should be Kurt's responsibility, but I wanted to talk to the owners first. Based on what I had just seen in the showroom, everything was coming together, but a little more marketing would not hurt anything.

Next, I prepared a list of "onboarding responsibilities" for Denise's first day in her new position, which was tomorrow. I wanted to make her first day special. I want her to feel at home in her new job. I knew that once Denise started doing her actual job responsibilities, she would be busy ten hours a day at work, probably for a couple of months. She would not be able to come up for air until mid-May!

I was going to have her attend the stand-up meeting so that I could introduce her to the whole management team. I planned to have Kurt, Ron, and Jordan take her to each of their departments and show her around. Jordan and Joshua could do the same with all the shop techs. Next, I was going to have her sit with Carole to fill out all the payroll and benefits paperwork, etc. Then, I would take her for a tour of the facility. Later, Brian, Jordan, and I would take her to lunch. We could fill her in on all that we were trying to accomplish in the next several months. I wanted her to know that we were in the middle of a turnaround of this company. Denise needed to feel that she was an integral part of this turnaround. I was hoping that she was up to the challenge of cleaning up the accounting department and getting all the work current.

Our new accounting manager was also going to have to deal with the calls from vendors that wanted a check immediately for ABC's delinquent payables. Since Denise had worked for a big success-ful dealership, she probably never had to cope with those kinds of issues before. Dealing with vendors was not an easy task when the company's cash flow was not good. I wanted to make sure she could handle this responsibility without getting stressed. The better she could contend with the vendors, the quicker ABC Off-Road Supply would go "From Red to Black."

I decided that I needed to talk to Brian and Jordan. I had to explain to them that Denise would be in a very stressful position until her department was current. My message was that they must not add additional stress to her workday. Brian and Jordan were in a good place right now because of the increase in sales. But I knew that they both had their "down" days. I knew that many times when cash is tight, small business owners would bite the head off the accounting manager. They believe that the weak cash position is their accounting manager's fault. In most cases, nothing could be further from the truth.

I developed a list of all the projects I would like Denise to work on and accomplish in my absence. She would be sitting with Carole the following day to get an understanding of what was going on in the accounting department. Once that was accomplished, I wanted her to work on the company's first weekly flash report. A flash report was essential for ABC based on their current financial situation. I printed Denise a copy of the report document as well as the instructions (see a copy of the report and instructions on pages 197 to 201).

"Onboarding" a new employee is not simple to accomplish, but it is essential. The onboarding process should start as early as possible, even before the employee starts the job. Ideally, onboarding should begin immediately after the candidate receives an offer letter and continue for at least a month after the new hire starts the job.

Once the candidate has accepted the job, signed the offer letter, and passed the background check and drug test, the company should prepare for the start date for the new employee. The future employee should be assigned a company email address and a phone number, and professional business cards should be ordered immediately. The candidate's workspace must be ready to make the employee feel at home on the first day.

An excellent onboarding policy is to send the new hire a photograph of each member of the existing management team and the candidate's future direct reports with bios for each employee. This procedure makes their first day on the job much more comfortable. When introducing the new employee to the managers and employees, the new hire will have a much easier time remembering faces and names. Also, during the introduction, the new hire's strengths and business experience should be highlighted. Everything shared during the conversation should be positive to help the new hire feel as comfortable as possible.

It is also a good idea to assign a mentor to the new hire. The mentor should be another manager or a long-term employee from the same department as the new employee. The mentoring employee should check in with the new employee regularly to help with growing the new hire's comfort level with the company's corporate culture.

The company's employees need to welcome the new hire. When hiring a new manager, each member of the senior management team should allocate at least a couple of hours in the first few days to sit and talk with the new person. The president/owner of the company, especially if the new person is an accounting manager, should schedule lunches in the first month with the newest member of the management team. The president should ask some of the other managers to join the lunches, which should break the ice for the new employee.

WEEKLY FLASH REPORT

When preparing the weekly flash report, use the key business indicators contained in the various financial and operating reports. The accounting manager is responsible for the overall coordination and preparation, but the management team provides all the data.

The Goals of the Flash Report

✦ To provide senior management with a current "snapshot" of the previous week's key business indicator statistics.

✦ To allow management to become proactive in reacting to changes in trends or areas needing attention.

✦ To establish common ground for management focus, to help ensure that the company achieves predetermined operating performance and financial results.

✦ To require participation from the sales & marketing, operational and financial functional areas to measure and monitor key operating statistics weekly rather than only when distributing financial statements.

ABC Off-Road Supply
WEEKLY FLASH REPORT
Week of: _____

Cash Activity	
Beginning Balance	
Plus: Receipts	
Cash Available	
Less:	
A/P Disbursements	
P/R Disbursements	
Debt Service Payments	
Ending Balance	

Line of Credit Activity	
Borrowing Base Calculation	
Current Line Usage	
Line Availability	
Percentage of Line Used	
Line of Credit Interest Rate	

Accounts Receivable Aging	Last Week $	%	Two Weeks Ago $	%	Three Weeks Ago $	%	Four Weeks Ago $	%
Current								
31 – 60 days (past due)								
61 – 90 days (past due)								
Over 90 days (past due)								
Grand Total								

Accounts Payable Aging	Last Week $	%	Two Weeks Ago $	%	Three Weeks Ago $	%	Four Weeks Ago $	%
Current								
31 – 60 days (past due)								
61 – 90 days (past due)								
Over 90 days (past due)								
Grand Total								

Payroll Summary	Last Week $	#	Two Weeks Ago $	#	Three Weeks Ago $	%	Four Weeks Ago $	#
Production Labor								
S, G & A Labor								
Grand Total								

Sales Summary	Last Week $	#	Two Weeks Ago $	#	Three Weeks Ago $	%	Four Weeks Ago $	#
Jobs Shipped								
Jobs Billed								
Quotes Prepared								
Customer Orders								
Backlog status								

Benefits of Weekly Flash Report

✦ Focusing senior management on key business indicator statistics by functional area of the company (sales and marketing, operations, financial, etc.) rather than an infrequent review of the company in total.

✦ Monitoring goals weekly to achieve preferred results.

✦ Reporting frequently creates a proactive as opposed to reactive management style.

✦ Initiating communication between senior management of all functional areas and focusing attention on the company's common goals and objectives.

✦ Giving each manager a view of the company's performance—successes or problem areas that should receive attention immediately.

✦ Helping to eliminate confusion and misinterpretation of the company's most current results of operations.

Weekly Flash Report Procedure

Reporting Frequency—Prepare the weekly flash report (page 198) from the financial and operational results of the company. The report is prepared immediately after the weekly payroll report is final for the prior week, Monday through Saturday. The report template format will be developed on Microsoft Excel and may be revised as senior management receives and adjusts the data to their customized needs. The report will contain information for the most current week ending and prior three weeks—providing a total of one month of history.

Information Included—The report includes six sections of information: cash activity, the line of credit, accounts receivable aging, accounts payable aging, company payroll (both dollars and headcount), sales trends, and any other information senior management desires.

The Information Reported Is:

Cash Activity—The cash data is a recap of the week's cash activity. Classify the disbursements into three types: accounts payable payments (A/P disbursements), payroll disbursements (P/R disbursements), and debt service. This information reflects the actual cash activity.

Line of Credit Activity—The line of credit data of the week's activity should include:

✦ The borrowing base calculation: The amount of borrowing available based on the assets required by the bank to collateralize the loan.

✦ The current line usage: The total amount of money borrowed by the company as of the date of report preparation.

✦ Line available: The subtraction of the current line usage from the borrowing base.

✦ The percentage used: The percent of the line of credit in use.

✦ Current borrowing interest rate.

Accounts Receivable Activity—Four weeks of accounts receivable aging information (current, 1 to 29 days, 30 days to 59, 60 to 89 days, and over 90 days) will be reported (both dollars and percentages).

Accounts Payable Activity—Four weeks of accounts payable aging information (current, 1 to 29 days, 30 days to 59, 60 to 89 days, and over 90 days) will be reported (both dollars and percentages).

Company Payroll Activity—Classify four weeks of gross payroll information into the production departments, selling, general and administrative. This information should be reported in dollars and by the headcount by category. The data is obtained from the payroll records and used in the flash report.

Sales Trends—Record the four different types of sales data, all obtained from the billing records and the estimating system. The information is:

- ✦ Jobs shipped
- ✦ Jobs billed
- ✦ Quotes prepared
- ✦ Customer orders received
- ✦ Current backlog status

Responsibilities
The accounting manager is responsible for creating the flash report.

Distribution
Distribute the report to the management team by noon each Monday.

Conclusion
Reporting of weekly information to the company management team will provide each of them with tools for quick and immediate decision-making, allowing each manager to keep their finger on the pulse of their respective departments.

I went to see Carole to thank her for the extra effort she had made the night before to get all the work done for the hiring of Joshua and Denise. I also wanted to ask her how long she would be available to work to get Denise familiar with everything in the accounting department. Carole assured me that she would not leave before Denise had a firm understanding of everything she needed to know to do her job as the accounting manager for ABC. She said that she would work full-time for two weeks to work with Denise. Carole shared that she felt she owed it to Brian and Jordan to leave only once Denise was well prepared to handle the responsibilities assigned to her. I thanked Carole and walked around her desk to shake her hand. She had done her absolute best for the company based upon her skills and abilities. Carole was a good person!

Chapter 9

THIS TURNAROUND
IS IN THE EARLY STAGES

"You never get a second chance to make a first impression."
—WILL ROGERS, AMERICAN HUMORIST, ACTOR AND AUTHOR

THURSDAY MORNING, I WOKE UP EARLY TO START PLANNING my day at ABC. This day was going to be a special one in the history of ABC Off-Road Supply. I had my fingers crossed that Denise would be a successful hire. I truly hoped she would show up to start her new position! I finished my outline of the tasks I wanted to accomplish before I flew home later that afternoon. Then I showered, dressed, and packed my suitcase. I went out to the front lobby to check out and get some breakfast.

* * *

It was 7:30 AM, and Brian and Jordan were already sitting at a table in the breakfast area. I was a little shocked they had shown up at the hotel this early for the free breakfast. When I saw them, I poured myself a cup of coffee. I looked over at Brian and Jordan, and I could clearly see the stress on their faces. I added cream to my coffee and walked over to the table. "Good morning, gentlemen! What is going on? You both look stressed!"

Brian said, "We are not stressed. What you are seeing is excitement! Did you see the sales total yesterday?"

"No, sir, I was so focused on dotting the *I's* and crossing the *T's* with our new hires. I did not hear anything about the sales totals yesterday."

"We had the most massive sales day in the history of the company. We did 43,000 dollars yesterday. That number is insane. We have *never* had a 35,000-dollar day, let alone 40,000-plus dollars!"

"Okay, so what is the problem? You are here very early—and you *do* look stressed."

"We came to talk to you this morning to encourage you to stay longer on this trip," Brian said. "We think that if you were here more often, the company would do better! Plus, we think being this is Denise's first day, you should be with her tomorrow and next week."

I took a seat and a sip of my coffee, and then I told them, "You don't understand. This company is not turning around because of me. You two are fixing the problems with ABC. It is you—the two of you. I did not make all these changes while I was in Fort Lauderdale. They were all accomplished by you, gentlemen."

Jordan said, "I understand what you are saying, Bob, but we would not have made any of the changes without your direction. Your leadership is magic. It brings customers through our front door. It makes the customers pull out their credit cards to buy our products and services. It is Bob Curry's direction that makes the techs finish a four-hour lift job in an hour and a half. It is your leadership that makes the sales staff get pumped up to double their all-time monthly sales total. We know that your leadership is turning this company around, and we are excited! We can see the light at the end of the tunnel. Before we called you, I just knew I was going to lose every cent I had accumulated over my career. Now I feel like I am going to be a millionaire in a few months."

"You guys are crazy," I told them. "This turnaround is still in the early stages. The three of us working together for two months doesn't mean that ABC is going to be profitable from now on. There is still a lot of broken stuff at your company that we need to fix. For example, we need to lower the inventory by 300,000 dollars. We need to load all the on-hand inventory balances on the accounting software. The annual sales should be at least 8 to 9 million by the end of this year. We need to sell all the old inventory in warehouse 2. The company must start keeping all the vendor payables current so that we can get better pricing from them. We must secure our inventory, so the employees do not steal it. The most critical issue, more important than the problems I just stated, is to have a strong management team manage the company. Today, we have a new accounting manager starting and, on Monday, a new service manager. We have a rookie—Ron— overseeing the two warehouses and shipping products for our internet sales. We need to support these people so that they get comfortable managing their respective areas in the future. They all need to start making good business decisions based upon the timely financial and operational reporting from the accounting department. Also, very important, Denise needs to upgrade the accounting department, as well as the reporting."

There was still a lot we needed to do, and I wanted them to understand that. "Guys, increasing sales is terrific, but we need policies, procedures, and reporting to manage this company successfully. Thank goodness sales are growing. That growth gives us time to fix all the other issues. Do you each understand?"

"That's exactly why we came here early this morning," Jordan said. "We want to talk to you about spending more time here to fix this comprehensive list of issues."

"It will all get done in due time," I assured them, but I had a different matter on my mind. "Before we finish here this morning and get to the office, there is an important issue I want to discuss with you about Denise starting today. I want you both to start right from the beginning to establish an excellent relationship with her. No employee in the past has done the job we are asking her to do for your company. Carole has not scratched the surface of the reporting required in the accounting department for the two of you. I will be working closely with Denise to create the financial reporting necessary to manage a 10-million-dollar, forty-employee company."

"Bob, if sales stay as strong as they are right now, we will not need any reporting!" Jordan exclaimed.

That concerned me. "Jordan," I said, "that statement could not be any more wrong. Regardless of the sales, every small company needs timely, accurate reporting weekly and monthly. Growing the sales will turn this company around. Good reporting will keep it turned around and profitable." I guessed this was a case where they "didn't know what they didn't know"!

Jordan and Brian seemed a little calmer, so I continued to put things in perspective for them: "In a few months, when Denise cleans up the considerable backlog of work in her department, you are going to start getting excellent reporting. That is something you have never seen before. Once you are used to getting these reports and using them to support your business decisions, you will wonder how you ever managed ABC without a fully functioning accounting department. Denise will be subject to a large amount of stress to get her department current. Please make life as easy as possible for her. Since she will be working long hours, I want her stress to be as minimal as possible. The last thing we need is for the accounting manager to give notice and leave in the next thirty days because the job is too overwhelming!"

"We hear you loud and clear!" Brian said. "We understand how important her work is to the success of the company. We will make that happen. We will do everything humanly possible to reduce her job-related stress."

I smiled. "Great, now let's get to work!"

* * *

Brian, Jordan, and I walked into the ABC building at 8:00 AM. I looked around the shop and saw techs working under all ten bays. I was delighted to witness them all at work so early. Brian said the guys had arrived at 7:00 AM because of the substantial increase in sales volume. We now had a backlog of work more significant than ever before!

My favorite tech, Joshua, saw us walking through the shop and grabbed a rag to clean the grease off his hands. He walked over to us and stuck out his hand for a shake.

Joshua said, "Mr. Curry, I owe you an apology. When we had the all-hands meeting here in the shop a couple of months ago, I asked you a few difficult questions. I suggested that you may not be qualified to turn this company around. I must tell you, I am humbled right now. I have never seen this shop so busy in my eight years here. In the past month, I have seen the volume of work increase every week. Your turnaround skills have made this group of technicians very happy. I am sure you know how to keep your shop techs happy in any company: give them more and more work! When this shop is slow, these guys are all grumpy because they are not making any money. I guarantee that every tech working in this facility has made more money in the past thirty days than they made any month in the past five years. So, sir, my long-winded message is: First, I am sorry for the sarcastic questions I asked at that meeting. And, second, thank you for doing a great job here. We are all benefiting from your expertise!"

I was taken back by Joshua's comments; they were completely unexpected. "Thank you, sir, for your kind words. They are sincerely appreciated," I replied. "Often, when I am doing my job, I forget that everything I do affects *all* the employees in the company. When employees come up to me and offer such a kind compliment, it hits me very hard. It makes the long days, flights across the country, sleeping in hotels, and time away from my wife and family all worth it."

We shook hands again, and Joshua went back to his bay to keep working on the vehicle up on the lift. Then I headed to my office.

* * *

My day's schedule was packed. I planned to spend most of my day with Denise to get her started on her job before I had to be at the airport for my 5:30 PM flight. When I got to my office, I hung up my parka and unpacked my backpack. A moment later, Denise showed up at my office door, holding a hot cup of coffee. I invited her in and asked her to have a seat at the table. I set up my computer across the table from Denise.

"Welcome, Denise. I am delighted you are here."

"Bob, as am I. I am ready to get to work. I was going crazy at home during my unemployment."

"Well, we have plenty of work for you to do. As I mentioned, Carole, the part-time bookkeeper, has only been working fifteen to twenty hours a week. Unfortunately, she does not have the skills to handle the responsibilities of managing the accounting department. That department demands a professionally skilled accounting manager who works at least forty-plus hours per week to keep all the work current."

Denise nodded and confirmed that I had told her about Carole's part-time efforts.

"Right now, the company is struggling financially," I went on. "The cash flow has put the vendor payables in a bad way. Many of the vendors are at sixty to ninety days past due. Several of the companies we purchase inventory from are on COD (cash on delivery) terms. Our inventory is way too high right now, causing our payable problems. We have approximately 150,000 dollars of older products in our warehouse 2 that have not been selling in the past several years. The last financial statements issued to the owners was in June of last year."

As I spoke, Denise took notes. She did not flinch as I told her about all the challenges she would be facing.

I continued, "We need to enter all the on-hand inventory balances into the accounting software."

"Bob, let me ask you a question about how you want me to handle catching up the monthly financial statements."

"Sure, ask away."

"Do you want me to close the books month by month on an accrual basis? As on option, I am suggesting doing a quick 'down-and-dirty' closing on a cash basis through November. Then I will do the December closing with accruals to make the year-end accurate. Starting January, I will do accruals monthly going forward."

"Denise, that is fine with me. I am good with your plan."

"Doing cash basis closings for the second half of the year should get the work done in about one half the time," she said.

"There are a couple of things that you need to check first," I told her. "Please make sure that Carole has reconciled all the bank and credit card statements. Also, check to ensure that she has been current on filing and paying the payroll and sales taxes. If she has not, we have to deal with those problems first."

"I am hoping that the tax returns are all filed timely and paid current," she said.

"As do I!" I replied.

"Bob, when are you flying home this week?" she asked.

Despite Jordan and Brian's request that morning, I was not going to extend my stay. "Unfortunately, I am leaving later this afternoon."

"Hmm . . . that is not what I was expecting to hear," Denise said with a twinge of concern.

I handed her my professional card with all my contact information and said, "Feel free to call or email me anytime with your questions. If you call me and I don't answer immediately, leave a voicemail. I will return the call as soon as I am free."

She tucked my card away and then said, "I am guessing I will be spending time with Carole while she is still here."

"Yes, you will!" I confirmed. "Yesterday, she promised me she would work two full-time weeks once you got here to help you become familiar with everything in the accounting department. Also, you will be going to lunch today with Brian, Jordan, and me. I want to get the owners comfortable with you so that they stay out of your sandbox until you get all the accounting department work caught up and current."

My phone alarm when off in my pocket.

I said to Denise, "Okay, we need to go attend your first stand-up meeting this morning in the conference room right now."

"What is a stand-up meeting?" she asked.

"You will see. It is a ten-minute meeting first thing every morning. The meeting's goal is to share important information with all the other managers. I always set the alarm on my phone to go off five minutes before each meeting so that I am not late. If you are late for the meeting, it will be over before you get there!"

Denise and I walked into the conference room together. The rest of the managers were there. I would say that everyone stood up when she walked into the room, but they were already standing! I immediately introduced Denise to each manager.

After the introductions, Brian said, "Denise, I want to be the first to welcome you to our company. We are all very excited to have you here. You should know that every person in the room and the employees who work for them are going to do everything they can do to support you from this day forward. We can talk more about this later today, if you are available to have lunch with Jordan, Bob, and me."

"Thank you, Brian. I look forward to having lunch with you gentlemen!"

"Okay, Kurt, you are up. What is going on in the sales department?"

Kurt answered, "First, Denise, welcome to the company. I am the sales manager. Please know that the sales department is going to do everything we can to help you get started with your new job here. If you have any problems at all with anyone on the sales team, please come and see me. I will handle the issue. Next, we had the greatest sales day yesterday in the history of the company. I am excited to follow up yesterday's day with another big sales day today. I distributed the new commission plan for the sale of the old products in warehouse 2. I think the plan will generate sales to get rid of all those older parts."

Jordan said, "Ron, you're up!"

"Denise, welcome! My team stayed after work last night and pulled all the parts for today's vehicles in the shop. We put all the products received yesterday in the racks. Finally, we are 100 percent current on shipping all the internet orders. I am proud of my team. They all did an awesome job yesterday!"

"Ron, great job," Jordan said. "I appreciate your team's hard work. Our current sales volume is going to test your team for a while. You need to keep your boys kicking butt every day now to stay current with the increase in order volume!"

"I am on it, boss!"

Brian was next and said, "The shop also had an amazing day yesterday. Each tech had between twelve and fourteen billable hours yesterday. Like the sales team, the techs in the shop had a record day also!"

As I stood there and listened, I realized this was an awesome meeting for Denise to attend on her first day. It is great for her to hear all the positive reports from the management team. My alarm vibrated in my pocket, and I ended the meeting by saying, "Go with confidence!"

Before everyone filed out of the conference room, I asked Ron and Kurt to stay behind because I needed to talk to them. I also requested that Denise wait so we could have a little chat.

Jordan turned to Kurt and Ron and said, "The last two times Bob and I talked to one of the managers after a meeting in this conference room, Brian fired them." He was referring to Scott and Jayson.

"Jordan, that is a terrible thing to say to these two guys," I quickly chimed in. "They are doing great jobs managing their departments! Ron, I would like you to take Denise to your department and introduce her to each one of the guys who report to you. Give her a fifty-cent tour of your warehouses. Tell her about all your current challenges and how you plan to resolve those problems. After you finish with her, walk Denise out to the sales area and pass her on to Kurt to do the same. Kurt, when you are finished with Denise, take her to Jordan. Jordan, you introduce Denise to the balance of the employees, including the shop guys, the ladies in purchasing, and then bring her to Carole. Carole needs to give Denise all the payroll and benefit forms to complete. Denise, when you are done with Carole, please come back to my office. We have more to talk about regarding operational reporting. Thank you, everyone, for your time and do a good job introducing Denise around."

"Denise, please follow me!" Ron said, and off they went.

* * *

I had a good feeling Denise would fit in well with this group. Carole was probably going to be very chatty with her, and that was okay with me! Brian showed up at my office door and tapped the door frame to get my attention. I motioned for him to come in.

He immediately echoed my sentiments about Denise and added, "Jordan told me all about her reference checks. I also made some phone calls to the people she worked with before. As you probably know, I know everyone in the auto industry in a hundred-mile radius of our facility. Everyone referred to her as a superstar. I am glad her son works here because that is one more reason for her to stay here long term. Bob, as a good friend of mine once said, *life is good!*"

I smiled in agreement. "Have you decided where we are going to lunch today?" I asked.

"Jordan decided we would take Denise to his favorite restaurant," he told me.

"Did Jordan even ask if Denise likes sushi?" I wondered aloud.

"Well, he said he did, but you never know with that guy. He might have said he did so that I would not try to pick a different place! That boy does love his sushi!"

* * *

While the four of us were sitting at the restaurant, Brian and Jordan peppered Denise with questions. I became uncomfortable after a while because I felt they were a little too aggressive with our new accounting manager on her first day. I was about to jump into the conversation, but then Denise sort of took the microphone.

She told the two owners about her career experience, which included joining the car dealership after it had filed for bankruptcy protection. She explained all the different rules of reporting when a company is in Chapter 13, bankruptcy. She said that the company had to do double reporting, once for the bankruptcy court and the other for the management team. She talked about the details for her first two years there until they finally got out of the bankruptcy. She had to submit a "workout plan" to the courts, which was a budget that showed how the company was going to be profitable, and the cash flow from the profits paid back the creditors. She explained how she worked six days a week, twelve hours per day.

The more Denise shared her story, the less Brian and Jordan talked. They quickly became confident that Denise was the right person for the job. The job title (accounting manager) and her compensation did not align with her skills and abilities, however. Denise's skills were at the controller or CFO level rather than an accounting manager. Her experience could earn her twice the salary in most other companies. I am not sure why she "settled" for this position and pay, but I thought it might have something to do with the fact that her son also worked for ABC.

By the time we all had our fill of sushi, we were ready to travel back to the office. Jordan paid the bill with the company American Express card.

Then Brian said, "Denise, I checked the references on your résumé. Everyone you worked for was quite impressed with your abilities and production in the accounting department. Jordan and I are pleased that you have joined our management team. I want you to know that if you ever have any problems at the company, see me immediately! I will be happy to refer you to Bob to fix whatever problems come your way."

Jordan and I laughed heartily.

"I am kidding, but I am also not kidding. I am sure you have figured out by now that Jordan and I hired Bob to turn this company around. We have had a great start. Sales have skyrocketed since he started with our company. Yesterday, we had the largest sales day in the history of ABC. I know that Bob recommended we hire you because he knows you can do an awesome job for us in the accounting department. I believe you can get the department's work and financial statements current soon."

Jordan chimed in, "Denise, what my long-winded partner is trying to say is welcome to ABC Off-Road Supply!"

"I am delighted!" Denise said.

"Okay, my long-winded friends, let's get back to the office and get some work done. I am flying home late this afternoon, and I still have a lot to accomplish before I leave."

* * *

Back in my office, I met with Denise again. She asked me a bunch of questions, and I was impressed by her professionalism. I did not doubt that she knew what she was doing in the accounting department. Even if the company were five times larger than ABC was currently, I knew she could handle it. I had great faith that she would be a long-term keeper.

Because I was leaving that afternoon to fly home and had achieved a good comfort level with this new employee, I sent her to meet with Carole for the balance of the afternoon. Denise knew what she needed to accomplish at ABC and certainly did not require me or anyone else to babysit her. I wanted to spend a few minutes with the other managers to answer any questions they had before I left for another ten days. I did not want any of these guys to flounder. I needed every department kicking butt while I was away to maintain the forward momentum.

Kurt was in the sales area with a customer. I did not want to interrupt him while he was with a customer, so I went to find Ron. Ron was in the warehouse area boxing up parts for internet orders. He looked busier than a one-armed paper hanger!

I walked over to him and asked, "Is everything going okay, Ron?"

"Yes, Bob, things are good, but sometime soon, I would like to talk to you about adding another employee to this department if the sales volume continues to be this strong."

"Ron, are you keeping statistics in your department? For example, how many packages you receive daily, how many returns to vendors your department processed, how many parts your team picked for the vehicles in the shop, and how many parts your team shipped for internet orders?"

Ron's eyes widened. "Unfortunately, I have not, but I will immediately start keeping a log of our daily production."

"Great idea, Ron! I wish I would have thought of that!" I joked.

"Are you okay if I give you a hug?" Ron asked in all seriousness. He seemed so relieved to have some direction.

"Sure, give me a hug, buddy!" I said, and we exchanged a quick "man hug."

"When is your next visit here?" he asked next, and I told him I would be back in ten days on a Monday. In response, he said, "I will have the production statistics for a week and a half when you return."

"Great, Ron, have a great balance of your day!"

I walked out into the shop area to find Jordan. He and Joshua were talking about a jeep suspension. It seemed that Joshua was having a problem with the vehicle on the lift in his bay. Jordan excused himself for a moment and asked if 3:30 would be good for me to leave for the airport.

"Yes, sir, that would be great! Are there any questions I can answer for you before we get out of here today?"

"Yes," he said immediately. "You never answered the question Brian and I asked you this morning."

"What question was that?" I asked.

"Don't you remember? We asked you to consider staying longer and not fly home today."

I shook my head. "My wife would kill me if I do not land in Fort Lauderdale on schedule!"

"Okay, we had to try. We definitely don't want your wife to be mad at us. She probably wouldn't let you return to Utah. But, hey, you never get anything unless you at least ask!"

"You are right, but in this case, I cannot do this. I will see you soon."

I looked at my watch; it was 3:00 PM. I went back to the sales area to see if Kurt had become available. He was standing behind Warren, helping him pick the right part for Warren's customer. The customer was standing on the other side of the sales counter listening to Warren and Kurt talk about his vehicle.

"Kurt, I am out of here in about thirty minutes. Do you have any questions I can answer before I leave?"

"Bob, I am all good. But I do want to give you my sincere thanks for everything you have done here. I now feel like this company is going to be very successful with all the changes you have put in place."

"Kurt, thank you. Here is one of my cards with my contact information. If you ever have a question that I can answer while I am in Fort Lauderdale, please do not hesitate to call me anytime!"

"Thank you again, Bob. I appreciate all your help! I also appreciate that you found Denise to clean up our accounting department."

"All is good, Kurt! I will see you on my next trip. I am depending on you to kick butt with these sales guys!"

"You can depend on that!" he assured me.

My next visit was with Denise and Carole. They were sitting in Carole's office, reviewing everything Carole did on a part-time basis. I walked into the office and asked how everything is going.

Carole looked more relaxed than I had ever seen her. "You hired a very smart lady, Bob. It is not going to take her very long to get control of this department."

"I agree with you," I said, and then added, "She is a lot smarter than me! Are there any questions I can answer for either of you ladies before I head home?"

Denise stood up and hugged me. "Bob, thank you for everything."

"Make me proud!" I replied.

"Will do," she said.

Then Carole asked, "If Denise picks up everything in the accounting department quickly, am I required to stay the whole two weeks?"

"Yes, you can work on the daily stuff, while Denise focuses on getting the financial statements current. Are you okay with that?"

"Yes, sir. I made a commitment to you that I would stay for two weeks. I will live up to my commitment."

"Thank you, Carole! You are the best! Be well, ladies! See you soon."

* * *

Brian was in the showroom behind the counter at his sales area. As I approached, I said, "I am out of here in about ten minutes."

He gave me an imploring look and asked, "We can't talk you into staying until next Friday?"

"That would be a big no!" I replied without hesitation.

Brian laughed. He then came around the counter and gave me a big hug. "Bob, thank you for everything you have done for us. Jordan and I are learning a ton from you about managing this company."

"That is what you are paying me for," I told him. "The turnaround is all free!"

"Travel safely, and I will see you when you return!"

I quickly shook hands with each salesperson and went to my office to pack up my stuff. When I walked back out to the showroom, Jordan was standing at the front door with his keys in his hand for his big, blue pickup truck.

The trip to the airport went very quickly because Jordan asked me a plethora of questions on the way there. Answering Jordan's questions was a good thing because the more the owners knew how to make good business decisions, the quicker this turnaround would be successful. Jordan dropped me off at the Delta Airlines Terminal. The flight was on time. As soon as the plane was in the air, I was fast asleep!

Chapter 10

GO WITH CONFIDENCE!

"If you can't measure it, you can't improve it."

—PETER DRUCKER, MANAGEMENT CONSULTANT,
EDUCATOR, AND AUTHOR

THE DAY WAS MONDAY, MAY 6. THIS TRIP WOULD BE MY EIGHTH to Utah for this client. As the plane was landing at the Salt Lake City International Airport, I noticed that the mountains were still snowcapped. When I got off the plane, it was 47 degrees, which was not that cold. When I got on the plane in Fort Lauderdale, just five hours earlier, it had been 87 degrees.

Brian picked me up outside of the Delta terminal. On the ride to the facility, he was in a great mood, much better than I had ever seen him since the day we first met. Brian had gone to the Moab Jeep Safari event with Jordan and three salespeople from Wednesday to Sunday. He shared with me that the time at Moab was very successful. His time out of the office to mingle with customers had worked out well. Brian said that our conversations about marketing several weeks ago had a big impact on his daily activities at ABC Off-Road Supply. He now looked at meeting with customers in the showroom as a marketing and sales opportunity.

In past years, Brian had approached the Moab Jeep Safari event as a fun time with a bunch of off-road vehicle owners. He explained how it was different this time:

"We have always set up an ABC Off-Road Supply booth for the week, but the company had no real marketing strategy. We received little value for the investment in going there. This year was different. We looked at every person we met as a 'sales and marketing opportunity.' The five of us worked very hard each of the five days that we were there. Our goal was to meet every person who attended the event. We tried to have an introductory conversation about ABC Off-Road Supply facility in Ogden without seeming too much like a 'salesperson.' We also talked about our website, where customers may order off-road parts at great prices. We handed out more than 500 ABC T-shirts. On the back of the black and gray T-shirt was our logo and the front, we put, 'I was at the Moab Jeep Safari!' People loved the shirts, and they were wearing them every day. We took hours and hours of videos. We took lots of photos, including the people who were wearing our T-shirts.

"Every evening, all five of us were posting videos and pictures on our website, Facebook, and Instagram. We saved the videos so we could have them streaming on the TV monitors in the showrooms. Bob, we paid 2,500 dollars for the ABC T-shirts. I am betting that the investment is going to get us at least 75,000 dollars of new business.

"I handed out 600 of my professional cards to pretty much every person who attended the event plus all the vendors. We had several vendors ask us if we could market and sell their products on our website. I have set up meetings this week to talk to those vendors. They are all going to come to our facility to discuss the partnership opportunity. I can see us charging these vendors a marketing allowance to sell their products, which could pay for the cost of the monthly website maintenance fees. I am pretty excited about the opportunity."

I was amazed by all of this, and so proud of the job that he and Jordan had done. I told him so. "You should be excited. You have done a great job. Congratulations."

My words put an even a bigger smile on Brian's face.

* * *

It was obvious to me that Brian had been going through a transformation since I had started coaching this company to profitability.

He was turning into a businessman managing an off-road supply company. There was a big difference between Brian and Jordan now, a very positive difference. Before I got here, they were both struggling to come up with the right answers on how to manage their company.

Brian was a salesman at heart. Year to date, his sales were 150 percent more than the top salesperson's numbers (Joshua). Brian's sales skyrocketed because he had started to visit all the dealerships in the area. He sold them installed lift kits for their pickup truck inventory. Those lifted pickup trucks sold much faster for the dealers than the vehicles without the lift kits. Because of Brian's sales skills, the dealers were now sending a steady flow of their trucks and jeeps to ABC. Now, Brian was getting a bunch of reoccurring sales without doing any selling.

When Brian's sales started hitting $160,000 per month, it motivated the other salespeople. He had proved to them that he could increase his sales by getting out of the office to visit potential customers at the car dealerships. Sitting on a stool behind the sales counter all day and being an "order taker" did not work if you wanted to make a good living as a salesman. "Order takers" never got within a $100,000 of Brian's monthly sales totals. His sales challenged the other salespeople's egos, which motivated them to do much better.

* * *

Brian pulled into the parking lot at ABC Off-Road Supply. I immediately noticed that the building had been painted dark gray and looked great.

"What do you think about the building?" Brian asked.

"It looks beautiful, and I love the color!" I said.

"Bob, I bartered the job by doing a lift kit for the painter's pickup truck for him to paint the building. The total cost of the lift kit, including the tech's labor, was 600 dollars. I had other quotes to paint the building for 1,500 to 2,000 dollars."

"The building looks really good! I am impressed." I looked up and saw his new sign.

Brian told me that the redo of the sign cost him nothing. Michelin Tire had paid for the total cost of upgrading the sign. "All I had to do is add their name on the bottom."

I said, "I can hardly see their name from here."

"I know, I was shocked when they approved the preliminary drawing for the sign."

"Good job, Brian! You are a great salesman!"

I looked around the parking lot. In front of the building were twenty-plus vehicles that all had off-road products. Four of the jeeps were on ramps to draw the attention of people driving past the dealership. "Even the parking lot looks professional!" I said. "The building looks brand new. The parked vehicles in front of the building are all free advertising for your company. Super job!"

"Kurt oversees the responsibility of the outside of the building. He has assigned each one of the salespeople to take ownership of the parking lot daily. The salespeople have been rolling up the sleeves and kicking butt recently. They have done an awesome job. Even though three salesmen, Jordan and I, were at Moab from Wednesday through Sunday, ABC ended the week with 180,000 dollars in sales. I honestly have no idea how they did it with only three salespeople in the showroom while we were gone."

"Brian, when you raise the bar for the sales staff, they tend to be more productive! Those three guys in the showroom were probably extremely happy all week. They got all the sales for the week rather than sharing the sales with another three salespeople."

"Bob, you are probably right."

"I noticed that those old jeeps that were in the south parking lot are gone. What happened to them?"

"Kurt said that those vehicles made our parking lot look like an old junkyard. I hated doing it, but I put a "for sale" on each one. Some guy came and bought all three jeeps for cash. He paid me the same price that I paid for them two years ago. I agree that the parking lot does look better without them sitting there, rusting away every day. Now that they are gone, and I have the money in the bank, I can see that it was a good decision to sell them."

When we walked into the showroom, there were customers everywhere!

"Brian, are all these people actors pretending to be customers?"

"No, Bob, they are all customers. The showroom has been like this for the past six weeks. I am not kidding!"

"Well, I am impressed."

"Bob, we have implemented *everything* you suggested. Our sales have grown every week. The graph for our daily and weekly sales numbers is pointing north!"

I thought to myself, *This sales growth is such a beautiful thing.* The thought that I had a client that precisely followed my direction during the turnaround gave me goosebumps!

The retail showroom looked beautiful and organized. Brian told me that each salesperson was assigned a day of the week to come in a half-hour early and clean the retail shelves. He explained that Kurt had come up with a system where each salesperson had something to do each morning before noon to either improve the appearance of the facility or drive sales. There was a chart of the day-by-day responsibilities for each salesperson in the room off the sales area. These guys realized that the better the showrooms and the parking lot looked to their customers, the more money they made each pay-day. The salesmen used to sit around and mope because they had nothing to do all day. Now they were much happier because they were busy all the time. They were making more money, and their day would go much faster. Brian told me they were constantly saying, "Hmm . . . where did the day go? It feels like I just got here, and now it is time to close!"

I urged Brian to keep talking. I really liked what I was hearing. He went on, "The sales team started advertising the old inventory on social media and the website, twenty-five SKUs at a time. Kurt suggested we set up a 'clearance table' in the front showroom and sell the products off the table. The idea has worked well. Funny thing, when the products are boxed up and stacked up in the warehouse racks in warehouse 2, we did not sell any of the old stuff. But when you display the products in the showroom with a clearance price, those old parts have moved quickly. Who would have thought that?"

Sometimes Brian was actually funny!

"We have sold a lot of the old stuff on Facebook, too! The way the old inventory is selling now, we should be sold out of those clearance items by the end of June. We are turning all that warehouse 2 inventory into cash and paying down our debt with our vendors. Not all the vendors are happy yet, but they are getting there. We have only a couple more vendors to get off the COD terms."

In the front showroom, I noticed that the old "army-looking" jeep was no longer there. I asked Brian what happened to it.

"Bob, when you put a 'for sale" sign on anything in our showrooms, it will sell."

I was very proud of Brian. I knew he did not want to sell that old jeep. He did because he finally agreed that it should not be taking up valuable selling space in the showroom. Plus, he used the cash from the sale to pay down more company debt.

Brian then asked me to follow him to the shop. He wanted me to see all the improvements since my last visit. As I passed the sales team, I noticed that Warren was clean-shaven. I patted him on the back and whispered in his ear, "Your sales have probably gone up since you started shaving, huh?"

He looked back at me and said, "Welcome back to Utah, Bob! I hate to admit it, but you are right!"

All the salespeople looked great. They all had on an ABC-logoed shirt and khaki pants. Every one of the salespeople looked much more professional than they had in the past visits.

In the room off the sales area, I saw the whiteboard with the list of tasks for each salesperson. I did not say anything, but I was impressed. This company just kept getting better. In the shop, the first thing I noticed was that it was looking materially better—clean, busy, and organized. Every tech was working under a vehicle. None of them looked "homeless" anymore. They all wore clean uniforms. There was a big sign on the wall: CONSECUTIVE SAFETY DAYS: 52. Below it was another sign: CONSECUTIVE ERROR FREE DAYS: 48.

Brian explained, "The shop is measuring our safety record and error-free days. We are focused on keeping this shop safe for the techs and delivering an 'error-free' vehicle back to our customers . . . every time. Bob, that quote you shared a few weeks ago by Peter Drucker really stuck with me: 'If you can't measure it, you can't improve it.'"

"I also believe that the opposite is true," I said. "If you *can* measure it, you *can* improve it!"

Brian smiled. "We started measuring a lot of things at this company. Not only are we measuring, but we are also improving our policies, procedures, and shop production. Once we get April's financial statements, I believe they are going to show another profitable month for this company!"

"You and Jordan should be very proud of yourselves and your teams."

Brian said, "Now, let's go see warehouse 2."

I wondered how warehouse 2 was going to look. I remembered when Scott had given me the fifty-cent tour of that warehouse all those months ago. After the first six feet, an employee had to crawl over pallets of inventory to get to the middle of the room, risking his or her life!

When Brian opened the warehouse door, I was shocked! There were storage racks around the perimeter of the room with inventory neatly stored in an organized manner. The tire busters were using the middle of the warehouse to install wheels and tires. The newly painted floor made the warehouse look a thousand times better than it had a couple of months earlier. This warehouse had transformed from a dump to an area of the company that generated a lot of revenue.

"Brian, awesome job cleaning up this warehouse!"

"Bob, this was one of Jordan's projects. He did do a very nice job with this warehouse. These guys install a lot of wheels and tires in the area."

When Brian and I got back to the showroom, he introduced me to Abbie. Abbie was a friend of Michael's, one of the salesmen. Michael had referred Abbie to Jordan and Brian because she had experience with posting social media.

Abbie was probably twenty-one years old. She was dressed in jeans and a sleeveless T-shirt, presumably to show off her tattoos. Because the sales were growing so much, Jordan also used her as a "driver" from time to time to pick up parts locally or deliver finished vehicles to the car dealerships.

When Brian introduced me to her, her first comment was, "Oh, you are *that* guy!"

"Abbie, what guy is that?"

She answered, "You're that guy that fixes everything in the company, right?"

"No, I am just the guy who makes the suggestions. Brian and Jordan are the ones who are responsible for fixing everything."

"Mr. Curry, that is not what I hear. Everyone says that you are the Turnaround Guy, and whenever you say jump, everyone here asks, 'How high?'"

"Well, Abbie, it is a pleasure to meet you!"

She responded, "Likewise!"

Jordan had agreed to hire her because he also needed her to do some of the other clerical jobs. For example, she was responsible for putting together the packages to give the customers when the shop finished their vehicles (the "Thank you for your business" card, the "10% off" on your next visit coupon, information on the 500-mile checkup, and the customer survey with the pre-addressed, pre-stamped envelope). According to Jordan, so far, Abbie had been a successful hire. She showed up for work every day on time and got her job done. I did mention to Jordan that she could look a little more professional if we had her wear an ABC-logoed long-sleeve shirt when she was in the showroom or delivering a vehicle to a car dealership.

Jordan answered, "Bob, you are right. I will make that happen right away."

When Kurt was free from working with a customer, he welcomed me back to Utah. "Thank you, Kurt, I appreciate that. How is everything going?"

"Bob, we have been crazy busy. I love it when this place is humming! The days go so quickly, it's amazing. You know that we are having our management meetings on Mondays now, right?"

"No, I did not. Why did the managers change the meeting day?"

"Because all the managers get their reporting done by Monday late morning for the prior week. It just makes sense to meet and react to the reporting on Monday at noon rather than having to wait until Wednesday."

"Hmm . . . that makes sense! Okay, I am assuming that the meeting is at noon in the conference room."

"Yes, sir!"

"Thank you for letting me know, Kurt. I don't ever want to be late for a management meeting!" I immediately pulled out my phone and set my alarm to go off at five minutes to noon.

I went to see Denise, but she had three people in her office. I decided I would catch up with her later when she was free. When she saw me, she waved and then continued her conversation with the people in her office. Since it was less than thirty minutes until the management meeting started, I decided to go to my office to prepare for the meeting. When my alarm went off, I got up and went to the conference room.

* * *

When I entered the conference room, I was shocked by the complete makeover. The carpeting looked brand new. Brian and Jordan had given everything in the company a critical look to see how they could improve it, which included the conference room. The big whiteboard was perfectly clean. There was a TV monitor mounted on the wall so that we could connect our computers to the screen and do presentations for everyone to see. Every manager walked through the door a few minutes to noon so that the meeting could start on time. The food was already delivered and waited for us in the middle of the table. Jordan grabbed the package and distributed the sandwiches and drinks to everyone.

The day before, Brian had emailed me the agenda for the meeting. I printed a copy and had it in front of me. I was impressed with everything I had seen so far! The meeting schedule was laid out professionally and was well-organized. Kurt was first on the list. He hooked his computer to the cable on the table and connected to the large computer monitor. He first showed a graph for the sales for April compared to last April.

Kurt said, "As you can all see, we finished the month of April up 17 percent over last April. I thought it was going to be a greater increase than that, but we had a large backlog of work that we were not able to get to for April sales total. The internet sales were up by 11 percent, and the sales team was up 20 percent. Year to date, the internet is up only by eight percent, the sales team by 11 percent, and total sales are up by 10 percent."

I listened intently, enjoying the professional way Kurt delivered the news, but I could see that he was not entirely pleased.

I realized I was spot on as Kurt continued, "I am not pleased with these numbers. I thought that we had a blowout April, especially since our sales set a record for the company. I am looking at these results knowing that we are going to set new records for the company in May."

Next, Kurt showed a graph of the monthly sales by a salesman of the older inventory stored in warehouse 2. He said, "We only started capturing these sales beginning February. We have doubled our sales total each month. Warren is doing a great job moving that older product. If we continue the sales at this rate, we will have sold all the inventory by the end of June."

Brian and Jordan applauded when Kurt showed that graph.

Jordan said, "Kurt, I think that we should give Warren a 100-dollar debit card to reward him for focusing on selling that old stuff in the warehouse."

"The sales contest this month is for the salesperson who sells the most warehouse 2 inventory. He will win a 200-dollar gift certificate to a restaurant of his choice! Do you want me to keep that or change it to something else?" Kurt asked.

Jordan shook his head no. "I am just suggesting that we reward Warren for doing a great job in April. When you give him the debit card, make sure you do it in front of all the other members of the sales team."

"Will do, sir!" Kurt said.

"Next, I want to make everyone aware that our next sales meeting is this Wednesday at 6:30 PM at Boston's Restaurant and Sports Bar," Jordan said. "They give us a discount on the food and drink because the manager is an off-roader himself. We will be giving out the rewards at the meeting for the sales contest for April and announcing May's competition. This meeting is going to be a good one. Please, everyone, come if possible. I want these salespeople to feel supported by the management team."

Kurt asked for the floor again. Jordan nodded, and he said, "Recently, I met a sales trainer who emailed me about sales training for our sales team. I wanted to run this by you all to see if there is interest in hiring this guy. He sent me a list of topics we may be interested in training our sales team. They are closing techniques, relationship selling, telephone sales, the importance of product knowledge, and using the internet to gain customers. Originally, I had planned to assign each of the salespeople a topic to research and train the other members of the sales team, but that did not work out. Our salespeople were not born to be sales trainers. It was quite obvious when Joshua did the first class. It was a crash and burn! The sales trainer said if we are interested, he will charge us 50 percent of his normal rate since he would not have to travel for our classes."

"Kurt, what are his normal fees?" I asked.

"Bob, according to his website, he charges 200 dollars per hour. The classes are each an hour long."

"I suggest you get a list of his current references and check them out," I commented.

"Good suggestion! Since I knew that you were going to suggest that, I already did. I called seven of his current clients and asked them five questions I had prepared beforehand. His clients all gave him excellent reviews. Three of the companies were car dealerships.

All the dealerships complemented his training skills. I believe car dealerships may be his sales training 'model' client."

I asked, "So are you saying that he will charge us 500 dollars for five training sessions?"

"Yes."

"When and where are the training sessions going to be?"

Kurt had a ready response: "Wednesdays at our sales meetings. I was thinking about asking him to join us at the sales meeting for dinner, and then the training classes would be after we ate. That way, he would be present for two hours rather than just one. We could ask him questions during dinner."

Brian said, "Kurt, if you think that these training classes are going to be valuable to your sales team, pull the trigger!"

"Thank you, sir, I will do that!" He paused for a moment before continuing. "I also want to update everyone about the phones and the calls we receive before we open our doors to customers. The salespeople are each coming in an hour early one day a week to answer any calls between eight and nine. Any emails from callers earlier than eight, the salesman will return the calls after nine. Does anyone have any questions?"

The room was silent.

Kurt continued, "This is the next to the last issue that I want to cover. It will be quick, I promise. We now have five off-road clubs who have agreed to meet in our upstairs conference room once or twice a month. They will meet every other week during the season and once a month during the off months. Their meetings are in the evenings from 6:30 to 8:00. The salesperson/shop technician who invited the club is going to be responsible for attending the meetings."

I asked, "Kurt, how many members are in these five clubs?"

"I believe there are about twenty members in each club."

"Which salesman closed the deal with the clubs?"

"Michael got two, and Warren had a friend in one club that he approached. Bob in the shop belongs to a club that he invited here for meetings and they accepted. I contacted a friend I knew was in a club. My friend and I met this past weekend. He said that meetings at our conference room would be ten times better than in his basement. His wife confirmed his decision because she hated his twenty 'best friends' tromping around in her finished basement with their muddy shoes."

Jordan said, "Great job, Kurt. This 'win' for us sounds like we may have just landed a hundred new loyal customers for our company. Should we buy food or snacks for the meetings as our way of saying thank you for holding their meetings at our facility?"

"That is not necessary," Kurt responded. "The clubs go to a bar after the meeting to eat burgers and drink beer. They are all looking at this like we are doing them a big favor, not the other way around. They all asked what the fee was for the conference room. When I told them there is no charge, they each said yes immediately."

Jordan commented, "We should do something nice for the groups so we can turn them all into our long-term customers."

Brian spoke up and said, "First, I would like to say, AWESOME JOB, Kurt! Second, I am looking at this like we just got a hundred new sales and marketing opportunities. These members are going to show up at our facility at least once a month, and some months, twice. Getting this many new customers for free is special! I am so glad we finished that conference room. It is going to be such an asset to this company. Kurt, this is very exciting! We will talk about this more. We need a plan on how to handle this opportunity. Kurt, please set up a meeting later today with Bob, and the three of us."

Kurt wrote a note on his white pad in front of him as a reminder.

Jordan asked me, "Do you think we should reward the salesperson for bringing the clubs into our facility?"

"Of course, I do! We should sit down with a calendar to see how many clubs a month we can handle. I know that the salesmen and Bob in the shop are donating their time for this, but I believe they are going to get a lot of future sales from these clubs, right, Kurt?"

"Yes, sir."

"The marketing cost to get a hundred new customers is pretty expensive. These clubs cost us nothing. Let's give the person responsible for bringing in the club a 250-dollar commission."

Brian and Jordan nodded their heads in approval.

I turned to Denise and said, "Please write a bonus check for Michael for 500 dollars, and 250 dollars each for Warren, Bob, and Kurt."

Denise wrote a note on the white pad in front of her.

I added, "Kurt, I want these checks handed out at the sales meeting on Wednesday. Jordan, you can give Bob the check since he will not be at the sales meeting. I want to send a crystal-clear message to our sales team: If you work hard and do the right things to bring sales into this company, you will get rewarded!"

Kurt asked, "Bob, can I ask you a favor? Please come to the meeting on Wednesday and hand out these checks. I would feel a little funny handing a check to myself."

"I will, sure, but maybe either Brian or Jordan want to do the honor?"

Jordan said, "No, Bob, you do it. You came up with the idea about the clubs meeting here and rewarding the people who got it done. You give out the rewards."

"Okay, I can do that, especially since I am getting a free meal out of the deal!"

Jordan laughed. "Bob, all your meals are free here!"

"Yeah, I know," I said, and I took a bite of my sandwich.

"Okay, finally, the last item on my list," Kurt announce. "I am passing out to all of you the 'vehicle checkout procedure.' Please review it and send me any comments you may have. I want to publish this with the sales team and the guys in the shop as soon as possible. It covers the information about the new marketing package we are giving our customers when the salesperson hands him his keys and the customer survey. Okay, now I am done."

I immediately reviewed the new policy. Kurt had done a nice job!

Brian said, "Thank you, Kurt, great job! Denise, you are next."

"Thank you, Brian!" Denise connected the cable to her computer so that everyone could see the statements on the monitor she would be reviewing. She showed the group March's income statement and balance sheet and began explaining what they were seeing. There were very few people in the meeting who understood the finances, but when she said, "ABC Off-Road Supply just had the highest sales total for one month in the history of the company," everyone clapped. Her next statement was that the company had made a nice profit for the month and year to date. "Plus," she added, "I believe the company may not have another loss in the month for the balance of the year."

Brian looked at me and asked, "Bob, does that mean that this company has turned around?"

"Well, Brian, that is one of the first signs of a company that has turned around."

"What other signs do we need to see?" he asked.

"That is a great question! There are several signs," I said, and then I covered each of the following:

✓ The company has a great management team with a professional manager in each functional area of the business.

✓ The company uses an operating budget to manage the business.

✓ The business has a detailed marketing plan to drive sales growth.

✓ The business has a strong system of internal controls to protect the company's assets.

✓ The company has timely, accurate financial and operational reporting.

✓ There is minimal employee turnover for the company during the year.

✓ The company has an excellent hiring policy and only hires "top-tier" candidates for each open position.

✓ The owner and senior managers are totally in sync with their goals for the business.

✓ The company never offers a person a job with the company before we do a complete and comprehensive background, criminal, drug, and credit check on the candidate.

✓ And, finally, the company hires the best people in the area, treats them with respect, gives them the tools to do their jobs, provides them an excellent environment to work in, and compensates them fairly.

"Brian, if you can look at your company and say all those statements are true in your business, your company has been turned around!"

Denise next put the weekly flash report on the computer screen. She handed Brian, Jordan, and me a hard copy of this week's report. I reviewed the document and was very happy with the information. The four weeks' statistics progressively got better each week. I complimented Denise for the great job she had done getting everything in the accounting department current and the quality of the reporting.

She smiled and said, "Thank you, Bob. It has not been easy, and I am glad I finished all the work."

I said, "Denise, now that everything is current, you can sit back and relax!"

"Bob, I don't think so, there is still a lot of work to do."

I answered, "I didn't know that! By the way, Denise, does this company have an operating budget yet?"

"Yes, it is done," she replied. "I was waiting for you to get here and bless it."

"Okay, I would like to have a meeting with this whole team to review all the numbers. Eventually, I would like these guys to develop the numbers for their departments, but on the first pass, this will work fine. Thank you, Denise! Every time you surprise me, it turns out to be a positive surprise!"

I asked, "Who's next?"

Ron raised his hand and said, "I am Bob."

Ron passed around a report showing the statistics from his department. "About six weeks ago, Bob asked me to start recording the daily statistics for my department. We recorded the number of packages we received, the number of parts that we returned to vendors, the number of parts we picked and delivered to the shop, and the number of customer orders that we shipped. The last two columns on the report are the total number of packages handled for the day and the packages we did not finish shipping until the next day. As you can all see, it shows our capacity in our department is pretty consistent."

Go with Confidence! ♦ 233

I asked Ron, "So, what you are telling me, Ron, is with your existing staff, you can move an average of 150 packages a day. That includes receiving the product, putting the products into the inventory, picking inventory for the shop or internet orders, then packing and shipping those customer orders. It also includes the RTVs, right?"

"Yes, sir, that is accurate."

"So, when the volume is higher than that, the orders roll over to the next day, right?"

"Yes, sir!"

"Therefore, if we want to make sure that all the customer orders get shipped within the same day, we must add either a part-time or full-time employee to your department. Is that what your analysis is showing?"

"Yes, sir!"

"Okay, I will talk to Brian and Jordan about adding staff to your department."

Ron said, "Thank you, Bob!"

Brian said, "Yes, I finally get to speak! I am just kidding. The three of you, Kurt, Denise, and Ron, are kicking butt. I am proud of all of you. I have a couple of things I want to talk about today. First, I have received a lot of customer surveys in the mail. The reviews are coming back with great ratings. I have recapped the evaluations for the six questions. In each case, our customers are saying that we are doing an excellent job. The answers compliment both the sales team and our techs. JB and Kurt, tell your teams that our customers are rating them an average of 4.8 out of a possible 5.0. That is not perfect, but damn close! I believe we have a lot of good employees. But it is better if our customers think we have a lot of excellent employees. That is what they are reporting so far. Congratulations to JB and Kurt!"

I asked, "Brian, who is JB?"

Brian laughed and said, "Bob, we already have two Joshuas who work here, so we started calling this Joshua "JB" to eliminate any confusion."

"Well, I am glad that there are not too many Bobs who work here. I would be afraid to find out what you would be calling me!"

The whole group laughed.

"Next, I want to share with everyone here our Google Analytics reports for the first four months of the year. You will note that the visits to our website have increased since we hired the new ad agency. That is indicated by the little line that starts going straight north beginning the first of March. Bob, thank you for the introduction to those guys. They are doing a much better job for us than our old friend, David. I also want to report that our new advertising agency is sending out email blasts using our extensive list of past customer email addresses. I believe that with all the marketing we are doing now, our sales are going to continue to grow expediently.

"I want to report that Kenny is doing an excellent job resolving all the customer order problems on our website, eBay, Amazon, and Facebook accounts. I expect when he finishes, we should have over 100,000 products on our website to sell to our customers. Okay, I'm at the bottom of my bullet points. It's your turn, JB, Joshua, or whatever your name is!"

With a big smile, JB stood up and handed out the shop productivity report for last week. "I will keep this short and sweet. If you look at the bottom right of the report, it says that the average hours billed for all the technicians was fifty-nine hours. The high amount billed was the "Other Joshua," with sixty-three hours, and the low was Cameron with forty hours. He would have been much higher, but he missed a day of work to pick up his mother from the hospital. Life is good in the shop. These guys are all happy when they are getting paid for fifty-nine hours and only working forty hours. Also, let me add that one of the reasons that they are so productive is because Ron's group is doing a wonderful job. The shop never has to wait for parts as we did in the past to finish the job. So, big kudos to Ron and his group."

Everyone gave Ron a little round of applause.

Jordan said, "I am next. I am not sure why I was not at the top of the list on the agenda. I have great news to report also. Our new software program that is keeping the on-hand inventory balances is up and running. The software is awesome. I cannot believe how easy it was to install and operate. It is completely compatible with QuickBooks. As most of you are aware, we took a physical inventory this weekend. And I agree, kudos to Ron's team. His department did an awesome job of taking the inventory this weekend. Our inventory now is down 220,500 dollars since the year-end. The ladies in purchasing have been doing a great job working with Ron's group to get that inventory balance down. If you people don't know, the reduction of the inventory has freed up cash to pay down our vendor accounts payables. We are now adding 'minimums and maximums' for all our SKUs. The goal is to keep the inventory balance low, but never have "out of stocks" that hold up our shop and shipments for our internet orders."

I looked at Jordan, and I could tell that he was very proud of himself. This inventory software and reduction of the inventory balance was a major win for ABC Off-Road Supply. Jordan, Ron, and the ladies in purchasing had done an unbelievable job getting this software installed and the inventory uploaded to the programs. Now that the software was operating as it was supposed to, we were receiving all the financial benefits. Life is good! When Jordan completed his presentation, I stood up and clapped, acknowledging that he had just knocked it out of the park for this company. Jordan also stood up and thanked everyone for their help with the project. I was next.

I said, "My turn! I have a question. Kurt, what is our current billing rate to our retail and wholesale customers?"

"Retail is 125 dollars, and wholesale is 60 or 65 dollars. Right, Brian?"

"Yes, most wholesale deals are now being charged 65 dollars an hour of labor," Brian replied.

"Okay, I want to move the retail customers up to 135 dollars and wholesale to 75 dollars," I said. "Brian, can you move your wholesale customers up 10 dollars per hour?"

"Bob, not right now. How about July first?" he asked.

"Sure, I will leave myself a note to remind you on the first of June to tell the customers that our prices are increasing on July first."

Kurt asked, "Bob, should we do the same for retail customers?"

"No, make the change today immediately after this meeting. If our customers are rating the shop work and sales team at 4.8 out of 5.0, they can pay a little more for our talented employees!"

"Bob, I love having you here," Jordan said. "I know that Brian and I would have never had our labor prices up this high if it was not for you being here."

I appreciated his comment, but I still had other comments I needed to make. I said, "It is now five minutes to one. This meeting is only supposed to last one hour. I have a few things to say, and we can get out of here on time. There has been a massive amount of work accomplished by this excellent management team and owners. I now cannot come up with a weakness in the company. We have a strong management team in this room. Every one of you is reporting the productivity in your respective departments. The reporting is showing positive results for last week. The reporting is timely— Monday at noon for the prior week's activities—and accurate. It is amazing how this team has raised the bar so quickly. Denise's financial statements are reporting that all your efforts are generating sales and profits. That was not true a few months ago. If fact, a few months ago, there was no reporting for each department, and financial statements were just a dream, not a reality. This organized meeting was efficient and well-managed."

Jordan said, "Bob, I have to interrupt you. You are not leading up to tell us that you will not be coming back to our company in the future, are you?"

"No, Jordan. I am using a lot of words to tell you a very simple message. You all are doing an incredible job here, and I am proud to say that I have the honor to work with such a talented management group. Thank you all for your hard work and for being so successful on the turnaround mission. Finally, Go with confidence! It is now one o'clock!"

Chapter 11

"AND NOW, THE REST OF THE STORY"

"The best executive is the one who has the sense enough to pick good men to do what he wants done, and self-restraint enough to keep from meddling with them while they do it."

—THEODORE ROOSEVELT, 26TH PRESIDENT OF THE UNITED STATES

ABC OFF-ROAD SUPPLY IN OGDEN, UTAH, WAS A SUCCESSFUL turnaround. One of the reasons it was so successful was because the owners of the business were both committed to growing as entrepreneurs, business people, and good managers of the employees. Brian and Jordan had transformed into successful business owners while working six very long days a week, for several months during the turnaround engagement. Both owners were good listeners; they both had high intelligence and grit! Brian and Jordan were wonderful to work with during the better part of a year. Their personal and professional growth was nothing short of amazing. Both owners transitioned from being off-road shop technicians to businesspeople managing an eight-million-dollar off-road supply company. I was confident that Brian and Jordan could now handle a $25 million company with their skills and abilities developed during the turnaround engagement. I was going to enjoy staying close to this client, and these two gentlemen to watch their business grow every year from this time forward.

The key components to the turnaround other than the professional growth of two owners were:

The "Total Makeover"

When I first walked through the front door of ABC, I knew that the whole company, including its employees, needed a total makeover! All the areas in the company that the public saw daily (the "junk-yard" parking lot, the building, the sign, the two showrooms, off-road vehicles, and the sales team) were all "no-brainers" to clean up immediately. It did not take any turnaround experience to make that decision. My goal was to improve the appearance of the company to its customers. That effort did not require a lot of money or time but had a very positive impact on both the customers and the employees. Right away, the sales for the company increased when the company looked more successful and professional.

The Management Team

When Scott picked me up at the airport on my first trip to Utah, he described the management team to me in detail. I knew I had to make some changes with the managers if this company was ever going to be profitable. The funny thing was when Scott was telling me all about how bad the managers were at ABC, he should have added his name to the list.

Wes, the service manager, who was managing the shop, and Carole, the bookkeeper, both asked me to replace them during my first interview with each of them.

When Brian and Jordan told me that Jayson was a great candidate to replace Wes, I should have never let them hire him before I was able to interview him face to face. That was a mistake. If I could, I would have turned back the calendar, but I couldn't. I know that if I had interviewed Jayson, I would not have recommended him.

Terminating Jayson quickly and replacing him with JB was a good decision and ultimately fixed the shop problems. JB, whose real name was Joshua, turned out to be a good manager for the group of techs who were mostly right around his age. The techs disliked Jayson immensely because he had poor management skills, but they liked and respected JB. JB was a young man with the skills and ability to manage the shop. He excelled in the position, especially when Jordan was spending more time in the shop and less time in the purchasing department. Jordan mentored JB, which was a perfect fit for both the guys. But, at the time, turning over three service managers in a matter of five months truly was not a good thing for this turnaround.

Replacing Carole, the bookkeeper with Denise, the new accounting manager, had many plusses attached to the hiring. Before Denise joined ABC, she was a skilled and experienced assistant controller who managed an accounting department for a large car dealership. The dealership was ten times the size of ABC. Finding her was lucky because ABC needed her advanced accounting and management skills to clean up the accounting department and get all the work and reporting current.

The Financial and Operational Reporting

Early in the consulting engagement, I needed current financial statements to help me successfully turn this company around. As soon as I had Denise sitting in Carole's chair, I then had the financial information I needed to make good business decisions for the company.

Denise worked very hard when she joined the organization to bring financial reporting up to date. A month after hiring Denise, she was able to get all the department's work current. Therefore, from that time forward, I had the information I needed to do my job. She prepared the weekly flash report (see page 197) right after she had the financial reporting up to date. Her work was timely and accurate. After the statements were current and the operational reporting distributed to the owners, the next project was the operating budget for the balance of the current year. Denise, Brian, Jordan, and I worked on producing the first budget ever for ABC for the current year and the next calendar year. Denise added the new budget, along with the prior year's actuals, for the current month and year-to-date to the financial statements.

I worked with Kurt on what I wanted the sales department's reports to look like when published for the owners. Kurt became passionate about his sales management position once he started issuing weekly sales reports. The weekly reporting documented that he and the sales team were now doing a great job. Each week, the company's sales were growing, and each member of the sales team was making his monthly sales quota.

JB created the shop productivity reports weekly. Those reports documented the number of billable hours each technician produced versus the total number of hours worked.

Ron, in the warehouse, created weekly reports showing all inventory movement, including the number of packages received daily, the number of returns to vendors, and the number of parts his team picked for the vehicles in the shop. The report also showed the number of orders his team shipped for internet sales. Later, Ron added the total labor hours used in his department to confirm the cost per piece that was received, picked, put in inventory, packed, and shipped.

There were three problem areas in Ron's department when I started with ABC back in January. They were returns to vendors (RTVs), the inventory on the customer pick-up racks, and orders not shipped during the same day the order was received. Once Ron added the additional columns for those issues in his report, the reporting automatically fixed those three problems. Going back to Peter Drucker's quote, "If you can't measure it, you can't improve it," when Ron's warehouse and shipping department started measuring the production, those three problem areas were cleaned up and resolved forever. The reports showed management the weaknesses and what they needed to do immediately fix the problems!

Recruiting, Hiring, and Onboarding

From day one of the consulting engagement, the owners and management team did not have a clue how to recruit, hire, and onboard quality candidates to fill open positions within the company. The owners had never done a background check, drug test, or checked references on a candidate before giving the person a job offer. They did not know what a "90-day probation policy" was. Basically, they rolled the dice with every candidate who was applying for a job with their organization. Without a procedure for recruiting, hiring, and onboarding, the company was going to lose the majority of the time!

After a few visits, I learned that Wes, Jayson, and JB were all rehired. They rehired Jayson to replace Wes, who was also was a rehire. Then they rehired JB to replace Jayson after two weeks when he turned out to be a train wreck of a shop manager.

Management turnover for a small company like ABC (three service managers in five months) is a very bad thing when the company is attempting to become profitable!

Onboarding is a very important process to bring on new employees and keep them. Intending to send a good "onboarding" message to Denise, we sent the new accounting manager a picture and bio of all the senior managers and the people reporting to her before her first day at ABC. Denise never commented that she appreciated the onboarding effort by the company, but I must believe that it made her first week or two at the company just a little bit better.

Communication

At the beginning of the turnaround, the owners and I met with all the employees at an all-hands meeting. The goal was to keep all employees aware of what they and I were attempting to accomplish during my visits to ABC Off-Road Supply. Our goal was to have the employees engaged in improving the company's performance and profitability. To achieve the goal, we continually kept them informed with everything that was going on, including the changes that were happening every day at the company.

The management team had meetings once a week for one hour to review the prior week's results for sales, warehouse, and shop productivity. Denise shared the weekly flash report with the team and the financial statements once a month. These weekly management meetings kept the managers informed of the company's operations so that the managers could keep their employees up to date with everything.

Every morning, Monday through Saturday, the management team had a stand-up meeting for ten minutes before opening the doors to the public. The daily ten-minute meetings were to review the previous day's results and the current day's goals. Every manager always participated in every one of these meetings.

The sales team and Kurt also had a stand-up meeting every morning at 8:30 to 8:40 AM. During these ten-minute meetings, Kurt briefly discussed any open sales issues before the day started with a steady flow of customers all day.

Wednesday nights, Kurt had their sales meeting after work at a local restaurant, which usually lasted from 6:30 to 8:30 PM.

Sales Production

During the engagement, I learned very early that Kurt was not a sales manager. He was more like a sales support employee. Brian gave Kurt the job as a sales manager, but he did not give him the power and authority to run the sales department. I decided that Kurt should either be accountable for the sales department or find a new job. I put pressure on Kurt to turn up the heat on every salesperson to improve their monthly sales production. I met with Kurt and told him that I wanted several improvements to the sales department. I told him that he needed to accomplish my sales department task list for him in the next ten days before my next visit. He thought that his job was on the line if he didn't get all the work done. He had a good understanding of my message because, if he didn't get it done, I would have been looking for a new sales manager. Kurt did an awesome job, and his efforts grew the department's sales. Kurt was to:

✦ Create a new sales commission plan.

✦ Create a list of monthly sales contests.

✦ Schedule daily stand-up meetings.

✦ Create a daily procedure for checking their customer pick-up inventory.

✦ Develop a list of topics that the sales team needs training to grow their sales skills. Kurt hired a sales trainer to teach the sales team to improve their selling skills.

✦ Schedule weekly sales meetings after work.

Kurt developed a system that each salesperson had something to do each morning before noon to either improve the appearance of the facility or drive sales. He assigned one salesperson per day to come in one hour early one day a week to receive any phone calls from a customer before 9:00 AM.

Brian's sales skyrocketed because he started to visit all the dealerships in the area.

Shop Labor Pricing

At my second visit to ABC, I increased the shop labor rate from $92.50 to $125.00 per hour, then two months later to $135.00. These increases improved the gross profit percent on every deal sold by the five salesmen. The increase in the billing labor rate, according to the sales team, did not impact their ability to ever close a sale with a customer. I watched the sales very closely after I increased the price because if we did get complaints from the customers, I would have adjusted the price down.

Marketing

I changed the marketing firm from David, the local guy, to XYZ Marketing to reduce the fees being charged ABC Off-Road Supply from 28 to 10 percent, thereby increasing the funds that could be invested in purchasing AdWords.

We implemented a new marketing program to increase sales to our existing customer base. When the customers received their keys back after the shop completed working on the customer's vehicle, the customer received a package with the following:

✦ A thank-you card to thank the customer for his business along with the salesperson's professional card.

✦ A coupon addressed to the customer giving him 10 percent off on his next purchase from ABC.

✦ A postcard to give the customer a free checkup for their vehicle after one month or 500 miles, whichever comes first.

✦ A customer survey with six questions for the customer to answer about the salesperson and the shop.

✦ A "request for a customer referral, prestamped postcard" that offered a reward to the customer if the referred customer purchased products or services at ABC.

Kurt managed the sales team to meet and offer off-road vehicle clubs to have their meetings at ABC's conference room.

The Inventory

The inventory at ABC was a major problem for many reasons, including 50 percent too much stock, on-hand balances not on the computer, no security, and the warehouses were a mess.

Putting the inventory on the computer and having control over the stock movement was a major "win" for this company. Getting rid of the old slow-moving products improved the cash flow and their payables with their vendors. Securing the inventory with a fence and security sent a message to the employees. The two investments in security would no longer allow any employee to steal stock from the company.

The whole company culture of ABC Off-Road Supply materially changed from a bunch of lazy employees and poor management team to a very profitable business with strong management and professional employees. The sales for the twelve months after the turnaround engagement started went from $6.3 million to $8.0 million.

ABC Off-Road Supply
INCOME STATEMENT
(2019 vs. 2018)

	2019		2018		Variance
	YTD	% of Sales	YTD	% of Sales	YTD
Ordinary Income/Expense					
Income	$ 7,984,901	100.0%	$ 6,330,195	100.0%	$ 1,654,705
Cost of Goods Sold	4,800,124	60.12%	4,224,044	66.73%	576,080
Gross Profit	3,184,776	39.89%	2,106,151	33.27%	1,078,625
Expenses					-
Advertising & Promotion	251,534	3.15%	262,331	4.14%	(10,797)
Automobile Expense	77,670	0.97%	65,667	1.04%	12,003
Bank Service Charges	91,508	1.15%	93,897	1.48%	(2,389)
Employee Relations	21,938	0.28%	19,893	0.31%	2,045
Computer & Internet Exp	40,626	0.51%	44,422	0.7%	(3,797)
Insurance Expense	42,624	0.53%	40,839	0.65%	1,785
Interest Expense	74,745	0.94%	65,658	1.04%	9,087
Meals & Entertainment	40,604	0.51%	35,498	0.56%	5,106
Office Expense	34,490	0.43%	32,286	0.51%	2,204
Payroll Expenses	1,360,938	17.04%	926,332	14.63%	434,606
Postage	70,347	0.88%	67,333	1.06%	3,014
Prof & Business Fees	297,275	3.72%	299,783	4.74%	(2,508)
Rent Expense	157,498	1.97%	154,777	2.45%	2,721
Repairs & Maintenance	34,288	0.43%	28,878	0.46%	5,410
Telephone & Internet Exp	14,760	0.19%	13,863	0.22%	897
Travel Expense	23,217	0.29%	20,327	0.32%	2,890
Uniforms	23,199	0.29%	20,392	0.32%	2,807
Utilities	35,144	0.44%	33,679	0.53%	1,465
Total Expense	2,692,403	33.72%	2,225,855	35.16%	466,548
Net Ordinary Income	492,373	6.17%	(119,704)	-1.89%	612,077
Other Income/Expense					-
Other Income	4,313	0.05%	3,434	0.05%	879
Other Expense	(14,640)	-0.18%	(13,131)	-0.21%	(1,509)
Net Other Income	18,953	0.24%	16,565	0.26%	2,388
Net Income	$ 511,327	6.4%	(103,139)	-1.63%	$ 614,465

EPILOGUE

AS OF THIS WRITING, IT HAS BEEN TEN MONTHS SINCE THE successful turnaround ended with ABC Off-Road Supply. It has also been six months since the start of the COVID-19 pandemic. After completing the ABC turnaround engagement, I have worked with two new turnaround clients, both in Texas. One was in Dallas and the other one was in Houston.

As soon as the coronavirus became a "national pandemic," I stopped all traveling. I feared it was too dangerous to be in an enclosed airplane with 180+ potentially coronavirus-infected passengers. My onsite turnaround consulting engagements became turnaround coaching using Zoom meetings rather than traveling to the clients' locations 1,300 to 2,500 miles away from Fort Lauderdale, Florida.

I have stayed in contact with Brian and Jordan at ABC Off-Road Supply, mostly in a casual relationship, rather than coaching them to continue to improve their business. When we spoke, I would always ask them about how their business is doing. I consistently got a generic answer: "Good, Bob." That was the total of the business conversation on our calls with the rest of the phone call sounding like three very good friends talking. I believed that if they needed to get more of my business advice, either Brian or Jordan would ask me specific questions about their company.

A few months after the start of the coronavirus pandemic, I became concerned that Brian and Jordan might be too proud to tell me if their business was suffering due to COVID-19.

They (Brian and Jordan) both have transitioned from two owners of a turnaround client into two friends—good friends for life. They also transitioned from two off-road guys running a business to two businesspeople managing a successful off-road supply company.

For the last several months, I have focused on other clients because they truly needed my help with saving their companies, especially since the coronavirus pandemic. One evening in early August, I received a surprise text message from Brian. The text was a picture of the ABC Off-Road Supply sales report for July.

When I started at ABC eighteen months earlier, the company was averaging $525,000 of sales per month or $6,300,000 for the prior twelve months. The report that Brian sent me showed sales of $1,031,570 for the preceding thirty-one days. Over $1 million in sales for one month for this company was extremely impressive. It was extraordinary to think that they grew the monthly sales to hit over $1 million when four of the last six months was during the pandemic.

I immediately called Brian to congratulate him on an amazing month of sales. Brian was flying high during our conversation, obviously feeling very proud of his company's sales performance. I asked one question, and Brian talked for almost 30 minutes, sharing information about his company. He commented that ABC was "hitting on all eight cylinders." That was apparently an off-road vehicle phrase, but I understood what Brian was saying.

Brian's passion grew as he continued to talk. A year ago, before the turnaround engagement, his company was close to filing for bankruptcy protection. Brian and Jordan are now enjoying the benefits of their successful company. When I finally got the opportunity to ask a few questions, I requested that Brian please send me the year-to-date income statement and the monthly sales reports.

There were several successes during this turnaround of ABC Off-Road Supply. By the end of the engagement, the owners and management team upgraded every department in the company. The management team improved the appearance of parking lot, the building, the showrooms, the shop, and the warehouses. By the end of the engagement, there was a strong management team running the company. I wish that I had taken "before" and "after" pictures of each area. No one, including myself, would have believed the dramatic changes in this business. All those changes created positive results in the profitability and cash flow of the business.

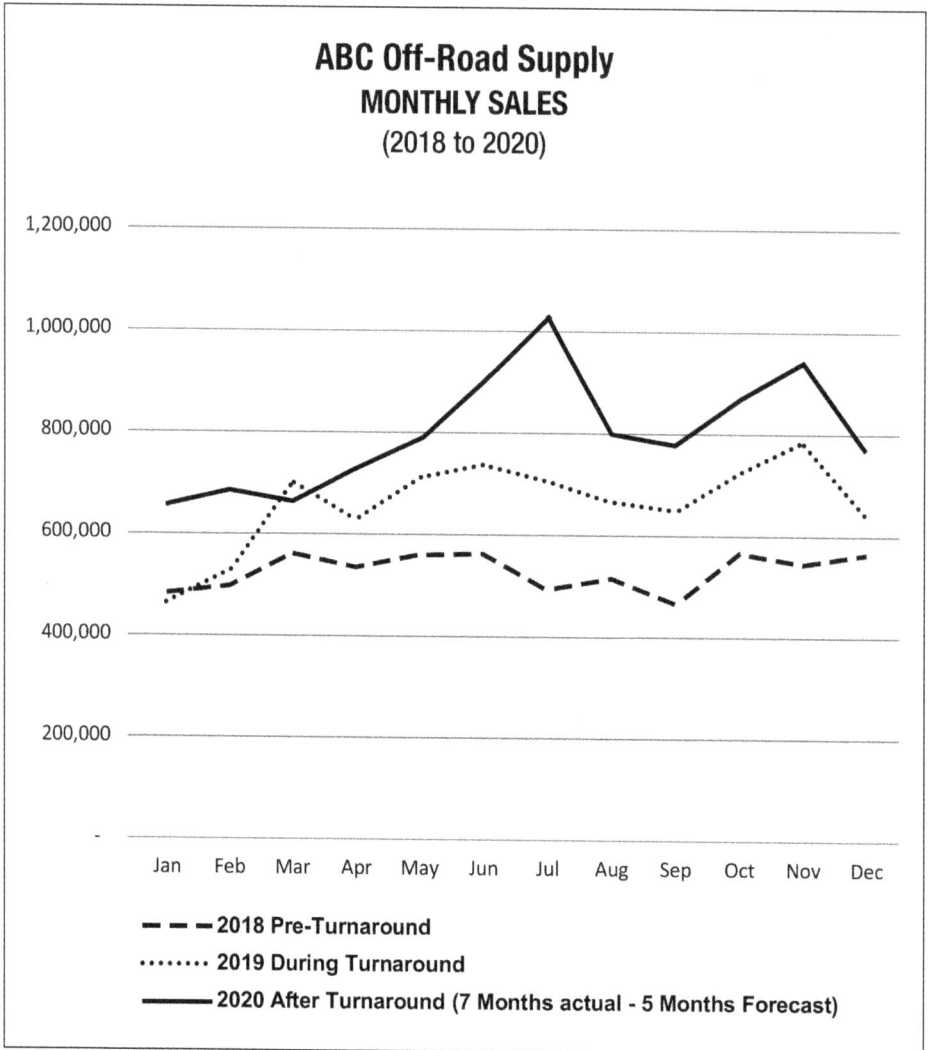

ABC Off-Road Supply
MONTHLY SALES
(2018 to 2020)

ABC Off-Road Supply
INCOME STATEMENT THROUGH JUNE 30, 2020

	20-Jan		20-Feb		20-Mar		20-Apr		20-May		20-Jun		Year to date Total	
	Month	% of Sales	Month	% of Sales	Month	% of Sales	Month	% of Sales	Month	% of Sales	Month	% of Sales	YTD	% of Sales
Ordinary Income/Expense														
Income	660,406	100.0%	689,663	100.0%	668,694	100.0%	733,905	100.0%	790,330	100.0%	907,138	100.0%	4,450,136	100.0%
Cost of Goods Sold	435,877	66.0%	434,244	62.97%	450,922	67.43%	445,601	60.72%	465,359	58.88%	538,905	59.41%	2,770,907	62.27%
Gross Profit	224,529	34.0%	255,420	37.04%	217,771	32.57%	288,304	39.28%	324,971	41.12%	368,233	40.59%	1,679,229	37.73%
Expenses														
Advertising & Promotion	18,066	2.74%	17,695	2.57%	17,664	2.64%	19,134	2.61%	21,256	2.69%	20,643	2.28%	114,459	2.57%
Automobile Expense	4,240	0.64%	2,052	0.3%	3,801	0.57%	3,108	0.42%	3,317	0.42%	2,873	0.32%	19,390	0.44%
Bank Service Charges	14,077	2.13%	11,771	1.71%	11,337	1.7%	11,585	1.58%	8,100	1.03%	10,393	1.15%	67,264	1.51%
Employee Relations	231	0.04%	46	0.01%	232	0.04%	-	0.0%	246	0.03%	633	0.07%	1,388	0.03%
Computer & Internet Exp	5,567	0.84%	5,003	0.73%	4,480	0.67%	7,297	0.99%	2,966	0.38%	3,033	0.33%	28,346	0.64%
Depreciation Expense	5,536	0.84%	5,536	0.8%	5,536	0.83%	5,536	0.75%	5,536	0.7%	5,536	0.61%	33,215	0.75%
Insurance Expense	(1,752)	-0.27%	6,645	0.96%	3,024	0.45%	3,024	0.41%	3,377	0.43%	6,627	0.73%	20,946	0.47%
Interest Expense	9,427	1.43%	9,418	1.37%	20,294	3.03%	8,793	1.2%	26,111	3.3%	22,747	2.51%	96,790	2.17%
Meals & Entertainment	1,215	0.18%	605	0.09%	1,335	0.2%	449	0.06%	478	0.06%	769	0.09%	4,850	0.11%
Office Expense	1,938	0.29%	875	0.13%	2,409	0.36%	800	0.11%	2,768	0.35%	1,979	0.22%	10,769	0.24%
Payroll Expenses	110,739	16.77%	124,769	18.09%	112,973	16.9%	119,715	16.31%	129,442	16.38%	122,599	13.52%	720,237	16.19%
Postage	1,141	0.17%	720	0.1%	311	0.05%	724	0.1%	78	0.01%	236	0.03%	3,211	0.07%
Prof & Business Fees	14,120	2.14%	11,747	1.7%	9,690	1.45%	11,000	1.5%	14,534	1.84%	20,200	2.23%	81,291	1.83%
Rent Expense	13,806	2.09%	13,556	1.97%	14,625	2.19%	13,556	1.85%	12,652	1.6%	13,556	1.49%	81,752	1.84%
Repairs & Maintenance	375	0.06%	305	0.04%	1,408	0.21%	86	0.01%	550	0.07%	6,444	0.71%	9,168	0.21%
Taxes	-	0.0%	-	0.0%	-	0.0%	-	0.0%	-	0.0%	11,201	1.23%	11,201	0.25%
Telephone & Internet Exp	829	0.13%	769	0.11%	402	0.06%	782	0.11%	1,404	0.18%	267	0.03%	4,453	0.1%
Travel Expense	1,845	0.28%	163	0.02%	404	0.06%	49	0.01%	269	0.03%	-	0.0%	2,730	0.06%
Uniforms	2,098	0.32%	1,653	0.24%	2,067	0.31%	1,913	0.26%	1,808	0.23%	2,204	0.24%	11,743	0.26%
Utilities	3,178	0.48%	4,062	0.59%	2,923	0.44%	3,189	0.44%	3,710	0.47%	3,116	0.34%	20,178	0.45%
Total Expense	206,675	31.3%	217,390	31.52%	214,915	32.14%	210,741	28.72%	238,602	30.19%	255,056	28.12%	1,343,378	30.19%
Net Ordinary Income	17,854	2.7%	38,029	5.51%	2,857	0.43%	77,563	10.57%	86,369	10.93%	113,177	12.48%	335,851	7.55%
Other Income/Expense														
Other Income	-	0.0%	-	0.0%	-	0.0%	-	0.0%	-	0.0%	-	0.0%	-	0.0%
Other Expense	(4,181)	-0.63%	(1)	0.0%	1,242	0.19%	(664)	-0.09%	5,575	0.71%	3,074	0.34%	5,047	0.11%
Net Other Income	4,181	0.63%	1	0.0%	(1,242)	-0.19%	664	0.09%	(5,575)	-0.71%	(3,074)	-0.34%	(5,047)	-0.11%
Net Income	22,035	3.34%	38,030	5.51%	1,614	0.24%	78,227	10.66%	80,794	10.22%	110,103	12.14%	330,804	7.43%

Comments about the Sales Graph (page 248)

✦ Sales for ABC Off-Road Supply during 2018 were $6,384,000 (Monthly average of $532,000) which was the year prior to the turnaround engagement.

✦ Sales for ABC during 2019 were $7,985,000 (monthly average of $665,000) during the year of the turnaround engagement. 2019 sales grew by 25% over 2018 sales.

✦ Sales during 2020 (January through July) was $5,482,000 (monthly average of $783,000) after the turnaround engagement. The forecasted sales for the whole year (2020) are $9,652,000 representing an increase over 2018 sales of 51% and an increase over 2019 sales by 21%.

Comments about the Income Statement for 2020 (page 249)

✦ ABC Off-Road Supply made a profit each of the first six months of the year.

✦ In June, the company reported a profit of $110,000 for the month. At the printing of this book, the company did not have the monthly closed done for July, but the sales for the month was $1,031,570 or $124,000 more than June.

✦ The company reported a profit for the first six months of the year of $330,800 or 7.43% of net sales.

✦ ABC's forecast for sales in 2020 is $9,652,000 and profits of $725,000. Profits for 2020 will be up by $214,000 over 2019 and up by $828,000 over 2018.

ABOUT THE AUTHOR

Robert S. Curry is a seasoned business coach and successful turnaround specialist. Early in his career, he served as a public accountant for two years before taking on the role of assistant controller, controller, and later CFO for a public retail company. Later, Bob served as president and CEO of three different companies ranging in size between one hundred million and one billion two hundred million in sales. All three businesses experienced successful turnarounds under his leadership and direction.

In the late 1990s, he started his own turnaround consulting firm, and for the past twenty-plus years, he has worked with more than 75 companies helping each to establish a strong management team and become profitable.

The Turnaround 2 is the third book in Bob's "From Loses to Profits" book series. All three books are written in a "story format" describing the turnaround of each company from the first day of the turnaround to the end of each successful consulting engagement.

Bob continues to turnarounds, business coaching and speaking engagements about his expertise: turnaround companies.

He resides in Fort Lauderdale, Florida, with his wife, Esther.

www.ingramcontent.com/pod-product-compliance
Lightning Source LLC
Chambersburg PA
CBHW041603220326
41597CB00057B/5095